THE LIVES AND DEATHS
OF SHELTER ANIMALS

THE LIVES AND DEATHS
OF SHELTER ANIMALS

Katja M. Guenther

Stanford University Press
Stanford, California

STANFORD UNIVERSITY PRESS
Stanford, California

©2020 by the Board of Trustees of the Leland Stanford Junior University.
All rights reserved.

Printed in the United States of America on acid-free, archival-quality paper

Library of Congress Cataloging-in-Publication Data available on request.

Cover design: Rob Ehle

Cover photo: Joe Adea

Typeset by Kevin Barrett Kane in 10.2/14.4 Minion Pro

Contents

Acknowledgments

My greatest gratitude goes to the nonhuman animals I met at the shelter I call
the Pacific Animal Welfare Center (PAW). The dogs and cats whose lives I
had the opportunity to witness there guided me toward new ways of thinking
about love, justice, and the future of human and nonhuman animals. This
book is about them and, ultimately, *for* them.

As animals outside the shelter, they are largely absent in this text, yet
the animals my wife and I fostered helped me to develop this analysis. They
enriched my understandings of care, vulnerability, and ability. I am particularly indebted to Aggie, Chet, Clover, Digby, Elphaba, Fergus, Gingersnap,
Kermit, Liesel, Maple, Marvel, Norton, Octavia, Opal, Peaches, and Trudy for
challenging and advancing my thinking. I also thank the two rescues which I
fostered for giving me the opportunity to know and love so many dogs.

Stella and Orla—both shelter animals—are the remarkable dogs who first
brought me to PAW. Without them, I would have lived a different, emptier
life. Orla, Ebert, Monkey, Kismet, Astrid, and Spätzle were with me almost
all the time when I was writing. They are my muses, and I hope to long be in
service to them.

I cannot thank the many volunteers, staff, and rescuers at PAW by name,
as doing so could violate their confidentiality. Thus I rely on a nonspecific
statement of tremendous thanks, and I trust that they know who they are
and that I immensely appreciate them and the work they do. I shared a lot of

laughter, anger, and frustration with fellow volunteers and rescue friends, and I am grateful for the various ways they supported me in negotiating those feelings so that I could continue with this project.

Claire Jean Kim was generous in her feedback on several chapters of this work through a critique session sponsored by the Center for Ideas and Society at the University of California, Riverside. I am grateful to her and all of the participants at this session. I also presented pieces of this work at various conferences, and I thank those who stimulated my thinking with their insights at those events.

I am indebted to Marcela Maxfield for her enthusiasm for this project, and to the two anonymous reviewers through Stanford University Press who provided thoughtful and important comments as I developed this book.

Dana Collins cheered me on in writing this book and faithfully reminded me to hear and write my voice. I am very fortunate to have such a friend. My family, especially my nephews Fox, Orson, and Wolfram, always encouraged me, as have so many other friends. Thank you. In the final stages, Tristan reminded me to be excited about my work when my energy flagged. I eagerly await when he can read this book.

My life companion, Tuppett, has been immensely patient with me in the development and writing of this work and has been an incredible partner in all things, including joining me in the pleasures and tribulations of fostering dozens of dogs from PAW and other area shelters. I am indescribably lucky that she is also a remarkably helpful editor, a wonderfully thoughtful sounding board, and, most importantly, an inspiration to me.

Some passages of chapters 4, 6, and 8 originally appeared in journal articles I authored. These include "How Volunteerism Inhibits Mobilization: A Case Study of Shelter Animal Advocates," published in *Social Movement Studies* (2017), copyright Taylor & Francis, Ltd., and available online at https://doi.org/10.1080/14742837.2016.1252668; "'Taking the Ghetto Out of the Dog': Reproducing Social Inequalities in Pit Bull Rescue," published in *Ethnic and Racial Studies* (2019), available online at https://doi.org/10.1080 /01419870.2019.1665695, copyright Taylor & Francis, Ltd.; and "Volunteers' Power and Resistance in the Struggle for Shelter Animal Survival," published in *Sociological Forum* (2017), available online at https://doi.org/10.1111/ socf.12376, copyright John Wiley & Sons.

Abbreviations

ASPCA American Society for the Prevention of Cruelty to Animals

BSL Breed-specific legislation

HSUS The Humane Society of the United States

PAW Pacific Animal Welfare Center

PDD Potentially dangerous dog

PTS Put to sleep

RVT Registered Veterinary Technician

SCAS Southern California Animal Services

TNR Trap, neuter, release

THE LIVES AND DEATHS
OF SHELTER ANIMALS

1 Monster's World

THE MUSCULAR GRAY DOG named Monster raised his square head, regarded me dispassionately with his amber eyes, and sank his head back down onto his enormous paws as if he knew that whether he got up to greet me or not made no difference whatsoever. His fate was already sealed. I knew the same as I knelt down and looked at him through the bent and rusted bars of the cage where he had been housed since arriving a few days earlier at the Pacific Animal Welfare Center (PAW), a high-intake public animal shelter in the Los Angeles metropolitan area. The next morning, he would join the seven or eight other dogs and fifteen or more cats put down each day at PAW. He would also become part of a much larger statistic as one of the three million companion animals who are put to sleep in animal shelters in the United States each year.[1]

Monster's death was the consequence of multiple social processes that I unpack in this book. He died because he lived in a community of lower-income people of color in which human residents face challenges that threaten their ability to maintain continuous, geographically proximal relationships with anyone, human or animal; this placed him at particular risk for entering an animal shelter. As a pit bull, Monster was also part of the group of dogs most likely to end up in a shelter and the least likely to leave alive because of breed discrimination that is itself grounded in racism and classism. Of course, his life would never have been at risk had he not lived in a society in which humans believe in their right to dominate and control what we see as the natural world, including nonhuman animals. This ideology—anthroparchy—is embedded in state-run shelters like the one where Monster found himself, giving shelters such as PAW license to kill animals whom they deem surplus or unadoptable.[2] Monster died because of who he was, who the humans he was attached to were, and how our society naturalizes and accepts the killing of animals.

■ ■ ■

The great hypocrisy of human's relationships with companion animals is that even as American society claims to cherish companion animals, we also embrace legal definitions of companion animals as property and widely accept the practice of killing them as a solution to what we construct as a market surplus. American's purported love for our companion animals also does not extend to other animals: the annual per capita consumption of nonmarine animal flesh is 220 pounds, making the US one of the top three highest per capita consumers of meat in the world.[3] Even as we endorse the brutality of intensive animal farming through our consumer choices, we howl over any instance of companion animal abuse. This hypocrisy informs what happens at PAW and how it happens, as the individual and institutional conflicts from competing beliefs pull PAW and its staff, volunteers, and public in different directions.

Animals' status as legal property is both a clear marker of their objectification in an anthroparchal state and a primary determinant of their life chances. In a society in which animals are owned by humans for purposes of consumption or companionship, the types of human communities to which they belong largely define animals' experiences. A chicken born to a so-called urban homesteader—or a typically white, educated, middle- or upper-middle-class household with members who want to reduce their reliance on agribusiness—leads a very different life than a chicken born in a chick-hatching facility that is part of the Tyson corporation, the largest producer of chicken flesh in the United States. One will likely enjoy ample sunshine and fresh air, a great deal of personalized attention from a human, veterinary care as needed, and appreciation from her human and chicken companions while she lives out her natural life and is then buried; the other will live a life of extreme confinement, neglect, physical pain, abuse, and an early, painful, and unnatural death, after which her body will be dismembered and sold as meat.[4]

The situation for companion animals in the United States is usually a less dramatic contrast, but the stratification becomes more apparent once an animal comes into a shelter. Those companion animals who live in affluent, predominantly white communities are likely to experience animal shelters that provide veterinary care and enrichment and where staff and management are deeply committed to reunification or adoption.[5] In contrast, companion animals who live in low-income and/or nonwhite communities are likely to enter shelters that have few resources for veterinary care or enrichment and where reunification or adoption is a much less likely outcome. Had Monster ended up in the privately managed shelter some twenty miles away from PAW in an affluent, predominantly white and Asian American area, his chances of survival would have been 95 percent, and, even if he had been among the unlucky 5 percent to die there, he would have enjoyed walks several times a day with volunteers, the stimulation of a training program, high-quality veterinary care, and likely months or even years at the shelter during efforts to find him a home.

At animal shelters, tensions between different approaches to animal keeping become visible, as do dynamics of power between institutions, volunteers, and clients. As living with companion animals has become a central activity for many Americans, middle-class norms of what constitutes proper care of such animals have given rise to a discourse of irresponsible owners, or people who lack the moral fitness to provide appropriate care to companion animals and who, at PAW, come from the shelter's predominantly nonwhite and low-income service area. Public animal shelters are the site for a wide range of functions related to companion animals, such as securing animal licenses, investigating noise complaints, classifying dogs as vicious and cats as feral, caring for stray animals, offering vaccination and spay/neuter services, and providing companion animal adoption and rescue, so people with disparate interests in animals come to shelters, where they interact with each other, with staff, and with impounded animals. At the shelter, humans with different animal practices, or expectations for human-animal relationships that guide human-animal interaction and that reflect group identity and history, come into close and routine contact.[6] The shelter's institutional practice of caging, for example, is an animal practice grounded in the shelter's belief that confinement without human contact is an acceptable strategy for housing companion animals. Shelter volunteers, however, reject this animal practice and manipulate, bend, break, and struggle against PAW's rules to take impounded dogs out into social areas so they can have a break from strict confinement, play, and receive individual attention. These kinds of conflicts over animal practices have the cumulative effect of solidifying group identities, maintaining existing inequalities, and sometimes shifting individual and institutional animal practices.

PAW offers limited freedoms to animals impounded there and exercises tight bureaucratic control over staff and volunteers. Such an atmosphere makes it a site for contestation over the meanings and practices of animal welfare and rights, responsible animal guardianship, risk and danger, and fairness and equity. As I unpack throughout this book, those meanings and practices themselves reflect socially rooted ideas and beliefs about race, class, gender, species, and breed.

PAW attempts to assert power over the lives of both human and nonhuman animals. Power, however, is never absolute or immutable and always coexists with resistance.[7] How do human and nonhuman animals resist the control of an institution that seems to have such complete control over them? Can animals—who are so often depicted as voiceless and powerless—be involved in resisting institutional control over their lives?

In this book, I engage with these questions to expose regimes of domination that try to manage and control the lives of animals and people, and to uncover how animals and people resist these efforts. I classify as resistance all attempts, irrespective of outcome, to challenge directives, actions, or discourses articulated by the shelter—whether directly stated by staff or conveyed through policies issued by unspecified managers.[8] Volunteers, rescuers, clients/subjects, and animals all engage in acts of everyday resistance, or routine acts that seek to undermine power.[9] Because resistance and power interact, they respond to each other: both power and resistance may be refined, reinvented, expanded, and/or repealed as an outcome of these interactions.

Within the shelter, animals become part of struggles around power. They are implicated in debates about humane animal care and are central to conflicts between staff and volunteers. Animals are also caught up in struggles between the shelter and the public, who may seek to adopt animals shelter staff think are unsuitable for adoption or who try to reclaim their companions when the shelter has deemed either the home or the animal unsuitable for reunification.

■ ■ ■

In this book, I analyze the social worlds of shelter animals—especially dogs—at PAW to make sense of what happened to Monster and what continues to happen to too many companion animals across the United States each day. I read Monster's story, and the stories of thousands of other animals I met, and hundreds who became my intimates, as a reflection of the junctures between social structures far larger than any animal shelter. The existence and reproduction of social inequalities; the use of state power to enforce behavioral norms on lower-income and nonwhite citizens; competing discourses and ideologies about animal sheltering, animal welfare, and what constitutes "humane" treatment; government policies and practices; and the growing move toward the privatization of public shelters all shape which animals end up in shelters and what they will experience once they get there. What happens at PAW—including human struggles over how animals at PAW live and if they die—is the outcome of everyday and sustained collisions of capitalism, anthroparchy, white supremacy, and patriarchy. These collisions reduce companion animals to expendable commodities; lace our views about which shelter animals deserve saving with ideas about race, class, gender, and ability; and ultimately allow the shelter to shift responsibility for the deaths of shelter animals onto the low-income minority community it purports to serve and onto the animals themselves.

I spent over three years conducting ethnography as a volunteer at PAW, watching, observing, and participating in the routine operations of the shelter and interacting with staff, other volunteers, and the many people who came to the shelter either in search of services or because PAW summoned them there to address some issue, such as an unlicensed animal. My analysis is guided by a desire to understand how and why an animal shelter like PAW asserts control over human and animal populations, how those humans and animals respond to and resist such control, and what the consequences of these dynamics of power and resistance are for companion animals impounded at PAW, and for all animals. I trace how these responses and strategies of resistance reflect the different social locations of the actors who interact at the shelter, including staff members, volunteers, animal rescuers, and clients/subjects (e.g., those seeking services like adoption or surrender of an animal, as well as the broader community subject to animal control regulations). Rather than viewing PAW as an isolated microcosm, I connect what happens at PAW to broader social structures and shifts, including inequalities of race, class, gender, species, and breed that shape shelter interactions and the likelihood of animal survival, as well as the broader backdrop of the politics of animal sheltering.

Analyzing PAW uncovers a swirl of discourses and practices around class, race, and gender. But these discourses and practices play out in myriad and often competing ways. Sometimes they work to undermine anthroparchal thinking, but they rarely engage with how the work of the shelter and of the volunteers and rescuers who try to get companion animals into homes they consider suitable reinforces capitalist logics of companion animals as commodities, white supremacist beliefs in the inferiority of racial-ethnic minorities as animal guardians and in the animality of Black bodies, patriarchal ideas that caring for companion animals is women's labor, and anthroparchal commitments to maintaining human domination over animals. In this book, I untangle these discourses and practices to understand better how social inequalities between human animals and between nonhuman animals are co-constituted in ways that significantly shape how animals live and when and how they die. I explore how these processes unfold and what they mean for dogs like Monster, who find themselves caught up in shelters that are increasingly in the crosshairs of debates about what shelters can do to reduce the risk of shelter death to companion animals.

ANIMAL SHELTERING IN THE UNITED STATES

Monster's experience at PAW reflects the history of animal sheltering in the United States, which has its roots in a public safety discourse that remains central to the animal practices at PAW. Claims about safety are regularly used to justify how the shelter treats impounded animals and why it kills so many of them. Importantly, animal sheltering in the United States is still undergoing a transformation from sovereign power to biopower, or techniques of power focused on subjugating bodies and controlling populations.[10] At PAW, threats to the sovereign—today most often couched in a discourse that emphasizes public safety—have resulted in sheltered animals being summarily killed. Gradually, there has been a shift toward a discourse in which governance of animals is described as being *in the interest of animals themselves.*[11] Animals cannot, under this new biopolitical logic, live safe and fulfilled lives if they are living on the street, nor can they do so if they are "warehoused" at the shelter (a favorite justification of shelter managers at PAW for why animals should stay at the shelter for only a limited amount of time before being killed). Likewise, vaccinating, spaying and neutering, and microchipping animals is largely done in the name of their own interests.

This is a marked change that has taken place in shelters across the nation starting in the late 1990s. The earliest animal control agencies in the United States had two primary goals: first, to protect the public from rabid or aggressive animals, and, second, to manage ownership disputes involving animals, particularly livestock. The fear of zoonotic contamination, especially of rabies, was a powerful motivator to capture and destroy unclaimed companion animals. The stray cats and dogs who found themselves picked up by animal control typically did not survive the encounter; until the end of the 1800s, close to 100 percent of animals picked up by animal control agencies were killed, often using brutal means, such as clubbing or mass drowning.[12] In mid-nineteenth-century New York City, dogcatchers were paid by the dog and placed up to several hundred stray dogs each day in large cages to drown them in the East River. Animal control was about taking animal life.

The idea that free-roaming animals are the mark of an uncivilized society remains dominant in the United States today, where it is widely believed that free-roaming dogs are an indicator of economic underdevelopment and are a nuisance and even a threat to public safety. Across the US, animal welfare agencies have zero tolerance for stray dogs and will seek to trap and impound such dogs. The Hollywood caricature of the dogcatcher as a burly, mean-looking man who jails dogs with the intent to kill them reasonably accurately captures the work of most dogcatchers through at least the 1980s. Across the United States, killing groups of stray animals in gas chambers was widely practiced through the 1980s.[13]

While America's early animal control agencies sought to protect public safety and prevent what they defined as nuisance animals, the birth of the animal welfare movement shifted the focus to providing compassionate care for animals and ensuring their protection from abuse. Animal shel-tering as we know it today emerged out of the efforts of mostly white, upper-class activists in the late 1800s who sought to protect animals from painful human experimentation and mistreatment. Henry Bergh, the wealthy heir to a shipbuilding fortune, founded the American Society to Prevent Cruelty to Animals (ASPCA), the first such organization in the US, in New York City in 1866. His observation of animal exploitation while working as a diplomat in Europe and his interactions with members of the Royal Society for the Prevention of Cruelty to Animals (RSPCA) in Britain, the world's first known anticruelty organization, founded in 1824, inspired Bergh to push for anticruelty statutes in the US. Activists within the RSPCA included clergymen, parliamentarians, and wealthy elites who used a combination of moral and religious arguments to promote kindness toward animals. Bergh and activists involved in establishing local societies to prevent cruelty to animals in US cities following the founding of the ASPCA similarly drew heavily on moral arguments about compassion and decency. Bergh and his associates enjoyed near-immediate legislative victories that established new parameters for policing cruelty to animals and penalizing offenders. A master of attracting publicity, Bergh routinely engaged in high-profile rescues of working horses and fighting dogs, which often functioned to highlight ethnic and class differences in animal prac-tices; in his efforts to reduce cruel animal practices among elites, he ap-pealed to their status as a basis for stopping the activity, arguing that "the greater the offender, the greater the offence."[14] Bergh also enjoyed wearing a uniform with a badge and asserting his authority as a legally empowered animal control officer.

Beginning in 1894—a few years after Bergh's death and fully twenty-four years after Caroline Earle White, another wealthy philanthropist, founded the Women's Pennsylvania SPCA, the first private animal shelter in the US—the ASPCA began operating animal shelters in New York City. The primary goal of the ASPCA shelter work in New York—as for SPCAs in other communities—was to preserve public safety by catching stray dogs and pro-viding them with a humane death, rather than clubbing them or drowning them, as had been the previous practice.[15] The ASPCA also investigated cases of animal cruelty and provided evidence to the relevant state authorities, with mixed outcomes: one of Henry Bergh's personal frustrations was that a judge ruled against using cruelty statutes to prosecute participants in the sport of pigeon shooting.[16]

In its first full year of operation in 1895, 95 percent of the 21,741 dogs and 24,140 cats who entered the ASPCA in New York were killed there.[17] Only after the Second World War did the percentage of animals put to death in shelters begin to decline as the issue of companion animal homelessness came to be seen as a social problem and shelter death as an undesirable outcome. The animal welfare movement was an active, entrenched part of US culture as early as the late nineteenth century, and, like Henry Bergh, animal welfare activists effectively deployed religious teachings about stewardship and American beliefs around morality to establish mercy toward animals as a core American value.[18] While much of the work of the animal welfare movement focused specifically on working animals such as horses, their efforts contributed to changing practices vis-à-vis all animals. Already by the 1920s, advocates for animal protection had started to change public views about blood sports (e.g., dogfighting, cockfighting, pigeon shooting, foxhunting), animal slaughter, and stray animals.

Norms of dog keeping especially shifted as the residents of the burgeoning post–Second World War American suburbia increasingly viewed their pets as their charges and family members. Allowing dogs to run loose and to reproduce repeatedly became less acceptable in the new suburbia and a marker of the lower classes. As standards of care rose for animals in homes, they also slowly started to rise for animals in shelters, which now had to provide at least basic veterinary care, appropriate caging, and an opportunity for reunification with a guardian or adoption to a new guardian. Legally, politically, and socially, the United States also began to recognize animal sentience, and this shift created pressures and conflicts within animal shelters to improve the standard of care and to increase the rate of live release, or the live exit of animals because of adoption, rescue, or return to their owner(s).

The practices of animal control agencies—public or private entities that contract with local governments—also began shifting in an effort to reduce the rate of incoming animals. Most importantly, animal shelters began sterilizing and vaccinating animals prior to release; beginning around 2006, animal control agencies also began routinely implanting microchips, which can help reunite lost animals and their guardians, in all released animals. As more people adopted animals from shelters, this meant that more companion animals were sterilized. Further, these services became more available to people who acquired animals outside shelters. While there have been ebbs and flows in the growth of spay/neuter access, the general trend in the US has been a steady increase in the availability of affordable sterilization services and the widespread acceptance that sterilization is the best option for cats and dogs.[19] The number of animals killed in US shelters began to decrease sharply after the 1970s, largely thanks to reductions in intake.[20]

The expectations for standards of care in shelters have risen substantially over the last thirty years: animal shelters are no longer places to warehouse street dogs and feral cats until they are put down and are instead expected to be friendly, comfortable environments that promote adoption. Maddie's Adoption Center in San Francisco, funded by technology billionaires David and Cheryl Duffield, became the nation's first cage-free, no-kill animal shelter in 1998.[21] Rather than being confined to kennels, animals at Maddie's Adoption Center live in home-style units complete with furniture and televisions. While even today some shelters in the United States continue to use gas chambers to end the lives of companion animals who are deemed unwanted or surplus, general standards in the late twentieth century held that chemical euthanasia (also called euthanasia by injection, or EBI) was the most humane method to kill unwanted companion animals, offering allegedly better deaths to those animals who did end up killed at shelters.

No-kill advocates, who have become a vocal presence in the animal-sheltering community since the early 1990s, hold that animal shelters should not put down any adoptable animals. The City of San Francisco was the pioneer for its embrace of a no-kill approach: in 1994, the city adopted a no-kill ordinance, and the then-director of its SPCA, Rich Avanzino, is largely viewed as the catalyst for no-kill sheltering in the US. In 2011, Austin, Texas, became the largest US city to adopt a no-kill practice. The City of Los Angeles is currently attempting to become no-kill; it reduced its rate of shelter death from 42 percent in 2011 to about 15 percent in 2014, and as of 2017, it declared itself no-kill for dogs but not for cats.

Even though no-kill sheltering originated in San Francisco, it has taken decades for other parts of California, including the Los Angeles area, to start to catch up. A number of factors help explain this lag, including a larger and more diverse human and animal population, Los Angeles's sprawling geography, local shelter systems known for their complex bureaucratic struc-tures and traditional views on animal sheltering (San Francisco Animal Care and Control, for instance, had one municipal shelter at the time San Francisco began moving toward no-kill, compared to the City of Los An-geles's five shelters, plus literally dozens more in adjacent communities like Hollywood, Santa Monica, Los Angeles County, Orange County, Riverside County, Ventura County, and beyond), and the absence of a major donor of the likes of the Duffields. The large numbers of shelter killings across California made the state the highest per capita and overall contributor to shelter killing nationally through 2018, when Texas may have eclipsed California by a few thousand animals.[22]

The spokespeople for the no-kill movement include white men advocates like Nathan Winograd, author and founder of the No Kill Advocacy Center, and Francis Battista and Gregory West, both leaders within Best Friends Animal Society, one of the nation's largest animal charities. Although no-kill advocates sometimes disagree with each other on how to define the approach, they share a focus on moving away from the practice of shelter killing and a commitment to ending shelter killing as a widespread "solu-tion" to homelessness among companion animals. Per the No Kill Advocacy Center, the shift to no-kill requires multiple programmatic changes within shelters, including high-volume sterilization of both shelter and community animals, progressive redemption policies so it is easy for guardians to re-claim companion animals who have ended up in a shelter, close relationships with nonprofit animal rescue organizations, foster programs for vulnerable animals such as unweaned kittens and puppies, and proactive behavior and medical intervention programs that benefit both animals in the shelter and animals in the community.[23]

No-kill advocates disagree on the details of the approach and even on what it means to achieve no-kill status. While there is no formal accreditation of no-kill shelters, the generally accepted standard within the sheltering com-munity is that shelters that put down fewer than 10 percent of impounded animals qualify as no-kill (and that the 10 percent should include a high pro-portion of animals who are not adoptable for veterinary reasons or because they pose a threat to public safety). Some no-kill advocates believe that a 100 percent live release rate should be an attainable goal. Strategy also varies: some no-kill advocates are eager to cooperate with notoriously difficult and institutionally inert shelter systems (as in Best Friends' partnership with the City of Los Angeles Animal Services), while others push for more aggressive tactics that are openly critical of public sheltering agencies. Winograd in particular has been harshly critical of many animal rights organizations, referring to divisions between grassroots advocacy by animal caregivers and large, national animal advocacy organizations. These divisions in part rest on the early resistance of national organizations to accept no-kill principles and/or practices, such as the reluctance of the Humane Society of the United States (HSUS) to support trap-neuter-release (TNR) for feral cats. The co-optation of some grassroots organizations by major animal welfare groups, such as the North Shore Animal League's takeover of grassroots Doing Things for Animals, which organized the first no-kill conference in 1995, further exacerbates tensions. Money also seems to be an issue, as the national groups often receive hundreds of millions of dollars in donations that no-kill critics feel are not used to benefit animals.[24] At the same time, the shift toward no-kill has resulted in increasingly cooperative relationships between animal control agencies and animal welfare organizations across locations.[25] With the advent of no-kill, shelters began partnering to move animals by van or plane to areas with better chances at adoption; the ASPCA, Best Friends Animal Society, and North Shore Animal League have all been active in coordinating and funding such efforts.

Among no-kill advocates, how to implement adoption programs and work with local communities also varies significantly. Some no-kill advocates, for example, support the need for adoption applications, whereas others push for less selective adoption policies to reduce barriers to adoption. Although these may sound like trivial matters, they are subject to extensive and often loud and angry debate within the animal-sheltering industry. At PAW, volunteers and staff often debate and disagree about how best to reduce shelter killing.

An important species divide exists in that dogs as a species fare much better than cats in the practices of contemporary shelters invested in at least lowering kill rates. Cats designated as feral are most likely to be killed in shelters. In the latter part of the twentieth century, some animal welfare agencies began developing programs for feral cats that reframe them as community cats and focus on eliminating their reproductive abilities while leaving them in their habitats as free-roaming cats. In 1990, Becky

Robinson developed TNR programs in Washington, DC, and founded Alley Cat Allies, the first national advocacy organization focused on the humane treatment of cats.[26] Through TNR programs, community cats are trapped, sterilized, clearly marked as sterilized (usually by clipping off the tip of one ear), and returned to where they were found. This way, the feline community stops growing, but those cats who are already part of it can continue to live out their lives. Many public shelters, however, do not engage in TNR: at PAW, for example, cats who demonstrate hostile behavior toward humans at intake are identified as feral and are killed when their legally mandated hold period is up. While the primary justification for killing feral cats is the protection of wild birds, PAW views them more broadly as public nuisances.[27] The death rate for cats at PAW during the research period was consistently much higher than that for dogs: in the 2014–15 fiscal year, for instance, the death rate for cats at PAW was 85 percent, compared to 19.5 percent for dogs (as per shelter statistics).

Tracing trends in shelter intakes and outcomes nationally remains a challenge because of a lack of data collection and coordination of data collection efforts across approximately five thousand public and private shelters in the United States.[28] The late 1960s are generally seen as the peak of the so-called pet overpopulation problem and the time when the highest numbers of shelter animals were killed. In the early 1970s, numbers begin to decline: in 1973, an estimated 13.5 million dogs and cats died in US shelters, but that figure dropped to an estimated 7.6 to 10 million animals in 1985 and has continued to decline.[29] In 2016, an estimated 4 to 5 million animals—but quite possibly as many as 7 million—entered US shelters, and close to 3 million were killed.[30] Undoubtedly, advocates for animals have much to celebrate in the decline in shelter death in the United States; no-kill advocates contend we need to continue working until no companion animals are killed.[31]

The introduction of the no-kill ethic in animal sheltering is an ongoing source of contention among those involved in animal sheltering and rescue. Some argue that no-kill shelters are abusive to impounded animals, who can end up living in shelters for months or even years. In the City of Los Angeles, which has been pushing for a goal of a 90 percent live release rate as part of its No-Kill Los Angeles (NKLA) initiative in partnership with Best Friends Animal Society, large dogs can be kenneled for well over a year, and some shelters have had to resort to using crates and other temporary kennels to accommodate all of the animals. Staff members in kill shelters assert that it's unfair for the public to criticize kill shelters when public resources are not made available to animal control agencies to provide services that would reduce shelter intakes.

Some shelter managers, including the five who ran PAW during the research period, see no-kill as an impossibility, no matter what the resources. From this perspective, as long as the flow of animals into shelters continues, and as long as public shelters are open-admission shelters that take in all animals, irrespective of health or behavior, some animals will necessarily need to be put down. PAW sits at the close edge of the push toward no-kill: several nearby shelters have moved toward the no-kill approach, and major animal welfare organizations have offered their services to PAW in pursuit of reducing shelter killing. Still, the shelter management has never endorsed the no-kill philosophy and has often opposed it, arguing that no-kill is inhumane and impossible. From the view of managers at PAW and Southern California Animal Services (SCAS), the multishelter animal control agency of which PAW is a part, many dogs like Monster cannot be saved: there are simply too many of them, produced by irresponsible owners, and without enough homes open to considering pit bulls and other undesirable (old, feline) animals.[32] Pit bulls and cats today are the animals that pose the greatest challenges to shelters like PAW that administer animal control in lower-income communities.

A CRITICAL FEMINIST PERSPECTIVE ON PAW

My examination of power and resistance at PAW speaks to, and is informed by, scholarship in critical animal studies, an interdisciplinary field that attends to intersections of human and animal inequalities and is committed to animal liberation.[33] The so-called animal turn in humanistic and, to a lesser degree, social scientific scholarship refers to growing concern about life beyond humans, an interest possibly triggered by massive changes in what humans see as the natural and technological worlds that require us to move away from anthrocentric thinking. While the earliest scholarship in animal studies, most famously Peter Singer's *Animal Liberation*, drew on rights-based discourses to argue for animal rights, much of the animal turn is less explicitly political and instead seeks to explore human-animal relationships and the role of animals in human life, including human expression.[34] As animals and other nonhumans have crept back into the narratives of many fields—notably history, literary studies, cultural studies, and anthropology—they have often done so as signifiers or as objects, rather than as active agents in their own right.

A strong branch of animal studies, however, focuses on the exploitation of animals and calls for an explicitly political engagement with animals.[35] This is the field known as critical animal studies. Critical animal studies emphasizes the need for nonhuman and human liberation through major social change. Core characteristics of this area of work include interdisciplinarity; attention to intersecting systems of inequality, such as race, class, gender, and species; and a commitment to using research and theory for the purposes of social change, or what is also referred to as activist scholarship.[36] Although scholars working in this field incorporate a diversity of theories, methods, and perspectives, they typically attend to domination and exploitation and integrate leading-edge approaches from the diverse disciplines from which critical animal studies draws (e.g., gender studies, queer theory, anthropology, philosophy, literary theory, and literary studies). Critical animal studies thus is a radical project, and often one at the fringes of academia because it presses on the boundaries of traditional (white, male, and human-dominated) knowledge production. This book fits squarely within this tradition by considering how systems of domination and exploitation shape the lives of human and nonhuman animals and by attending to dynamics of power and resistance within a space that is a core battleground over human-animal relationships and especially violence against animals.

Like much of critical animal studies, this book seeks to denaturalize human activities vis-à-vis nonhumans that we mostly take for granted, namely the keeping and the sheltering of companion animals.[37] Relatively little social scientific and humanistic scholarship has examined animal shelters in the United States. This is surprising given how visible animal control agencies and their representatives are in the cultural landscape of the United States—the dogcatcher is usually among the first figures children in the United States learn to fear on the basis of depictions from children's films and books, and journalistic accounts of animal rescue abound[38]—and how popular it has become for people to "rescue" a companion animal by adopting them from a shelter or rescue organization. Over three million dogs and cats from shelters (in roughly equal shares) move into private homes each year through adoption, with some estimates suggesting that as many as 80 percent of companion animals are adopted through shelters or nonprofit rescue organizations or as strays.[39] Still, most of what we "know" about animal sheltering is assumptive or comes from research conducted at smaller shelters and/or private rescue groups.[40] This book offers a rich ethnographic account of routine activity at a high-intake, open-admission, public shelter, the type of shelter in which companion animals in the United States are most likely to find themselves should they become unwanted or stray from their home.[41]

A biopolitical approach considers how biological life is subject to regulation.[42] *Biopolitics* refers to the extension of political control over biological and social processes and is accomplished through regimes of knowledge and authority that expand state power into bodies and selves. Per Michel Foucault's genealogies of power, biopower is an *addition* to repression and violence. Biopower occupies diverse regimes of authority, including medicine, social work, public health, and more, and can "foster life or disallow it to the point of death."[43] Foucaultian thinking is highly influential in critical animal studies, where scholars have extended ideas about biopolitics from the human to the animal. The emphasis on biopolitical governance in animal studies draws attention "to the way in which the same violent biopolitical forces that shape the governance of animals are closely mirrored in human relations of power. There is here the largely unexplored potential for a shared politics between human and nonhuman interests."[44] Indeed, my engagement in this book is precisely with the aim of showing the connections between human and nonhuman interests and how contemporary regimes of power harm humans and animals alike.

One appearance of these connections is in structures and ideologies of race. Animals are central to the construction of difference and similarity among humans. That animals have been constituted as nonhuman along with racialized humans has serious implications for their welfare and survival. Animality is central to the construction of racial difference.[45] In Western thought, animals and raced people form two stable counterparts to the human.[46] While their experiences are not analogous, both Black people and animals endured intensive exploitation in the development of American capitalism, with such exploitation justified by the idea that neither Black people nor animals had the feeling or intellect to care for themselves or achieve self-fulfillment (itself an idea white human animals have laid sole claim to).

Echoing the mechanics of Giorgio Agamben's theory of the anthropological machine, Claire Jean Kim argues that

> slavery produces and bequeaths to us an entire zoologo-racial order . . . in which everything "human" depends on keeping the relationships between the "black" and the "animal" *unspeakably close and perpetually open.* We cannot stop posing the question, "*Is the black animal?*" It is not the answer to this question but rather the infinite deferral of the answer that fixes the closed loop of meaning in which both imagined entities—"black" and "animal"—are produced *as indeterminate relative to each other.* The ontological certainty of the "human" turns out to depend on the ontological uncertainty of "black" and "animal."[47]

This ontological uncertainty means that Black people fall at the margins of the human.

Women, too, are seen as outside culture and within nature, although, depending on their race, class, and sexuality, they may stand closer to culture or to nature. The logics that place white women at the bounds of the human are different from the logics that leave Black people in the realm of the animal. White women's animality is neither savage nor beastly nor dangerous unless carefully controlled; it is, instead, part of women's closeness to the natural world.[48] Patriarchal discourses have justified women's subordination on the basis of the view that, with monthly cycles seemingly tied to those of the moon and the sea, and the ostensible naturalness of birthing, women's bodies and spirits are more closely tied to nature than to culture. Women of all races have also been constructed as animal-like in their lesser intelligence and limited abilities to reason compared to men, a conclusion that in turn justifies women's exclusion from power.

Feminist animal studies emphasizes the importance of seeing the connections between the oppression of women and other people and nonhuman animals. Violence against animals normalizes violence against humans, especially women who have been constructed as animal-like in the sense that they are voiceless and victimizable.[49] Like animals, women have endured a long history of being silenced, devalued, and subjected to violence. Women's bodies have been commodified and butchered like animals', leaving both women and animals to occupy spaces as objects rather than subjects.[50] The suffering of women and animals is justified through claims about their lack of reason and inherent violability—claims that are used to justify violence against and exploitation of all women and that make poor women and women of color uniquely vulnerable to violence.[51]

Volunteering with animals is powerfully gendered and reflects women's socialization to care for others, as well as their particular familiarity with the vulnerabilities and abuses animals experience.[52] Women volunteers also build queer intimacies with shelter animals—queer in that they deviate from the norms of heterosexual family life in the United States through their fluidity and lack of commitment and the particular types of physical intimacy.[53] For volunteers, these forms of kinship and multispecies intimacy typically involve only adults and animals: almost all women volunteers who have children are retirees whose children are adults, and no active volunteer had a young child or gave birth during the period of research. This is not to say that animals become "substitute children," as is often implied about child-free women who are guardians to companion animals. Rather, women volunteers at PAW develop preferred and voluntary relationships with animals both because they find these relationships more satisfying than those with humans and as a way to maintain connection to other adults and to be part of a purposeful community of caring.[54]

In the following chapters, gender emerges as important in at least four ways. First, women constitute almost all volunteers at PAW, as well as almost all rescuers. (By *almost all*, I mean that during the research period I was aware of four men who were regular PAW volunteers, compared to several dozen women; I met the same number of men involved in dog rescue and dozens of women.) This gender composition tells us a great deal about women's social roles and about their caregiving relationships with companion animals. Second, these women form various bonds with shelter animals and engage in queer practices of kinship and intimacy, practices that fall outside the usual ordering of sex, intimacy, and reproduction.[55] Third, animal sheltering is concerned with animal reproduction, particularly the purported need to curb the population of surplus companion animals, which in turn involves the assertion of human control over animals. Reproduction is a routine site of conflict between the shelter and the human community it serves, and it reflects gendered and racialized meanings of both human and animal bodies. Finally, ideologies about animality and Black and brown men's masculinities link these men to particular kinds of animals and particular types of relationships with animals.

In spite of the centrality of gender in human-animal relationships, the key linkages between the exploitation of women and of animals, and the particular role women have taken on in animal rights activism, feminist animal studies remains marginal within feminism, just as animal studies remains largely peripheral in many disciplines in the social sciences and humanities. The marginalization in scholarship and other social institutions of the study of animals as sentient and exploited subjects also mirrors the resistance to the study of women and their subjugation. This marginalization is the outcome of anthroparchy and misogyny: too often, mainstream masculine academia dismisses feminist animal studies as overly emotional or sentimental or political or feminine, while feminist scholars dismiss animal studies as less valuable because it focuses on nonhuman animals rather than on human animals. The only way for us to move forward in our relationships to nonhuman animals—and to all that we construct as "natural" more broadly—is to continue interrogating how human practices and ideologies toward animals reify and reinforce our practices and ideologies toward different groups of humans. We cannot expect to abolish prisons or to reduce gender-based (or any) violence in a society that cages and tortures billions of animals. The liberation of people will not be achieved without the liberation of animals.

Examining our relationships with animals, and especially our preoccupation with delineating what is natural and what is aberrant, can also produce fruitful frameworks for exploring dynamics among humans. Discourses of what is natural and unnatural are wielded in different ways to oppress particular populations. Similar to trans, disabled, and other humans whose bodies do not conform to dominant expectations, those animals at PAW who violate human expectations of companion animal behavior are seen as aberrant, and all animals are seen as needing a human—that is, a more rational, powerful, competent animal—to lead them. Ultimately, women, people of color, the poor, the disabled, gender-nonconforming humans, and companion animals all occupy what Kim calls a borderland between human and animal, "a fraught zone of ambiguity, menace, and transgression," and thus are rendered particularly vulnerable to violence and exclusion.[56]

The analytic and empirical connections between the exploitation and marginalization of human minorities and animals are overwhelmingly abundant. Yet our entrenchment in carnism—the powerful ideology that legitimizes our consumption of animals, especially in the form of meat— makes it deeply challenging for feminists, antiracists, anticapitalists, and other liberationists to see these connections.[57] My goal with this book is not to shatter carnism: a good deal of writing and activism has already sought to do that.[58] But I do hope to show readers the connections between different forms of social inequalities as they exist in a space occupied primarily by animals, where humans and animals share in marginalization. I destabilize the idea that animals are objects and reveal one of many social milieus in which animals' fates hinge on the replication of human inequalities. Throughout this work, I query how impounded animals are situated within human struggles for power and also how the very conditions of their confinement reflect a particular set of worldviews about animal care, human-animal relations, and incarceration. Throughout, I move away from human exceptionalism, or the belief that humans are inherently different from nonhuman animals and therefore more deserving of survival than nonhuman animals.

I explore these complexities of species, race, and gender through a feminist multispecies ethnography, or an ethnography that "centers on how a multitude of organisms' livelihoods shape and are shaped by political, economic, and cultural forces," particularly those forces that distribute power and resources unequally on the basis of race, class, gender, and/or species.[59] Multispecies ethnographers focus on multispecies encounters, or those sites where various types of animals (human and non-) interact and often cocreate social worlds. Through these interactions, human and nonhuman animals engage with one another and may even form particular relationships, like kinship bonds.[60]

Multispecies ethnography becomes an intersectional feminist project by attending to issues of power and inequality within human-animal relationships at both individual and structural levels. A feminist approach opens doorways to querying how human-animal relationships are raced, classed, and gendered; how the race, class, and gender associations of both humans and animals shape their life chances; and how identities of race, class, gender, and/or species are deployed in efforts to resist institutional power. A feminist approach also carefully attends to issues of power in examining how human and nonhuman animals cocreate social spaces.[61]

One important tool in turning away from human exceptionalism and toward embracing feminist multispecies ethnography is a commitment to witnessing animals and integrating their knowledges and experiences into the analysis.[62] Reflecting feminist concerns with relations of power and how they are reproduced, witnessing, which deliberately engages with animals emotionally, offers a political alternative to observation. Rather than seeking to record and categorize behavior, witnessing asks the researcher to probe what the animal is communicating.[63] How are they feeling? How are they communicating this feeling? What do they care about? To whom are they bonded, human or nonhuman? How are their lives part of the social world around them?

Witnessing involves a moment of recognition of nonhuman animals in ways that draw our attention to the power imbalance between human and nonhuman animals and require us to rethink our multispecies lifeworlds.[64] It moves away from epistemological anthropocentrism and epistemic violence to develop knowledge projects grounded in animal perspectives.[65] Rather than looking away from painful or uncomfortable moments, witnessing asks that we consider how animals came to be in situations that cause pain or discomfort. In this way, witnessing bridges the individual and the structural—so it moves us beyond bearing witness to another's life to an explicitly political project of trying to change the conditions of that life.

Witnessing also resists the erasure of individual animals: in a shelter like PAW, where over fifteen thousand to twenty thousand animals passed through each year during my fieldwork, it's relatively easy for the impounded animals to become part of a faceless mass and for those who interact with them to see them as "a population of refugees rather than as individual pets."[66] This is referred to as "scale-blocking," which involves focusing on the general and on the broader pattern to avoid the immediate, the individual, the intimate.[67] Witnessing, in contrast, requires being deliberately present with the intimate and purposefully seeking connection and seeing each of these animals—something that I no doubt did imperfectly but always tried to do. In so doing, witnessing builds on entangled empathy, or "a type of caring perception focused on attending to another's experience of wellbeing . . . [and] an experiential process involving a blend of emotion and cognition in which we recognize we are in relationships with others and are called upon to be responsive and responsible in these relationships by attending to another's needs, interests, desires, vulnerabilities, hopes, and sensitivities."[68]

Witnessing importantly attends to the political potential of emotion. Emotions and the emotional connections between human and nonhuman animals can be transformative, propelling people to engage in efforts to protect animals. Too often, feminist animal studies (and animal studies in general) have been dismissed as "soft" and overly emotional. This accusation reflects sexist beliefs about what constitutes "real" knowledge *and* negates the critical role emotions play in humans' massive web of relationships with nonhuman animals, and in our lifeworlds in general. People have strong feelings about nonhuman animals—especially companion animals—and thus emotions figure centrally in this book. That women volunteers working to reform a masculinist animal welfare system most often express emotions only drives home how deeply embedded gender and sexism are in the dismissive views many hold of those who advocate for nonhuman animals.

Finally, witnessing is about telling stories of what has transpired and who was there. Animal shelters are at once public and opaque: while visitors can see the animals in a shelter (unlike those in the typical American factory farm, where it is generally illegal to enter without permission and where those people who do enter without authorization face severe penalties, thanks to so-called Ag-Gag laws), PAW's most contentious practice—killing animals—takes place outside public view and is thus rendered largely invisible to outsiders, even as it remains a core site of conflict within PAW itself. I worked to see PAW from multiple perspectives, to explore its many nuances, contradictions, and tensions, to make visible the different life forms there, and to recognize the feelings, thoughts, ideologies, and actions of members of different groups (e.g., staff, volunteers, dogs, cats). Many volunteers at PAW commemorate the lives of the animals who died there. For volunteers, witnessing is a way to honor these animals through memory, to give meaning to their existence, and to use memories of them to fuel continued action and resistance. To make visible a life otherwise invisible, to hold onto a memory, and to insist that this life mattered is itself a political act that subverts the dominant discourse in the United States—even in the era of exaggerated pet parenting—of shelter animals as disposable victims.[69]

AN INVITATION TO PAW

In the coming chapters, I invite the reader to join me at PAW as I knew it during the research period from 2014 until the end of 2017. My analysis draws on my experiences as a participant-observer at PAW, where I served as a volunteer. I first began volunteering at PAW in the winter of 2012 and continued to do so after finishing fieldwork; I limit the period of active research to 2014–17. I had not started out intending to conduct research at PAW; rather, as I became embedded in the shelter environment, I began to see issues and patterns that intrigued me and that I wanted to explore further. My fieldwork included spending anywhere from ten to sixty hours per month at PAW, where I participated in the routine activities of the shelter, such as cleaning kennels, helping prospective adopters and rescuers to select animals, and taking dogs out to the designated play areas for individual attention. While I include cats and other types of animals who moved through PAW during my time there, my analysis skews toward dogs. This is primarily because, although I share my home with three indoor cats, I am significantly allergic to cats and found working in the kennel buildings for cats for more than thirty minutes quite immiserating, even when I was using allergy medication. I have spent time with the cats at PAW and have also interacted at length with staff and volunteers who work with cats, but the scope of my experience with cats is more limited than with dogs.

During my fieldwork, I was among a cadre of about a half-dozen volunteers who had continuously volunteered for two or more years. Volunteer attrition at PAW is very high: in my training group of over thirty new volunteer trainees, only two of us were still volunteering six months later, and a year later it was just me. Those volunteers who are long-termers like me generally earn acceptance and respect from other volunteers and from staff. We also accumulate a great deal of knowledge about how the institutions of PAW and SCAS operate, as well as about animal-sheltering practices more broadly. As an astute observer of organizations, I was able to quickly learn the formal and informal rules at PAW, which also increased my status there. Furthermore, I developed strong ties to the local and regional animal rescue community and worked with a program coordinated by an outside nonprofit organization to help attract more adopters to the shelter. Because I was a key player in saving hundreds of dogs, mostly pit bulls, from the shelter, and fostered dozens of dogs myself for two local rescue organizations, I was a credible part of the shelter community and enjoyed a degree of freedom that newer volunteers do not always have—including the freedom to ask tough questions of staff during routine interactions. While at PAW, I became a "go-to" person with issues or complaints other volunteers had, and I often found myself in the role of volunteer spokeswoman. I suspect this happened because of my ability to write and speak eloquently, as well as my willingness to stand up to SCAS management. This was not a role I sought out, although I freely admit that rather than taking a noninterventionist approach to my research site, I continuously attempted to find ways for volunteers to be more effective in advocating for humane shelter practices at PAW and through SCAS. At the same time, in spite of the different forms of capital I brought into the shelter and the long period of my volunteerism, I remained—like all volunteers—disempowered in decision-making at PAW and shut out from staff authority. This book thus represents research from many angles, for I have viewed PAW both as a sociological researcher with a tenured position and a high degree of autonomy in my professional life *and* as a lowly volunteer, relegated to following shelter rules that almost always frustrated my desire to help animals and effect change at PAW.

I was trained in sociology, a discipline that emphasizes impartiality and the need to systematize observations and analysis in ways that distance the researcher from the researched. I deliberately turn away from these tendencies and instead embrace the messy possibilities of being a researcher with complex ties to the social setting I am analyzing. Following Donna Haraway's instruction on how to talk about animals, I gladly embraced becoming "dirty and knowledgeable," letting myself attach to, care about, and develop intimacies with both humans and animals I encountered at PAW.[70] I have the opportunity to bring deep insider knowledge to an analysis that is necessarily rife with contradictions and in which it is not possible for me to be impartial (if it is ever possible for any researcher, which I doubt). My own experience within the social world of the shelter is a powerful starting point for reflection and analysis. Being part of the social world of PAW involves building alliances, making friendships with humans and animals, and pushing for change. While there are volunteers who simply come to the shelter and clean kennels and pet the animals without ever asking for anything to be different, I find it unethical to be aware of and involved in PAW without seeking to change it, particularly given that the social capital I possess makes me aware of other ways of organizing an animal shelter and knowledgeable about how to effect social change. As an outspoken advocate at PAW for improved treatment of animals impounded there, I am undoubtedly a good distance away from the ideal type of the impartial researcher. I was embedded and engaged in multiple ways, through my political commitments to change and my personal relationships with other volunteers and staff.

Throughout my research, I tried to let other volunteers know on an individual basis that I was working on a research project focused on the shelter; only one of them ever asked me to elaborate.[71] I never sought to make any staff member at PAW aware of my intentions as a researcher (although many staff were aware that I was a university faculty member) because I was concerned that if higher-level managers learned I was doing research of any kind they would throw me out; no staff member ever asked me about whether I was conducting research.[72] SCAS has a strong reputation as an opaque organization and has a punitive relationship with volunteers; the retaliatory firing of staff and volunteers (though not for taking notes on routine activities at PAW) before and during my fieldwork reinforced my doubts about being open about my research at PAW. I would have liked to have crafted a more participatory model of research, yet even now, after some time not in the field, I am unable to pinpoint alternatives that would not have posed an undue burden on already overworked staff and volunteers and that would have allowed me to complete this work, which is important. Public institutions, including animal shelters like PAW, need analysis.

I augmented my ethnographic work with public web-based materials, including websites and social media pages, such as those for rescue and animal welfare organizations working at PAW or rescuing animals from PAW. These sources of data didn't play a major role in my research or analysis but were useful in verifying some themes, and I occasionally use materials from these sources in the chapters that follow. I do not include in my analysis observations that took place outside shelter settings, but I recognize that my extrashelter contact with volunteers (such as through private social media and in social settings) likely shaped my ultimate analyses.

In this book, I use pseudonyms to talk about PAW and SCAS, as well as when discussing any volunteer or staff member. I also use pseudonyms for animals when using their real names could be problematic for a human and generally when they were in the care of PAW rather than in my care. While these are imperfect measures in that they do little to ensure relational confidentiality, or the ability of persons depicted in this work to recognize other such persons, they are intended to protect the identities of individuals as much as possible, with a particular concern about retaliation from SCAS.[73] I have been especially attentive to avoid presentation of any details that could be deleterious to the employment or volunteer status of a staff member or volunteer, even when the omission of such details renders my arguments less compelling.

The perspective of this book skews toward those of volunteers and of animals. This is for two reasons. One is that I am a volunteer and the book reflects my experiences, including that my most frequent contact was with volunteers, as volunteers and staff often engage in separate activities. Second, I focus on volunteers and animals because every existing analysis of animal shelters centers staff members and, if animals fall within the research purview at all, considers animals only as objects (for example, research on what characteristics adopters find most important in adopting a companion animal or why companion animals are brought into the shelter). I seek to restore voice and agency to volunteers—who are almost entirely women—and animals, to show the shelter from their point of view. I attend to those groups—volunteers and animals—whose experiences and voices have rarely, if ever, been included in research on animal sheltering.

I recognize that my experiences as a volunteer are not necessarily universal, and to that end I seek specifically to question and examine those experiences that differ from mine. The volunteers at PAW, while overwhelmingly women, were diverse in their backgrounds and in their specific ideas about what should change at PAW, and I strove to be mindful of these differences and to seek to understand their significance.

I also spent a significant amount of time working with, talking to, and observing staff, and their experiences are important to my analysis of PAW. At PAW, staff and volunteers comingled freely in workspaces like the kennels, the many courtyards between buildings, the play areas out with dogs, and the large, shared offices/workrooms where many staff completed their computer-based work. Sometimes I was the only volunteer with a pair or group of staff; other times, I was in a mixed group of staff and volunteers. More rarely was I alone with a staff person. Given that I observed staff crying, complaining about other staff or volunteers not present, laughing, sleeping on the job, having inappropriate cell phone conversations with intimate partners, yelling at each other, and discussing illegal/illicit activities (like drug and alcohol use outside work), I do not believe that my presence had a major influence on staff behavior. I had friendly, open relationships with many staff members (especially lower-level workers) and more distant or even conflictual relationships with a few. Whatever my relationship with individual staff members, I tried to consider the shelter from the perspective of the staff and to account for how and why they followed particular courses of action; in fact, this line of reasoning is what brought me to develop chapter 4, which problematizes how volunteers use their more privileged status outside the shelter in their efforts to undermine staff authority in the shelter. I feel less able to represent the staff perspective than the volunteer perspective (and becoming a staff member would have been an impossibility given my lack of qualifications, disability status, and ethical concerns about taking a paid job from someone who needed it and in an institution actively engaged in killing animals). Still, I work to make staff visible in this book, since all too often lower-income and less-educated people are the ones tasked with the labor of caring for and killing animals. We need to recognize animal care work as classed and raced labor in the way we already recognize child and elder care as gendered and raced labor. Animal care work is underappreciated and undercompensated, reflecting the low standing that animals and the workers who labor with them have in our society.

As a fieldworker, I have sought to move beyond my own experiences to embrace and analyze those of others, both human and animal. An animal shelter is a multispecies contact zone, or a place where species who do not share the same languages or ways of communicating intermingle and are entangled with one another.[74] Learning to observe nonhuman animals and their interactions with human animals was something quite different from my previous fieldwork experiences focused only on observing humans. Doing so with companion animals may have provided me with particular advantages, yet also created particular pitfalls, as we humans are very quick to assume we "know" dogs and cats. Although we may feel connected to these animals who so often live their lives close to ours, dogs and cats communicate differently than humans, and my fieldwork required learning (and unlearning, and relearning) ways of thinking about animal communication. I have lived my entire life with dogs, and all of my adult life with cats, which I believed helped prepare me for this fieldwork. Still, I found I had to employ new skills to get to know shelter animals, who often approached me and volunteers and staff differently than the companion animals in my home did, and to whom I also often responded differently (including, sometimes, with feelings of fear, revulsion, or pity, feelings I've rarely had for companion animals in my own home).

Ultimately, my approach to multispecies ethnography echoes what Lisa-Jeane Moore and Mary Kosut call intraspecies mindfulness, or "a practice of speculation about non-human species that strives to resist anthropomorphic reflections. It is an attempt at getting at, and with, another species in order to move outside of our human selves—while also recognizing that both 'human and 'other' are cultural constructions."[75] I also had to be open to the many different ways humans communicate with animals and be aware of how observing interactions between humans and animals is different from observing humans with other humans—in part because I can never ask the animal a follow-up question about what an interaction meant to them. Learning to forget my reliance on human language and my socialization in a society that generally adheres to behaviorism, or the idea that behavior is the outcome of conditioning and not of thoughts or feelings, in explaining why animals do what they do has often challenged me and opened up new possibilities for seeing and understanding the thousands of animals I have met, watched, touched, restrained, guided, talked with, held, stroked, kissed, worried about, tried to save, and mourned at PAW.

LOOKING AHEAD

This project exposes regimes of domination that attempt to manage and control the lives of companion animals and people.[76] Throughout the book, I use terms that warrant explanation because some of my usage may be confusing or contentious. First, I call what happens to animals at PAW who are injected with lethal doses of barbiturates to end their lives *killing*. Many workers in the sheltering industry prefer to call this practice euthanasia, while some animal rights supporters might argue in favor of identifying what happens at PAW as murder. Dictionaries agree that euthanasia is the practice of ending human or animal life to relieve incurable pain or suffering. What happens in most animal shelters—and certainly at PAW—does not meet this definition. As I discuss in greater detail in chapters ahead, the overwhelming majority of animals whose lives end at PAW are selected for death because staff feel that they have been there too long or that they have poor chances of adoption or rescue. Much less frequently does PAW receive an animal who is so badly injured or so severely ill that euthanasia is used, and when I discuss such incidents in this book I use the term *euthanasia*. For all other shelter deaths, I do employ the term *killing*. I recognize that *murder* is also a potentially appropriate way to describe these deaths, even though definitions of murder often center on legality, and it is, unfortunately, legal for animal shelters to kill impounded animals. At present, in the United States, companion animals are murderable only *outside* animal shelters. Yet, although very much aware of the analytic slipperiness between killing and murder, I use the term *killing* because it aligns with existing work in the field and in the hopes that it may be less alienating to readers who approach this work from the animal-sheltering industry.[77]

Second, I avoid the use of the terms *pet* and *owner* in favor of *companion animal* and *guardian*. *Pet* has been widely criticized as a belittling and infantilizing term, and it also distances companion animals too much from other animals. *Owner* rightly reflects the property-based model of the human-companion animal relationship in the US. However, turning away from *owner* carries with it the emancipatory possibility that animals may have relationships to humans other than as products or as property.[78] While PAW maintains an ownership culture, as does our broader society, I use *guardian* to decenter and problematize our thinking about the relationship between humans and companion animals with whom we share our lives. When discussing the discourse around irresponsible owners in chapter 3, I do use the language of ownership because that is central to the discourse.

In the subsequent chapters, I invite readers behind the fences at PAW, describing its institutional logics and introducing the staff, volunteers, rescuers, and animals that work or live there. Chapters discuss various outcomes of interactions between the human and nonhuman animals that cross PAW's doorstep, including the narratives spun about humans in the surrounding community, the way death is made sense of and commemorated, responses to breed discrimination, and, finally, resistance to the various forms of control. In the concluding chapter, I reflect on the implications of this multispecies ethnography for rethinking social justice to include

animals. Achieving a society that treats companion animals humanely requires radically rethinking the organization and practices of public animal
shelters like PAW. As long as animal control agencies engage punitively
with lower-income animal guardians, homelessness among companion
animals will continue. The animal-sheltering community must participate
in broader efforts at social change if it wants to continue to reduce or even
eliminate the need for animal shelters and to give dogs like Monster a real
chance at living out their natural lives in a home. If we can't achieve justice
for companion animals like Monster, it is improbable that we will achieve
justice for any kind of animal. Conversely, justice for animals will require
justice for *all* humans and could play a major role in saving the planet from
humans' destructive activities.

2   Helping/Policing/Killing

WHEN I STARTED volunteering at PAW, I had a hard time finding the facility. PAW hides at the end of a bumpy dead-end street in an industrial area with only a small, easy-to-miss sign pointing drivers up the road. The rear of the facility butts up against a high concrete block wall that keeps people and animals away from the adjacent train tracks, and the sides of the property run along a bus depot and truck yards. Staff, volunteers, and members of the public enter the shelter through the lobby. The Impound Window, where people can turn in animals they have found as strays or no longer want at any time of day or night, is located on the outside wall facing the parking lot so people bringing in animals don't actually enter the facility. The rest of us—people working at PAW, those trying to help animals at PAW by volunteering, individuals and families hoping to adopt an animal or with other business at the shelter—walk past those waiting at the Impound Window, into a narrow lobby where staff assist people during business hours.

Beyond the lobby are seven other buildings, six of which house animals. I learned how to navigate these buildings early on as a volunteer, shortcutting through side entrances, massaging a sticky kennel lock, getting the attention of a staff member busy doing something else, and guiding animal bodies as I moved with them through the many sounds and smells that permeate the facility. My work helping kennel attendant Oscar one hot summer afternoon reveals much about the shelter's organization and operations. Summer is always the period of peak intakes, and he and I struggled to catch up with the flow of incoming animals. Without access to the shelter's computer system as a volunteer, I could not enter the information that would become an animal's official record of impound, but I could help Oscar by moving animals from one space into another as they were evaluated, checked for identification, photographed, vaccinated, and placed in kennels.

For impounded animals, the experience of coming to PAW starts with one of two points of entry: either a member of public comes to the shelter and surrenders an animal at the Impound Window, or a field officer picks up an animal as a stray in an SCAS vehicle and brings them back to the shelter. Once at PAW, each animal is subject to the disciplinary power of SCAS, a subjection I learned about in detail during the many hours I spent assisting Oscar and other kennel attendants with the impound process.

Oscar sat in a small office staff called the Impound Room at the far back of the shelter, a space that kennel attendants enjoy retreating to because, while the room has an overwhelming smell of stale animal urine, it also has particularly effective air conditioning and is quiet and private. I moved the animals into the cages in the Impound Room, held them while Oscar photographed them, cajoled them onto the shelter's cold metal scale to document their weight, and wrote their impound numbers on their new shelter-issued plastic collars while Oscar read the numbers off to me from the computer. Most of the animals were cooperative or completely passive. A few tried to scratch or growled at me. Others were elated at my company and licked my face happily or curled purring into my arms. Oscar taught me practical skills not covered in the shelter's volunteer training, like how to swaddle a small dog who was trying to nip, how to move cats between cages without having any physical contact with them, and how to use the shelter's plastic slip leads to make an instant muzzle around a dog's snout. Each of these skills was a tool for managing animal bodies and for preventing injury to me or others.

For every animal, Oscar and I went through the same set of steps. Yet although rote in many ways, Oscar's work was hardly trivial, as the kennel attendant impounding any given animal sets that animal on a particular path at PAW. Assigning characteristics like breed, age, sex, and—for cats— whether an animal is social or feral shapes the life chances of that animal at PAW. Those animals whom intake staff identify as any one of fifteen types of dog breeds SCAS considers "dominant breeds," for instance, will have a different experience at PAW and a lower chance of survival than animals not labeled as such.[1] Cats whom staff classify as feral have almost no chance of exiting the shelter alive.

As I learned from helping with impounds, staff make assessments quickly, focusing on efficiency over accuracy. To establish a cat's age, they give a cursory glance into the cat's mouth; if a cat bites or hisses, kennel attendants like Oscar or sometimes registered veterinary technicians (RVTs) assign an age based on their sense of the animal's overall condition, or label them as having "no age," a tag that can stay with an animal throughout their stay. Kennel attendants are also the first to promote compliance with SCAS's views of health. They or the RVTs, who work in an adjacent office, administer initial vaccines.[2] The kennel attendant also notes any significant health abnormalities, which are subsequently evaluated by the RVTs, who establish if and how the animal's body conforms with, or deviates from, SCAS's norms of health and appearance. The kennel attendant—or the volunteer helping them, like me—takes the animal to a cage and places the kennel card—which includes the animal's photograph, impound number, date of impound, and age, sex, and breed—inside a plastic cover on the door of that cage so that visitors, staff, and volunteers can see the animal's basic information.

At the moment when I closed each cage door to lock in a newly impounded animal, the animal lived under the control of SCAS but as the legal property of their original human guardian. Their remaining time with a legally recognized guardian varies: under California law, animals surrendered by their guardians become the shelter's property after one day, while stray animals with no identification or microchip become shelter property after four days, and stray animals with identification or a microchip after ten days.[3] While the animal is still on their "hold period," SCAS cannot adopt the animal out or put the animal down unless the animal is "irremediably suffering" (a condition not clearly defined in California law). Once the animal becomes SCAS's legal property, the staff at PAW may decide to put the animal down at any time.

As PAW takes in animals and interacts with the public, it engages in multiple activities. One core activity is *helping* animals (and sometimes people) in distress: providing shelter and food to lost or abandoned animals while trying to find them homes, picking up injured and dead animals from roadways, removing wild or free-roaming animals from areas where they are considered hazardous to themselves or others, and offering low-cost vaccinations to companion animals in the community. A second core activity is *policing* human-animal relationships by enforcing who may have what kinds of animals, where, and in what conditions. Field officers and canvassers (the latter of who work for SCAS but do not have offices at PAW) visit neighborhoods and homes to make sure residents are following local regulations and issue citations to those not in compliance. A third activity is managing the population of unhoused animals by *killing* animals whom the shelter sees as surplus, suffering, unsafe, or unadoptable to the community because of health or behavior.

While some of these activities take place in the communities in which PAW is responsible for providing animal control—a general location that staff refer to as "in the field"—PAW's small campus is the nexus of its work of helping, policing, and killing. Previous scholarship that focuses on how workers at animal shelters cope with putting down animals refers to the "caring/killing" paradox that shelter workers must navigate as they both provide care for animals and participate in ending their lives.[4] But such scholarship doesn't explain the origins of this paradox. Why do we have workers who both care for *and* kill animals, particularly in the context of animal shelters, which ostensibly seek to help animals? Here, I explain the antecedents to the caring/killing paradox. I examine helping/policing/killing to make these regimes of domination and their *interconnectedness* visible. The overlaps among helping, policing, and killing are empirical examples of the tensions in biopolitics itself: biopolitics can hinge on domination, exploitation, and violence, but it is also centered on care and providing care.[5]

Helping, policing, and killing operate together as the nexus of three branches of contemporary state power that regulate humans and animals: the welfare state, the carceral state, and anthroparchal state. The welfare state engages in interventions intended to promote the social and economic well-being of a citizenry and to regulate inequality. Welfare state practices include redistributing resources through cash transfers and tax breaks, providing affordable housing to low-income people, serving school lunches to poor children, and feeding and housing companion animals who have been lost or abandoned. The carceral state relies on law and criminal justice, penal institutions, punishment—including caging—and the threat of punishment, and administrative processes to exert control over the population. Carceral state practices include surveilling, policing, prosecuting, shaming, and jailing both people and animals. The anthroparchal state involves a web of state policies and practices that seek to secure and maintain humans' domination over nature, including nonhuman animals.[6] Anthroparchal state practices include the denial of animal personhood and the maintenance of animals as legal property, the building of projects to control or contain nature such as dams and wildlife tunnels, legal protections of agribusiness that facilitate the suffering and slaughter of farmed animals, and the use of caging and shelter killing as solutions to homelessness among companion animals. All three involve control over bodies and efforts to manage behavior—and thus are attempts at subjectification, or self-governance, of both humans and animals.

Staff call PAW a "homeless shelter for animals," invoking an idea of providing safety and basic resources to those in dire need, a temporary stop on the way to a more permanent home. Even PAW's name—"welfare center"—invokes preserving animal welfare. Members of the public, rescuers, and volunteers, however, much more often refer to PAW in carceral terms, calling it a "jail," "prison," "lockup," or "concentration camp." Less commonly, I hear people invoke anthroparchy when they refer to the shelter as "a slaughterhouse." These perceptions point to the overlapping and interdependent operations of the welfare, carceral, and anthroparchal states.

Detailing routine activities at PAW reveals how this animal shelter provides needed help (welfare), polices animals and low-income people of color (carceral), and controls and kills animals in the name of human needs (anthroparchal). While typically examined as separate systems of state power, welfare, carceral, and anthroparchal state power operate together in settings like PAW both to legitimate and to disguise each other. Sometimes it's difficult to establish whether a particular action is one or the other: for instance, when a field officer catches a dog running loose on the street and brings her to the shelter, that officer may be helping the animal by reducing her risk of injury or assisting the community by preventing the dog from slowing traffic or knocking people over on the sidewalk; but the officer is also policing the community and the dog by enforcing the rule that dogs running loose are dogs out of place. The caging and killing are often done in the name of helping; forced sterilization involves subjecting animals to discourses and practices of helping, policing, and killing. In addressing them each in turn, I seek to break down ubiquitous state power over human and animal bodies at PAW into its component parts to understand better how power operates vis-à-vis companion animals. Animal welfare is part of the state and its regimes of domination, and attending to helping, policing, and killing reveals the range of the shelter's work, the scope of its power, and the conflicts that exist within public shelters from the outset. Further, by recognizing PAW's hybridity, I am able to reveal the various (and sometimes contradictory) motives for what PAW does: PAW attempts to ameliorate animal suffering, seeks to police and regulate human-animal interactions, and works to maintain and reinforce human dominance over animals.

In conceptualizing PAW as a hybrid institution, I build on the work of critical geographers who have explored the similarities between carceral institutions for human and nonhuman animals. Karen Morin, for instance, examines similarities between prisons, zoos, execution chambers, and slaughterhouses, pointing to ways that these institutions share key logics of domination and violence.[7] Animal shelters as institutions also share many similarities with these other institutions. In zoos, prisons, and animal shelters, humans or animals are kept in cages under the auspices of maintaining the safety of the public and the lines of sight of guards/keepers/attendants. The caged people and animals lose the ability to engage in normal social interaction or activity and suffer from isolation and sensory deprivation. They experience intense surveillance with little or no privacy. They are forced to forfeit virtually all social rights. These institutions all operate in relative secrecy, with the court system often proving to be the only meaningful pathway for reform. Incarcerated humans and animals experience a type of social death, becoming "completely unmoored from social life and conditions that make for a live-able life," and often also literal death.[8] The animals are subject to logics of intensive confinement—and therefore the attendant corporeal experiences—that are strikingly similar to those of mega-hog and -cow farms, including enclosure and partitioning, surveillance, discipline, and record keeping.[9] Once a dog or cat is impounded at PAW, they are immediately exiled from any normal life for either species.

However, even as this social and physical death occurs, it is done in the name of human and/or animal welfare. Here we see the welfare, carceral, and anthroparchal state collide.

THE ORGANIZATION OF PAW

PAW is part of a nested structure that asserts control over the relationships between humans and (mostly) domesticated animals in its service area. Local policy makers—including the statewide, county, and city governments—create codes and laws that SCAS in turn is tasked to enforce. Managers at SCAS's regional office then translate those codes and laws into agency-wide policies with a set of desired practices. These are transmitted to SCAS's multiple shelters, including PAW, through policy manuals, training, and routine verbal and email contact. The director of SCAS is the ultimate authority and arbiter of disputes about animal care (other than the courts, and members of the public do periodically engage in legal struggles with SCAS). The director visits the shelter occasionally; more frequently, the regional director, who is one step down from the director in the hierarchy and who is responsible for overseeing PAW and other SCAS shelters in the vicinity, communicates with PAW's manager and visits the shelter. Lower-level staff and volunteers rarely have direct contact with the director or regional director but may occasionally appeal to one or both of them, particularly via email, regarding an issue with a specific animal or a policy practice at PAW. Volunteers more regularly hear from SCAS's system-wide volunteer coordinator, although mostly via general announcements to all volunteers. Personal emails from the system-wide volunteer coordinator occur only if the volunteer has made a complaint to them or if the volunteer has allegedly violated policy practice.

Through the multiple layers of governance, individuals interpret and reinterpret codes, laws, and policies in various ways that result in variation in how specific staff, or staff at different facilities, execute SCAS policies. The highest authority on site at PAW is the general manager. That person sets the tone for the shelter, but underlings may still resist their decisions. Further, when the general managers change, practices often do too. One general manager at PAW, for instance, allowed specific volunteers to interview and approve prospective adopters for dogs that the shelter designates as dominant breeds; although there was no change in SCAS policy, the manager's successor rescinded this privilege.[10] Another general manager implemented a practice that dogs should be fed only once per day to reduce the amount of staff time spent feeding, a practice that was abandoned by the next general manager. I conducted fieldwork during a period of high turnover among the managers at PAW. A long-term manager left a few months after I began fieldwork and was succeeded by a series of interim managers and two managers who were meant to be permanent but each lasted barely a year at PAW.

The organization of PAW and SCAS is bureaucratic and hierarchical. Everything is documented: times are clocked in and out; health and behavior notes on dogs and interactions with the public are documented in the computer system. Policies and procedures are extensive, and most staff follow them to the letter. Kennel attendants occupy the bottom rungs among those staff who work with animals, while clerical staff occupy the bottom of the hierarchy among office workers; however, for both classes of workers there is a short career ladder, so that some kennel attendants and clerical workers hold higher ranks than others. Increases in rank are generally associated with higher compensation and more responsibilities. Field officers and midlevel managers have greater authority and responsibility than kennel attendants or clerical workers; most midlevel managers supervise these other workers. At the top of PAW's hierarchy is the general manager. Irrespective of their role at PAW, all staff members are involved in different ways in the projects of helping and policing. Only some workers are directly involved in the work of killing, but all workers participate in validating the idea that PAW must use killing as a strategy to manage its population of animals.

HELPING

PAW is an open-admission shelter responsible for animal control services in nearly two dozen primarily lower- and working-class bedroom communities of Los Angeles with many residents who are nonwhite or recent immigrants or both. PAW's service area stretches across nearly three hundred square miles that are home to about half a million people and, using conservative population estimates of animals, around 290,000 dogs and *at least* 320,000 cats (although I would estimate much higher given the high rate of feral or community cats in this area).[11] This is a substantial area to cover, and with fifty employees and a physical space that was in a state of deterioration when I began in 2012, the shelter faces very real constraints in providing services.[12]

PAW's service area has a diverse population with an overrepresentation of Latinx and Asian American people compared to the City of Los Angeles. Of the seventy-five thousand people who reside in the city in which PAW is located, which is one of the more affluent the shelter serves, almost 80 percent are Latinx (compared to 38 percent statewide and 47 percent in the City of Los Angeles), 16 percent are Asian (compared to 13 percent statewide and 11 percent in the City of Los Angeles), and barely 4 percent are white (compared to 38 percent statewide and 30 percent in the City of Los Angeles). Forty-five percent of residents are foreign born, compared to about a quarter of California residents as a whole and just under 40 percent in the City of Los Angeles. Home values, educational attainment, and household incomes are lower than state averages and far lower than in wealthier, whiter suburbs of Los Angeles.

The city that produces the highest rate and number of intakes for PAW has 115,000 human residents, only 4 percent of whom are white, and their median annual income is more than $20,000 below the statewide median. Here 50 percent of residents were born outside of the United States, and nearly as many identify themselves as not speaking English well. The poverty rate is 24 percent, compared to a statewide rate of about 17 percent. Volunteers refer to this city as "the stray dog capital of America" because so many dogs come into the shelter from this town alone. I have never driven through this community without seeing at least a few free-roaming dogs, something I never see in the more affluent community where I live ten miles away.

PAW is service provider, enforcer, and arbiter over life and death to the communities for which it is responsible. Central to PAW's mission and work is helping animals who do not have homes. This help includes providing shelter, food, water, and health care—so meeting companion animals' basic needs as they await another home. The shelter also helps reunite some companion animals with their guardians and facilitates new guardians' bringing companion animals into their homes. Services for existing animal guardians are limited to providing a monthly low-cost vaccination clinic at which demand regularly exceeds supply, as well as providing a physical site for people to comply with municipal regulations pertaining to their companion animals, such as licensing.

SCAS managers assert that one of their primary goals is caring for animals in a humane way. While companion animals are near the top of the species hierarchy, those in shelters lose the status conferred upon them through their connection with a human guardian; as members of common species, they also are not afforded the level of specialized care typical in accredited zoos.[13] Further, at a shelter like PAW, where most of the animals come from low-income communities, the animals experience a higher degree of confinement and a lower quality of care than animals impounded at other California shelters serving higher-income populations.

Whether PAW *is* helping impounded animals or people is subject to debate within and outside the shelter. Many volunteers with whom I interacted believe that dogs are better off in the shelter than they are on the street; as volunteer Maria asserted, "At least here [at PAW] they are safe—they won't get hit by a car or starve." Others feel that free-roaming dogs and most especially free-roaming cats have a better life than dogs and cats impounded at PAW and that their chances of survival and finding a home are just as good, if not better, than for animals impounded at PAW, who face high levels of policing and the risk of shelter death. Volunteer Annie, one of the most dedicated volunteers working with cats, routinely expressed frustration with the many people she saw who had trapped feral cats and brought them to the shelter: "Why catch them just so they can be killed here?"

PAW has followed trends in the animal-sheltering industry and moved toward working to find homes for animals the shelter deems adoptable and, as space and resources permit, per SCAS's own determinations. Between the 2011–12 fiscal year and the 2014–15 fiscal year, the death rate at the shelter dropped from 60 percent to 54 percent; by 2016–17, the death rate had dropped substantially further, to 38 percent, although some volunteers and rescuers question these figures.[14] Just as important, the overall intake dropped from 19,744 animals when I started my fieldwork to slightly under 15,000 animals in 2016–17. While a small part of the reduction in intakes can be explained by some cities moving their contracts from SCAS to another shelter system, this cannot account for the full reduction, suggesting that more companion animals are staying in their homes or that more are being adopted into new homes or taken into rescues without ever entering the shelter.

The decrease in shelter killing reflects a number of initiatives, many of which do not stem from PAW itself but do require the permission of SCAS and some degree of cooperation. First, SCAS partnered with a major national animal welfare organization that I call Humane America to offer a web of services, including a mobile spay/neuter clinic that offers low-cost sterilization surgeries to residents of the shelter's service area, a shelter intervention program that works to keep companion animals out of the shelter by reaching out to guardians surrendering animals to discuss other options and provide support such as veterinary vouchers, and a program transporting animals to low-kill or no-kill shelters in other parts of the United States, especially the Pacific Northwest. Simultaneously, several rescue organizations not affiliated with PAW or SCAS began offering low-cost or free spay/neuter surgeries and vaccines through mobile clinics in the area. One of these rescues also engages in community outreach that has been helpful in redirecting to rescue organizations some animals who might have ended up at the shelter as owner surrenders. While volunteers soundly criticize PAW and SCAS for their ineffectiveness in utilizing off-site adoption events, the shelter has participated in some widely publicized adoption events on- and off-site that are sponsored and coordinated by other organizations or businesses, such as the annual No-Kill Los Angeles (NKLA) Super Adoption event in Los Angeles.[15] Participation in these events may also have increased live releases. Taken together, these various initiatives increase availability of services to human guardians of animals, including adoption services, and to animals themselves.

Rescue organizations also take animals from SCAS shelters. SCAS staff state they have aggressively sought out new rescue partners, although I have no evidence to suggest that the rescue rate increased during my research period, other than through Humane America transports, which count toward the total number of animals considered rescued. In fact, many rescuers and volunteers report that the rate of local rescues taking animals from PAW declined as a result of the NKLA initiative, which excluded SCAS shelters from a financial incentive provided to rescue organizations that take animals from other shelters.

Volunteers understand their role as one of service to animals, not service to PAW or SCAS, by helping animals cope better with the conditions of confinement at the shelter and leave the shelter alive. Volunteers eschew staff entreaties to help with cleaning and instead focus on promoting adoptions (for example, by helping adopters, using social media to spread the word about adoptable animals, and working with rescue groups) and on supporting animals by offering companionship and care. Because staff are often too busy to spend time one on one with animals, volunteers are the primary group to take dogs out for time in the shelter's small play areas or to help dogs in the medical ward, who are kept in much smaller cages than other dogs, get out for bathroom breaks. In the cat house, volunteers distribute catnip and cat toys, play with the cats, and, for those cats who enjoy it, pet the cats and offer them attention.

The shelter discourse varies in how much it emphasizes helping or policing. The organizational mission statement speaks of promoting compassionate care and responsible pet ownership; it also repeatedly refers to the purposes of maintaining public safety and enforcing animal welfare law. A tension thus exists between helping animals and maintaining public safety. These two goals generally stand in opposition at PAW, rather than operating complementarily, and public safety trumps helping animals. The discourse of public safety at PAW is primarily employed to explain and justify policing and killing animals rather than helping humans or animals.

Health is another domain in which helping, policing, and killing collide. PAW exercises power in some ways that echo what Foucault identifies as pastoral power, or a power of care.[16] Describing pastoral care through the analogy of a shepherd, Foucault reminds us that a shepherd must care both for each individual animal and for the flock as a whole, a role that creates dilemmas when the interests of the individual and the group collide. Similarly, PAW must make decisions that balance the needs and wants of individual animals with the needs of the population of impounded animals.[17] This can result in controversial and sometimes contradictory actions that are often grounded in the practice of shelter medicine, a specialized type of veterinary care that functions as the key mechanism for regulating biological life in the shelter.[18] Staff members are encouraged to notice and report any signs of illness among impounded animals. Such reports trigger visits from the RVT and possibly the shelter veterinarian, who, on the basis of physical examinations alone (as the shelter has limited diagnostic equipment) determine what an animal may be suffering from and whether that illness poses a threat to others. In this way, animal bodies are subject to constant surveillance of their visible well-being and are policed if they show signs of illness. Many ultimately are killed because the RVTs or veterinarian establish their condition to pose a threat to other animals or, rarely, to the staff.[19]

PAW routinely asserts that the well-being of the population trumps that of individuals: this resulted in thousands of cats and dogs being killed during my fieldwork in a purported effort to control the spread of communicable diseases. Here helping collides with killing, as killing is routinely done in the name of helping, whether to end the suffering of one specific animal or to try to slow the spread of disease.[20] Further, as the following sections on policing and killing reveal, PAW's work is not only about giving care. It is also about confining, caging, punishing, inflicting suffering, denying natural behaviors, repressing resistance, and killing.

POLICING IN THE COMMUNITY

"These people won't let me keep my dog!" the woman wailed in heavily accented English. Fellow volunteer Alice grimaced and asked the woman to elaborate. "They say I can't have them all. Not more than three! But they are small! And quiet!" she replied. "How many dogs do you have?" Alice asked gently. "Just four," answered the woman, her voice lowering as she sensed Alice's engagement with her. Alice pursed her lips, thinking. "This happens a lot," she said. "Do you have anyone else who could take your dog? A friend, or a family member?" The woman shook her head, her eyes filling with tears again. "No, I already asked everyone . . ." she said, her voice trailing. "I just don't understand, because there is no problems [sic] with the dogs. Just too many."

PAW has a range of administrative tools at its disposal to enforce particular practices of animal keeping. The local state makes a normalizing judgment about what an appropriate number of companion animals is per household through ordinances limiting the number of animals per household. If SCAS agents discover a household is in excess of the legal limit, SCAS may seize the surplus animal(s), as happened to the distraught woman that Alice tried to help at the shelter. Like welfare state agencies focused exclusively on humans, PAW is a site for imposing dominant animal practices on animal guardians, although the anthroparchal state largely permits humans to do as they wish with animals considered their property. While limited by laws and ordinances that empower animal guardians, the shelter has capacities to enforce desired norms of animal keeping through formal and informal mechanisms and practices. SCAS and its staff at PAW are engaged in the work of examining the animal practices of the public and making judgments about members of this public that sometimes result in disciplinary action being taken. Thus those animal guardians whose irresponsibility is visible can be subject to interventions, including fines and the seizure of their companion animals.

Policing work at and by PAW is considerable and involves regulating how people treat animals and how animals treat people. SCAS and the field officers at PAW are responsible for enforcing codes related to animals across this geographically large area with a diverse and often disadvantaged population. Common issues include too many animals at one address per local code, free-roaming dogs and cats, unlicensed animals, and complaints about noise or odors from neighbors.[21] The shelter also handles cases of neglect, hoarding, and abuse. Neglect and hoarding are relatively common, although the shelter can do very little to help neglected animals other than encourage a guardian to change their practices. Many forms of neglect are not considered abuse under the law, and prosecution of cases that involve failure to provide veterinary care or grooming is rare. Hoarding cases occurred a few times each year while I was at PAW. Some of these cases were clearly ones of overwhelmed guardians, like a woman in her eighties who was given a pair of rabbits by neighbors when they moved away and soon had over twenty rabbits in her small home. Abuse cases involving animals who were brought to the shelter rarely occurred during my fieldwork. Of the few cases of abuse that I am aware were prosecuted, most involved extreme neglect; only one that I know of involved someone deliberately trying to hurt an animal.

Staff and volunteers are often frustrated that codes and laws tend to set a very low bar for animal care. Most staff and seemingly all volunteers find the practice of keeping dogs entirely outdoors problematic and irresponsible, yet it is not a violation of any law or code in PAW's service area to keep a dog living entirely outdoors as long as the animal has access to food, water, and shelter. This means that even though PAW can and does refuse to allow dogs to be adopted into homes when it knows the animals are intended to be kept exclusively outdoors, field officers are basically powerless to assist dogs who are already living entirely outdoors.

So-called yard dogs constitute the largest group of victims of guardians whom staff and volunteers see as so-called irresponsible owners, who are the focus of the next chapter. Forced to live entirely outdoors, these dogs often seem to develop barrier aggression (that is, aggression when they see or hear dogs and/or people on the other side of a fence) or other forms of aggression toward other dogs or people. They are usually bored and understimulated, so they may bark incessantly or dig holes, chew through fences, or find other ways to escape their enclosures and bother (or even hurt) others. They are often physically neglected, arriving at the shelter with ears that have no fur due to fly strike.[22] Many have fleas or mange as well. They of course don't know how to walk on leash, are not housebroken, and have no experience living indoors, making them quite undesirable to most prospective adopters. They are often dumped at the shelter when they are "too old" to serve as guard dogs anymore or when age or medical neglect leads to serious health issues their owners don't want to or can't pay to treat. Staff and volunteers look upon the guardians of these dogs with particular disdain, arguing that someone must be completely indifferent to an animal's needs and suffering to leave them outdoors around-the-clock. "Bringing your dog into the house at night is free," one staff member groused to me after negotiating with a guardian reclaiming his German Shepherd whose ear tips were naked and partially missing from fly strike, thus stressing that poverty is not a reason to keep dogs outdoors.

When enforcing laws and codes, staff use mechanisms of the law and the legal system such as anticruelty statutes and the district attorney's office to conduct cruelty or neglect cases, which can result in clear disciplinary actions, including fines or imprisonment. Much more commonly, staff give guardians of companion animals instructions on issues guardians need to "correct" in order to be deemed worthy of reclaiming their companion animal. This often involves securing their yard or seeking veterinary or grooming care for their animal. When a guardian's home must be modified to reclaim their animal, SCAS field officers visit the guardian's home to ensure that changes have been made through a practice known as property checks, a process that can take weeks. For veterinary or grooming care, guardians typically need to submit paperwork to SCAS showing they have completed the tasks asked of them. In all of these situations, guardians are subjected to normative judgments about the standard of care to be provided.

It is not uncommon for guardians simply to surrender their animal to PAW rather than attempt to negotiate the requirements imposed upon them. Some guardians also misunderstand what is at stake or who is asking for compliance. The staff who work in the field, like many classes of SCAS workers, have an air of authority thanks to their formal uniforms and badges. I met one man at the shelter who was visiting a dog he had surrendered to PAW. Puzzled about his relinquishment, since he seemed to care deeply for his dog, I asked him why he had given up his animal. He replied that "the policeman who came to my house told me it would be better for me to just sign him over." That "policeman" was, in fact, a PAW field officer, not a police officer, responding to a barking complaint; the man interpreted him as an agent of the law and was persuaded that giving up his dog was a better route than trying to resolve the barking issue.

An order to comply, an enforceable legal order, thus provides staff with a mechanism for addressing concerns about an animal's welfare when staff do not believe, on the basis of their understanding of the law, that the case for neglect is strong enough for the district attorney to take action. For the owner, these warnings are an indicator of their failure to care for their companion animal in a way seen as humane and appropriate by the state. For example, when an owner came to PAW to reclaim a Shih Tzu mix—a breed of long-haired small dog that requires frequent brushing and hair trimming—who was so poorly cared for that her fur had grown into massive mats, making it difficult for her to see, walk, or even go to the bathroom, staff returned the animal to the guardian with an order to comply requiring that the guardian take the dog to a groomer within twenty-four hours. (While poor grooming may sound like a trivial matter, during my fieldwork at PAW I became aware of several cases of Shih Tzus, Lhaso Apsos, and similar long-haired dogs who had to have limbs amputated at the shelter because the blood supply to their limb was strangled by matted fur. Staff thus see inadequate grooming as a potentially serious threat to the health of an animal.) While it's not known to me how often guardians comply with these orders, PAW communicates the expectation and conveys to the guardian that they are failing to provide adequately for the companion animal in their care.

PAW also polices the activities of animals themselves, and it is here that its work is often the most punitive. According to PAW, the only appropriate site for an animal is in or on the property of a human guardian or in another area designated for companion animals such as a dog park. Dogs are not to roam free, and while cats may do so, if they are injured, bother neighbors in some way, or are (mis)identified as feral, they also risk impoundment and, in the case of feral cats, certain death at PAW. PAW's strong stance against free-roaming animals is the norm in the animal-sheltering industry, whose origins lie in controlling and culling free-roaming companion animals and livestock.[23] Companion animals who are off their guardian's property are bodies out of place, markers of disruption and, in PAW's view, potential threats to themselves, to other animals, and, most especially, to people.[24] They thus must be stopped and brought to the shelter for their own protection and that of the community. Once the animals are there, shelter staff may intervene in animals' relationships with their guardians and require that the guardians meet specific requirements to reclaim their companion animals, a process I discuss further in the next chapter. Once the animals enter PAW, they become subject to the institution's methods of assessment of health and behavior, and the guardian—if they appear—becomes subject to the institution's assessment of moral fitness for keeping an animal companion. The outcomes of these assessments can jeopardize an animal's chance of returning to a human guardian, or even continuing to live at all.

POLICING IN THE SHELTER

Policing takes place inside the shelter as well as outside it. The physical space of PAW is organized around specific functions that reflect the nexus of helping/policing/killing: (1) to house homeless animals; (2) to facilitate the release of live animals to guardians, adopters, or rescues that PAW determines are appropriate parties for animal guardianship; (3) to complete tasks related to the regulation of relationships between humans and (mostly) companion animals; and (4) to kill animals deemed surplus, problematic, or otherwise unnecessary.[25] For visitors to the shelter, the most striking aspect of the physical space of the shelter is the caging. Visitors pass cages filled with dogs who are often barking, pacing, or jumping at the kennel doors. The cat kenneling area is lined with stacked cat cages. Coming to the shelter is a visual, auditory, and olfactory experience: visitors see an unusually large number of dogs and cats in a small overall space, hear the sounds of animals and humans comingling at often painful volumes, and experience the stench from animal feces, urine, vomit, and wet fur.

The practices of caging and administration are central to maintaining human control over this environment and enforcing PAW's expectations of animals and people. Caging involves keeping impounded animals in tightly confined spaces. That they are in a cage is ostensibly for their own protection and to minimize the risk of injury to workers (paid and volunteer) and members of the public—so their welfare and that of the public are used as a basis to justify the caging of animals. That their cages are small is to minimize construction and maintenance costs (including the complexity of daily cleaning), maximize the number of animals who can be kept, enhance the ease with which the kennels can be observed, and increase the efficiency with which animals can be cared for (i.e., fed, taken out, etc.). Caging facilitates the shelter staff's work of administration, which includes knowing which animal is where at all times and how long they have been there, information that guides the performance of routine activities like feeding, and of killing.

The general design at PAW reflects the mid-twentieth-century vision of the animal shelter as a place to store wayward animals for a few days only. The shelter's location at the end of a narrow and eroding dead-end road in an industrial neighborhood suggests the low priority that public access played in the original construction of the shelter in the 1950s and the limited funding allocated for a shelter. The lot on which PAW sits is tiny, hemmed in by trains passing behind and transit and truck yards on the remaining three sides, presumably all spewing diesel particulate into the shelter's air.

PAW itself is a compound, with nine buildings and multiple sheds and storage containers. The buildings are connected by a maze of driveways and pathways that control outsiders' access into human workspaces and areas with animals. There is remarkably little green space: almost every surface is paved over, and the small play areas for dogs are lined with artificial grass or dirt. Within the compound, different areas are designated for specific activities, with well over half of the space dedicated to the caging of animals.

PAW has four kennel buildings for dogs and two for cats. Excluding restricted areas, the kennels are open to visitors for seven hours each day, seven days a week (except on state holidays). Three of the kennel buildings for dogs are built identically, and a fourth, somewhat newer building, shares the same general design with a few minor differences. The dog kennels have epoxied cinderblock exterior and interior walls and cement floors. Each building has a central corridor leading down the middle, and the kennels face the interior hallway on one side ("the inside") and the outdoors ("the outside") on the other. This means staff, volunteers, and visitors can look into the kennels from both the inside and the outside, and access to the individual kennels is also possible from both sides for those with keys. The two halves of each kennel are separated by an opening that can be closed with a guillotine door controlled by a weighted pulley on the interior side. This allows staff and volunteers to confine a dog to either the indoor or outdoor half of the kennel, as is necessary for cleaning of the kennels and sometimes for other reasons; on a few occasions, the shelter was so full that one large dog would be housed on the inside half of a kennel and another on the outside half.

The kennel doors are made out of metal and chain link, while the side walls dividing the kennels are cinderblock for about four feet with chain link up to the ceiling; very tall or athletic dogs can attempt to jump at each other at the chain-link top. Gutters run along the floor just outside both sides of the kennels so that when the kennels are cleaned, dirty water flushes down the gutters to an often-clogged main drain. To enter or exit a kennel, staff, volunteers, and animals must step over the gutter and the lower lip of the kennel door, which is about eight inches high. As a volunteer, I quickly learned that most smaller dogs have to be carried to negotiate this lip, whereas many larger dogs would jump out of their kennel happily to walk with me but upon return would refuse to go back in so that I (sometimes with the help of another volunteer or staff member) would have to heave them back into the kennel.[26] Buildings A and C each have one exterior side that does not face other kennels, so these are the preferred sides for taking animals out; all other kennel doors in A, B, and C face another row of kennels, so when a dog is being taken in or out, the barking from other dogs can be very loud.

Companion and feral cats are segregated into two separate buildings. The cats who are friendly with people inhabit cages that are roughly two-foot cubes, stacked from the floor to close to the ceiling in a building known as the Cat House. Rabbits, guinea pigs, and other small pets—including reptiles, who are frequently at the shelter—are also kenneled here. The building is just a single room with its own sink and feeding area. Although the cages are small, the room is bright and quite airy. One of the exterior walls has garage door–type panels so that the Cat House can be opened to the outdoors to let in fresh air and give at least some of the cats exposure to natural light and something new to see. During the hotter months, the building has excellent air conditioning, making it a popular resting spot for volunteers. Several times during my fieldwork, it was closed to anyone but staff because of outbreaks of the highly contagious and often fatal viral feline disease panleukopenia.

Feral cats are sent to an area in a building referred to as Building E, which houses multiple spaces, including the RVT office, the Impound Room, a small grooming room, the area for sick and injured small dogs and cats, and the room designated for shelter killing, or the Euth Room. This building is kept locked and inaccessible to the public; except for the Euth Room, volunteers may enter this building. The feral cats are caged in a room without air conditioning, so the air can be stifling in hot weather, even with industrial fans blowing. The narrow, awkward spaces of Building E are a high-traffic zone because animals move from the room where staff process their impound through to the office where the RVTs conduct a veterinary check. Shelter medicine experts urge shelters not to allow cats and dogs to see or even hear one another because of the stress such interspecies encounters can cause cats; at PAW, however, cats are regularly exposed to the sounds and sights of dogs, and this building in particular is a zone of frequent interspecies contact.

Policing the animals at PAW happens through routine interactions. Kennel attendants and sometimes other staff are present on a regular basis in the kennels, where they observe and interact with impounded animals. Kennel attendants, volunteers, and CalWorks and community service workers also enter the kennels:[27] they come in twice each day for feeding and once each day for cleaning.[28] So at least three times each day animals have the opportunity to bite or lunge at a human, greet them with a wagging tail and a kiss, or ignore them completely. Responses considered aberrant—such as biting or growling—are usually documented in the computer system, although volunteers are loath to report concerns and may not always do so.

Animals at PAW spend almost the entire day, every day, in their cages. Dogs may come out of their kennels to one of the shelter's small play areas if a prospective adopter wants to meet them or if a staff member or volunteer wants to give them a chance to run around. This break in caging normally lasts somewhere between five and thirty minutes. Cats have no such respite: they stay in their cages unless they are being moved to go to the veterinarian.

Even when outside their cages, the animals at PAW have limited freedom of movement, as they are on a leash or in a transit cage. Staff at PAW are trained to approach animals as potential threats, and their first step in dealing with any animal they want to take out of a kennel is threat assessment; while many volunteers reject this approach, staff encourage volunteers to engage with animals the same way. Does the animal show signs of hostility through body language, vocalization, and/or positioning? How does the animal react as the staff or volunteer member advances? Any perceived behavior issues are to be noted in the computer system, which can result in an animal being flagged as difficult, aggressive, and/or unadoptable.

Like police, who are often trained to use a range of tools to defuse confrontations, staff at the shelter are trained to try different approaches with animals who are unwilling to be moved or touched. With small dogs, staff can use towels, wrapping one arm with a towel so that the dog cannot bite through it and using that arm to grab the dog; small dogs who growl, show their teeth, or snap often become completely subdued once they are held. Staff also routinely turn to force, leashing both small and large dogs and simply pulling them along at arm's length. The only leashes used at PAW are slip leads, or single-piece ropes that slide over an animal's head and put pressure on the neck if the animal pulls away from the human at the other end of the line. When animals are significantly resistant to following the lead of the human, they will start to choke. Sometimes two staff members will leash an unruly large dog, one on each side with one leash each, and keep the animal almost suspended between them. This prevents the dog from being able to bite either staff member. The shelter also has rolling cages in a range of sizes so that a dog can be tricked or scared into entering the cage and then can be moved from one location to another in the rolling cage.

While considered least desirable because the sight of it upsets volunteers and some members of the public, catchpoles, the traditional tool of dog catchers that features a wire lasso at the end of a metal pole, can also be used, enabling staff members to catch a dog around the neck and then move the dog, but with the dog at a distance from them of at least five or six feet. According to staff I have asked about it, catchpoles are widely used in the field; in the shelter, I saw staff use catchpoles in only a handful of instances. Volunteers learn to use a catchpole only if they receive a purportedly mandatory safety training, as a catchpole can be used as a tool to stop a dog attack.[29]

Each of these approaches involves the assertion of human dominance over animals. PAW thus follows prominent masculinist models of human-animal relationships in which humans are to be the master or, in the gentler, seemingly more species-appropriate language of contemporary "dog psychology," the pack leader. PAW staff never use treats as lures or rewards because treats are understood as being a potential trigger for aggressive behavior. Nor are animals ever given the opportunity to consent to being leashed, caged, or uncaged. Although staff and volunteers may be trying to help an animal by moving them, that movement also involves the maintenance of human control through watching, containing, and leashing. Animal bodies are at the mercy of what staff and volunteers want to do with them.

The computer system helps organize information used to help, police, and kill animals. The location and history of each animal at PAW are documented in the computer system, which all staff can access but which almost no volunteers can.[30] The computer system also holds notes about each animal's health and behavior, and each day the command staff reviews a list of animals who have a health or behavior issue, as well as a list of animals by the number of days they have been at the shelter. These two lists are used to establish which animals will be "reviewed" on what date; after the review, animals are usually killed. The kennel manager (who is ranked lower than the shelter manager) is also expected to walk through the kennels at the beginning of their shift and make notes in the computer system about any issues they observe with the animals. The computer system thus plays an important role in facilitating the policing and killing of animals.

While volunteers are generally resigned to being denied access to the computer system, they have been more resistant when PAW managers have attempted to curtail their access to physical spaces that animals occupy. Space is political at PAW, and therefore a site of conflict, because staff and management restrict who may be where when. This limits the freedoms of volunteers, the public, and the impounded animals and restricts the capacity of volunteers to help impounded animals while it increases the capacity of shelter staff to police and to kill without interference. During the period of fieldwork, the use of space at PAW changed frequently, as did access to space.

For example, one spatial shift during my fieldwork was in where and how quarantined dogs were placed. When I first began volunteering at PAW, the back half of Building A was used to house quarantined dogs. These are dogs who are being investigated as "potentially dangerous dogs" (PDDs) because they have allegedly been involved in biting humans or fighting with other dogs. The quarantine area also includes dogs who are being held as part of a rabies quarantine, again either because of biting others or sometimes because they have been bitten by free-roaming animals, most often coyotes or raccoons. Occasionally, SCAS investigates a cruelty case and must hold a dog as evidence; these animals are also sometimes housed in the quarantine area. When quarantined dogs were housed in Building A, the building was divided in half on the inside, with the back half secured with a locked gate so that members of the public could not walk down the back half of the central corridor. Staff and volunteers had keys that granted them access to the interior corridor. On both the inside and outside, the kennels had reinforced steel bars so thick it was difficult even to see the animals in the kennels. Still, volunteers could see and interact with these dogs.

In late 2015, Building D became the new home for these dogs, as well as for dogs slated to go on rescue transports, and the entire building became locked and inaccessible to the public and to volunteers. No changes were made to the kennel design, but SCAS erected an eight-foot-high chain-link fence around the outside of the building so that it was no longer possible to even see the animals who were in Building D. The closing of Building D to the public and volunteers created substantial consternation among volunteers because it was unclear how members of the public seeking lost pets would find their companions if they could not access a quarter of the impounded dogs. Volunteers also wanted to be able to document the existence of these dogs—including through photographs and video they would place on social media—and try to help them if appropriate, but they were barred from entering without a staff member accompanying them (a policy many volunteers violated, since this was easy to do given that our general kennel keys opened the now-locked door to Building D). About a year later, without explanation, Building D became unlocked again, although the chain-link enclosure built around the sides of the building remained intact, albeit with no apparent purpose.

Ultimately, access to space—and therefore to animals—is controlled by managerial staff, and volunteers feel that they have few avenues for resisting being shut out of spaces. Being shut out raises a number of issues for volunteers, including concerns about the animals they can't access and the feeling that staff are sometimes arbitrarily asserting control over them. Access to space is closely tied up with the politics of sight. As in Timothy Pachirat's analysis of a slaughterhouse, concealment and visibility work together.[31] On the one hand, the shelter welcomes the public and volunteers into its spaces and in fact is dependent on these visitors to help do the work of caring for animals and to adopt and rescue animals. On the other hand, the shelter operates under a logic of concealment. Modern societies hide that which we find distasteful, such as the killing of companion animals.[32] The Euth Room is thus closed off to volunteers and the public, and, during the time when Building D was closed to volunteers and the public, so were those animals most likely to die at the shelter. Volunteers do sometimes see dead animals, but PAW has worked toward making this less and less likely, recognizing that volunteers' reports to the general public—including through social media—can damage the shelter's reputation.

Time is also implicated in issues of sight: the shelter is closed to the public for seventeen hours out of every twenty-four-hour period, and to volunteers for fifteen hours. During this time, staff members continue their work: the shelter is staffed around the clock, and even key managers have shifts that typically start hours before the shelter opens to the public or to volunteers. The hours when the shelter is closed to the public give the shelter staff time and opportunity to engage in activities PAW and SCAS prefer they conceal. While animals may not be aware of this, their time alone with the staff is when they are most at risk for death or rough handling, or even abuse. Staff generally use the time when the shelter is closed to kill animals and to move difficult dogs, such as those who can be handled only with a catchpole. Staff almost always put animals down during hours when neither the public nor volunteers are present at the shelter. The labor of killing is thus made invisible from those most likely to attempt to interrupt it.

Even when protected from the eyes of the public and volunteers, staff members work under surveillance and can be hailed at any time. All staff carry radios and are accountable to supervisors who may call them with specific requests or inquire about their whereabouts. The shelter also has a surveillance system: there are cameras behind black orbs in each of the kennel buildings, as well as in most office spaces. Animals, workers, and volunteers live under these watchful eyes. On several occasions, staff and volunteers were reprimanded or even dismissed on the basis of video evidence.

Importantly, when the shelter is closed to the public and to volunteers, impounded animals experience markedly less activity and surveillance. During open hours, volunteers and members of the public walk through the kennels, peering at the animals and often attempting to interact with them. This stimulation is welcomed by some animals and bothers or even terrifies others. The closed times give the animals time away from the intrusion of so many human voices and hands reaching into their kennels. I have visited the shelter many times both when it has been open to the public and when it has been closed. The difference in noise is remarkable: during the public open hours the barking comes in long, loud waves, coupled with the sounds of feeding and cleaning and the voices of people as they try to shout above the din. When the shelter is closed, it is almost entirely quiet. The dogs do not bark, and their silence is both calming and eerie. Dogs lie in their beds or stretch out in the sun. During the cooler months, the exterior doors to Buildings A-D are closed and the heat is turned on, creating a cozy environment in the interior of the buildings. In the cat house, cats who have been hiding in the back of their cages during open hours come out to eat and use the litter box and stretch when the shelter is closed to the public. Their entire energy shifts from being frightened and unhappy to seeming relaxed and curious. Closed time provides welcome privacy and quiet for the impounded animals. Thus, while on the one hand the closed times offer concealment of contentious activities, like drawing up euthanasia lists and actually killing animals, closing the space to visitors also gives impounded animals a needed break from the intrusions of humans.

For some animals, this time can also be a respite from staff policing, an opportunity to break rules (with the consent of staff) and enjoy it. Over the years, several dogs have routinely escaped their kennels during closed hours, and if they are cooperative and friendly, the staff let them stay out of their kennels and just poke around the facility. One pit bull became a shelter celebrity because he slept under a bush alongside one of the buildings each night and then returned to his kennel at opening time. Another dog preferred to break out of her kennel and climb into kennels with other dogs and then sleep with them. When the shelter is open to the public, staff operate as police, treating loose dogs as a threat to their own safety and the safety of the public, anxiously yelling out, "Loose dog!" When the shelter is closed to the public, fears dissipate and rules relax.

KILLING

Anthroparchal logic runs through everything that PAW does. At each opportunity, PAW asserts human dominance over animals, whether in making choices for animals about their activities, location, health, or continued survival. Anthroparchal control is evident in PAW's management of animals' bodies through the practice of caging, the methods of interaction between staff and animals, the medicalization of animal bodies, and the assessment of which animals are adoptable and which are not. The most severe example of anthroparchal logic is the practice of killing. PAW ends the lives of animals whom it deems unadoptable, whose physical condition is conceptualized as a threat to other animals (i.e., animals with upper respiratory infections or other contagious illnesses), who have been at the shelter "too long," or who have characteristics that lead staff to think they will not likely be adopted.

While in another context the actions at PAW could be considered animal abuse, the anthroparchal state has created laws and codes that permit the killing of animals when this is deemed necessary according to human priorities—in this case, to save the resources and time that would be required if the institution were to attempt to rehome all animals, even those who might be less appealing to adopters in a culture that has turned companion animals into commodities with differential value based on age, health, appearance, and behavior. The shelter is an exceptionary space, one where the state suspends the laws by which the rest of the population must abide.[33] By taking the lives of animals, PAW reasserts the right of humans, and of the state, to control all aspects of animals' lives.

To select animals to be killed, the kennel manager or a midlevel manager reviews each day a list of animals who have been at the shelter beyond their legally mandated hold or who have been flagged as somehow problematic because they are sick or considered unadoptable. As per the shelter's policy manual, the computer system generates the list of animals eligible to be killed, automating the first stage of the process:

> The list of animals that may be considered for euthanasia is generated out of [the computer system] by the following procedure:
>
> 1. Standard login
> 2. Go to Reports, under Reports (run a report or F3) and scroll down to Adoption Evaluation Report and click on it.
> 3. Under "Value," type in the date and press Enter. The system will automatically show all animals that may be considered for euthanasia.
> 4. Print the list.

The manager reviewing the daily list need not authorize any animals to be killed that day. The staff member tasked with reviewing the daily list decides how many animals and which ones on the basis of instructions from the shelter manager and veterinarian, which in turn are informed by the flow of animals into and out of the shelter (i.e., crowding), staffing levels, considerations for the health of the shelter population, and notes that may have been made in the computer about specific animals (e.g., that an animal is unfriendly or a volunteer favorite). Following a series of checks to make sure that no one is seeking to adopt, rescue, or reclaim these animals, the animals selected will then be placed on a list of animals to be killed that day.

A kennel attendant and an RVT normally work together to kill an animal. When Monster died, a kennel attendant would have gone to retrieve him from his kennel. I would like to think Monster was happy to see the worker and enjoyed the walk, but I and other volunteers have also seen dogs sitting on their haunches as they are led to the Euth Room. Monster would have been alone with two staff members in the small room, maybe more if he was struggling a lot (animals are not to see other animals being killed or dead, so each animal enters alone and each body is removed before the next animal comes into the room). Once the staff had control of him, they would have administered an intravenous injection of a lethal dose of sodium pentobarbital. The drugs would have stopped Monster's heart and lungs. His muscles would have gone limp. Once he was declared dead, the staff members present would have placed his body in an oil drum in the rear courtyard. Most of the drums are stored in a cooler the size of a large garden shed, but when the shelter is very full there are oil drums outside the freezer as well. Monster's body, and those of days or weeks of other killed animals, would remain in these drums until the truck from the rendering plant came to retrieve them.

Sometimes the oil drums are left open and volunteers see the dead animals. I remember the first time I saw an animal who had been killed at PAW, a regal German Shepherd whose body was positioned so that the top of her head looked out over the edge of the barrel and one of her feet was resting on the edge of the drum, as if she were offering me her paw. I grimaced at the sight of her but then proceeded to wash stacks of dirty stainless steel bowls at the sink about twenty feet away, under her deadened gaze. Killing at PAW is at once deeply contentious and completely routine.

CONTROLLING REPRODUCTION

The most widespread strategy for trying to reduce shelter intakes and shelter killing in the United States is spaying and neutering companion animals. Since the 1980s, spaying and neutering animals prior to releasing them from animal shelters has become an industry practice. The logic behind this practice is to reduce rates of reproduction among companion animals so that fewer animals end up unwanted and therefore in shelters. Practicing sterilization is supported by claims that it is in the best interest of both currently living and nonliving animals: if fewer new companion animals are born, more people will choose to adopt adult animals, and fewer animals will end up in the shelter as unwanted in the future, thereby reducing suffering for both animals who are already alive and those who could yet be born. Advocates also maintain that spaying and neutering reduce the risks of certain health and behavior issues, although the research findings on this are mixed and suggest that for male dogs and for very young animals sterilization increases health risks.[34]

Shelter control over reproduction is a powerful example of the intersections of helping, policing, and killing. While the narrative of improving the welfare of animals dominates discourses about spaying and neutering at PAW, enforcing spaying and neutering is also a practice of policing animal bodies and human activities, and sometimes of killing. As Krithika Srinivasan notes, "Irrespective of what the actual benefits or harms of neutering might be, castrating or removing the ovaries and uterus of an otherwise healthy animal is certainly a biopolitical act in that it intervenes in basic life processes—sexuality and reproduction—on the basis of a set of truth discourses about the regulation of the wellbeing of dog individuals and populations."[35] Each unsterilized animal becomes a case at risk for unwanted reproduction. Animals lose control over their reproductive capacities and are denied the opportunity to engage in what seems to be a typical behavior for them. Animal practices that do not involve spaying and neutering are vilified. Finally, the politics of animal reproduction are such that fetuses and even very young animals are routinely killed at PAW in the name of minimizing overpopulation.

PAW, like most other shelters, spays and neuters all animals who are healthy enough to undergo surgery.[36] Captive wild and domesticated species routinely experience human-caused disruption to their sexual behaviors.[37] Because humans have shaped the reproductive behaviors of many domesticated animals for millennia, it's not always clear exactly what their "normal" reproductive behavior would be, nor what role this behavior has in providing animals with a fulfilled sense of self. Many shelter volunteers assert that female dogs and cats in particular are being "spared" unwanted motherhood through the large-scale sterilization of both male and female dogs. They also often refer to sexual intercourse between animals as "rape," suggesting that female animals are unable to consent to sex. Female dogs who enter the shelter with puppies, pregnant, or with clear evidence of breeding are among the most pitied of animals; volunteers and many staff see them as victims of humans seeking to profit from them or at least not caring about them enough to ensure they don't get pregnant.

Staff and volunteers widely support spaying and neutering companion animals and see failure to do so as a mark of an irresponsible owner. To say that commitment to spaying and neutering is comparable to zealous religious devotion for shelter workers and volunteers is not an overstatement: these humans are deeply committed to trying to end homelessness among companion animals by reducing the size of the population of companion animals.

This is true even though in human worlds forced or coerced sterilization is considered a violation of basic human rights. The reproductive justice movement focuses on ending practices of forced or coerced sterilization and birth control among all women.[38] It's less clear whether animals share the same right to reproduce that feminists argue that women have, particularly given humans' inability to ask them and understand their response. That there is not even a question that animals should be spayed and neutered at PAW, and that those guardians who refuse to do so are quickly labeled as bad people, reveals the willingness of humans to embrace anthroparchal thinking uncritically, in part by assuming different standards for animals' rights and bodily autonomy than for humans'. This logic is couched in the language of helping: humans promoting sterilization are benevolent actors who claim to be doing what is best for companion animals. However, the mandate of spaying and neutering is also a powerful form of policing the bodies of companion animals and the animal practices of animal guardians.

Sterilization also involves killing. While staff and volunteers at PAW enthusiastically support the practice of spaying and neutering, abortion and the killing of unweaned juveniles is highly contentious. It is PAW's practice to abort in cases when pregnant females are not at full term (although what constitutes "full term" is unclear—on at least one occasion, an upset RVT told volunteers that the puppies removed from a pregnant mother dog were viable and had to be killed separately with the usual injection of barbiturates used for adult dogs). Volunteers, irrespective of their views around reproductive choice for human women, argue that pregnant dogs should be allowed to complete their pregnancies normally. This is a curious contradiction with their otherwise unrelenting promotion of spaying and neutering and their dedication to the idea that there are too many companion animals. I also never heard arguments in favor of allowing pregnant cats to carry their pregnancies to term. With 85 percent of cats killed at the shelter, aborting feline pregnancies or killing pregnant cats does not incite moral outrage from volunteers or rescuers, who largely see cats as having an excessive surplus.

Volunteers strenuously object to the shelter's practice of routinely killing unweaned puppies and kittens who come into the shelter without their mothers; until 2017, these animals were usually killed within a few hours of their impound because the shelter lacked the resources to bottle-feed unweaned animals.[39] Volunteers see this practice as unnecessary and accuse PAW of doing too little to establish necessary infrastructure to help unweaned animals. Each spring, as "Kitten Season" goes into full swing, the shelter receives multiple families of unweaned kittens each day, usually brought to the shelter in cardboard boxes or laundry baskets.[40] Unweaned animals can survive with bottle feeding, but until 2017 PAW had only a few volunteers and staff members willing and trained to bottle-feed, and consequently the majority of these unweaned animals were killed shortly after intake. Volunteers find this morally outrageous, blaming both the people who brought juvenile animals to the shelter without their mothers and the shelter for their callous disregard for the lives of vulnerable young animals. Here volunteers' opposition to shelter killing trumps their commitment to reducing the population of unwanted companion animals—so opposition to killing overrides a commitment to reproductive policing.

In a public animal shelter like PAW, helping, policing, and killing operate in overlapping ways, sometimes creating contradictions—for example, when the shelter kills animals under the auspices of helping them. Staff and volunteers must negotiate and cope with these contradictions, usually emphasizing their efforts to support the welfare of animals and communities over acknowledging the centrality of policing and killing at the shelter. Yet this work of helping also involves the assertion of biopower over animal bodies, judging animals for temperament and health while simultaneously subjecting animal guardians to normalizing judgments about animal practices.

3   The Myth of the Irresponsible Owner

IN MARCH 2013, one of PAW's field officers picked up a nearly hairless fawn-and-white male pit bull from a small community within PAW's service area. The neighborhood is home to working-class Latinx families living mostly in small, plain, and tidy ranch houses sandwiched between industrial areas and major freeway interchanges. Given the proximity the suburban-seeming side streets in this community have to major roadways, including six-lane surface streets and ten-lane highways, it seemed fortunate for the dog that he had been plucked off the street into the security of one of SCAS's trucks.

The dog needed veterinary attention. He was suffering from a severe case of demodectic mange, a noncontagious overpopulation of skin mites, and he had only a few patches of fur clinging to his flanks. His skin was bright pink and crusty with inflammation from secondary infections of bacteria and fungi that were taking advantage of his weakened immune system.

The kennel attendant processing impounds named the dog Digby. Digby entered PAW at a time when pit bulls routinely were given only a day or two beyond the time frame set by California law to be reclaimed, adopted, or rescued before being put down.[1] Although mange is generally quite inexpensive to treat, its appearance unsurprisingly alarms many people, including prospective adopters. Coupled with being an adult pit bull, Digby's mange meant his chances of adoption were slim, and staff and volunteers feared for him.

Luckily, a senior staff member had a soft spot for Digby and protected him for a month, even managing to include him in an off-site adoption event where dogs have good chances of being adopted. Alas, he was one of the few dogs to come back from the adoption event without a home. My wife and I discussed the situation and decided we would rescue him. That weekend, we brought Digby home as a foster dog.[2]

Digby's gentle nature won us over immediately. When first introduced to one of our cats, he wagged his tail in a relaxed circle and licked her head. He made fast friends with our dogs, especially our female dog, with whom he would engage in seemingly endless games of tug-of-war and chase. Digby loved to swim, and as spring moved into summer we looked forward to daily swims in our pool with Digby paddling enthusiastically beside us. At night, he snuggled up beside us in bed, and we became accustomed to the powerfully yeasty smell—or so-called mange stink—of his warm, hairless body. Everyone in our home—human, canine, and feline—loved him. Online, we set up a Facebook page for him and received frequent messages from well-wishers who watched videos of him playing with our dogs, swimming, and cuddling.

Life with Digby also involved a lot of work because of his skin condition. In addition to daily medications, he needed regular medicated baths that required keeping the shampoo on for fifteen minutes—an eternity in the mind of a wet dog. When Digby failed to respond to the initial treatment protocol, the rescue's veterinarian suggested an alternative approach that required dropping him off in the morning at the veterinarian's office well over half an hour away once every week and then making the trip again in the afternoon rush hour to pick him up. Soon after we started this treatment, however, his fur began to sprout, and within a few weeks a velvety peach coat replaced his once bald, swollen skin. His recovery was a true labor of love, but seeing his health restored was well worth the effort.

In July, Digby was finally mange-free, which meant both that we needed to step up our efforts at finding him a permanent home and that he could finally be neutered. (Because veterinarians believe mange is related to immune issues, and because surgery can trigger such issues, dogs with mange are released from SCAS shelters without being spayed or neutered and are usually fixed once recovered.) Here Digby's happy ending abruptly stopped. Neuter surgeries are usually uneventful, but, as with any surgery, the risk of complication is always present. The morning following his surgery, I awoke to find Digby shivering on his dog bed, his lips a pale blue. I rushed him back to the veterinary clinic. He was bleeding internally, but the veterinarian could not find the source of the bleeding with an ultrasound. He gave Digby a blood transfusion and hoped the bleeding might resolve with the support of a compression bandage around his abdomen. Instead, Digby's abdominal cavity swelled with blood. Our choices were to do nothing and hope the bleeding stopped (which seemed unlikely), or subject him to an exploratory surgery that might reveal the source of the bleeding and thus enable the veterinarian to stop the bleeding.

We opted for the surgery. A few hours after the surgery began, the veterinarian called us, confused and sad: he had been unable to find any specific source of bleeding, and Digby was not regaining consciousness. We rushed to his side. Hours after the veterinary clinic had closed on a Saturday night, my wife and I stood beside Digby's quiet body on the operating table as the veterinary technician turned off the respirator and disconnected the intubation. Digby's eyes remained half-closed, and his chest stopped moving. Digby slipped away from us, for no reason anyone could offer. A bucket half-filled with blood stood in the corner; the veterinarian, exhausted and overwhelmed, shook his head and told us, "He just bled and bled . . . It wouldn't stop."

Digby was a foster dog, part of our lives for only four months, and yet I was devastated by his unexpected death. In a world filled with injustices, I was enraged that Digby should have come so close to having a perfect life only to have it ripped away for no known reason (the veterinarian could only conjecture about problems with Digby's ability to clot, although no abnormalities showed in his laboratory work). I also blamed myself for decisions made in his final two days. What if we had tried a different approach? Taken him to a specialist? Operated sooner? Or not at all? I mourned for him more than for my own dogs who had died. I have always considered myself a fair, loving, and compassionate guardian to companion animals, but Digby's death made me question my judgment. I felt I had failed him. I suddenly saw myself as a bad dog guardian.

I was startled a year later when I received a message from someone I didn't know, a man named Alvado who identified himself as Digby's former guardian. I quickly established communication with Alvado and learned about Digby's history. As I had always suspected, he was a loved and wanted companion. Alvado had chosen him from a litter of puppies born to the dog of a friend of his cousin. Alvado named him Beso, Spanish for "kiss." Smitten with Beso's snubby face, Alvado bought him a collar and leash and made Beso a central part of his life, teaching him how to walk on a leash and house-training him. Beso developed mange as a puppy (when it often starts in pit bulls), but Alvado took him to a local veterinarian for care, and Beso thrived. Because I asked how old Beso was, Alvado sent me pictures of all of his veterinary records, and I could see from those records that Alvado took excellent care of Beso, seeking out regular veterinary care and purchasing needed medications and treatments.[3] In the pictures Alvado sent me, Beso is healthy and his fur is lustrous with no obvious signs of mange at all. In one of the images, Alvado sits in front of a Christmas tree with one arm around a small child and his other arm arced around Beso, holding up a new collar and leash set that are Beso's holiday gift. Alvado also sent me a picture of Beso in his doghouse, a custom-built two-story structure designed to look like a Norman castle, which Beso personalized with his chew marks. Beso was clearly happy with Alvado's family, which included kids and small dogs.

In the spring of 2013, Alvado had a serious health issue and had to be hospitalized for an extended period. During that time, Beso was in the care of Alvado's family and he escaped from the yard. When Alvado finally came home, he looked everywhere for Beso without success. A family member thought to look on PetFinder, a website where people seeking to adopt dogs can search through listings posted by shelters and rescues, and found Digby's listing there, which included a link to the Facebook page for him. Alvado could not believe he had found Beso, and he didn't know what to do. Ultimately, he decided, "Beso seemed to live a better life with you guys and he seemed happy and that's all that mattered to me." Although he did not say so, I suspect that Alvado was continuing to struggle financially after missing so much work as a manual laborer and felt that we were better able to care for Beso than he was.

Alvado and Beso shared a close bond that was ruptured by an accidental separation preempted by a crisis outside of anyone's control. Alvado did what he could to ensure Beso's care while he was in the hospital, but his family didn't succeed in containing Beso. When Alvado faced the possibility of trying to reclaim Beso, he decided Beso's new life looked too good to interrupt, an act that seems selfless. He was not an irresponsible dog owner, but rather someone who was caught up in a personal crisis made more complicated by a lack of resources; he could not afford, for example, to pay to board Beso at a secure facility while he was in the hospital. Beso was not a neglected dog, or one heartlessly abandoned at the shelter for being sick or old or annoying. In his life, he had known only love.

Beso's story illuminates how companion animals can end up at PAW because of the precarious lives their human guardians have. When a low-income Latinx man lands in the hospital, or must care for a relative in his country of origin, or loses his home to eviction or foreclosure, what resources does he have to protect and care for his dog? Because Alvado lacked the safety net of people who could be reliable caregivers for his dog or the financial resources to pay for secure boarding, a sequence of events started for Beso that brought him to the shelter and sadly and painfully ended a few months later on the operating table, an outcome of bad luck and the choices I—not someone who would be readily identified as an irresponsible owner because of my race (white), class (upper), and gender (woman)—made for him.

The discourse of irresponsible owners obscures the complex reasons why animals end up in shelters in favor of an individualistic narrative that blames these so-called irresponsible owners for their lack of personal responsibility to their companion animals. When Digby was at the shelter, staff and volunteers would look at his inflamed skin and wonder aloud, "*Who* could let their dog get like that?" Their unspoken answer was an irresponsible owner: someone uncaring and indifferent to the suffering of their companion animal, someone too lazy or greedy to pay for veterinary care, someone who would rather let their sick dog loose on the street than take responsibility for his well-being.

At PAW, the irresponsible owner is always imagined as a placed person, as someone from "around here"—so a member of the local community and thus *not* a white person—and as a man, particularly when the dog in question is a larger dog. Further, shelter volunteers and staff reserve their harshest condemnations for the irresponsible owners of pit bulls. In a circular logic, pit bulls are assumed to be disproportionately owned by irresponsible owners, and irresponsible owners are assumed to disproportionately own pit bulls.[4] Staff and volunteers regard every man who comes to PAW with a pit bull as suspect, and single men from the local community are never considered appropriate adopters for any dog, especially not for a pit bull.[5]

PAW and SCAS assert power over the public and companion animals through two regulatory discourses. One of these discourses centers on irresponsible owners and is the focus of this chapter; I address the other, public safety, in greater detail in chapter 6. In the discourse of irresponsible owners, irresponsible owners demonstrate one or more of several behaviors: (1) they view their dog as a thing, not as a family member, rendering the animal disposable and replaceable; (2) they do not spay or neuter their companion animal, allowing them to reproduce and/or develop reproductive cancers; (3) they fail to provide their dog with proper training and socialization and/or keep their dog living entirely outdoors so that they develop behavioral problems that make them nuisances or even safety threats in their communities and that may render them difficult to adopt out once at the shelter; (4) they allow their companion animals to roam in their neighborhood, placing the animal and possibly people or other animals at risk for injury; (5) they abandon their dogs at the shelter if the dogs demonstrate a behavior the owner doesn't like, rather than seeking out assistance from trainers or other qualified professionals; (6) they bring their companion animals to the shelter when they encounter a life setback rather than seek out alternatives. Viewed in terms of a set of characteristics rather than behaviors, irresponsible owners are, of course, irresponsible but also indifferent, lazy, lacking compassion, freeloaders, unable to shoulder normal adult responsibilities, egoistic, and/or seeking the easiest way out of life's problems—many of the same characteristics associated with negative stereotypes of poor people and welfare recipients in the US.[6] Notably, while responsibility with dogs is often fleeting—for instance, an otherwise responsible dog guardian can lose control of a dog for a moment and become briefly irresponsible—the category of irresponsible owners is fixed.[7] While there are possibilities for atonement and redemption, an irresponsible owner occupies a relatively stable position.

The discourse of irresponsible ownership has three powerful and interrelated consequences. First, focusing on individual humans as irresponsible obscures the structural conditions that facilitate the entry of so many animals from low-income communities into animal shelters. This in turn contributes to misguided interventions—especially punitive approaches to animal control—and reinforces existing, but seemingly incorrect, ideas about the factors that lead to homelessness among companion animals. Second, placing blame for an animal's entry into the animal shelter onto the guardian allows shelter workers to deflect responsibility for what happens to those animals away from the institution, its workers, and the broader community and society onto the former guardians of the animal. That animals die at the shelter is thus a problem created by irresponsible owners, not by the shelter or, more broadly, the society. This in turn also allows shelter workers to deflect complaints about the shelter from volunteers and the public: according to PAW, irresponsible owners cause shelter killing, not the shelter or the taxpayers who fund the shelter or the broader society that endorses the killing of animals. Third, coupled with the act of leaving an animal at the shelter, the racial and class dynamics of the discourse of irresponsible owners enable staff and volunteers to see themselves as different from the former guardians of impounded animals, thereby limiting possibilities for compassion toward people unable to keep their companion animals and expanding opportunities for punitive treatment of guardians. Taken together, these consequences undercut critical engagement with structural inequality and with the shelter practice of killing, and thus link race, class, and animal death together in ways that justify the shelter's assertion of power and control over the animals of poor people of color and, by extension, over the lives of poor people of color themselves.

HOW POOR PEOPLE'S COMPANIONS
END UP AT PAW

The narrative of irresponsible owners views animals' entry into the shelter as the outcome of individual-level behaviors when in fact animals come into the shelter primarily because of population-level issues. While certainly some animal guardians *are* indifferent, neglectful, or even abusive toward animals in their purported care, the main reason animals end up at PAW is that structural inequalities make it extremely difficult for many people to care for and hold on to animal companion animals even when they want to. The guardians whose dogs end up at PAW are disproportionately lower-income people of color who are subject to population-level conditions of control and power that make them vulnerable to losing their animals to the shelter system, including precariousness in housing and employment and high police and animal control presence. In the communities that make up PAW's service area, human and animal residents routinely find themselves up against mechanisms of structural inequality that disrupt their lives and those of their animals and often severely restrict the life chances of both. PAW's interference in relationships between poor people of color and their companion animals is yet another way of enacting state violence against them.

My analysis here is importantly different from previous work examining how companion animals end up at shelters and why humans leave them there. First, my work is more current: most existing work looking at why humans surrender animals to shelters is from the 1990s or early 2000s.[8] Given shifts in the US economy and the rise of the no-kill approach to sheltering, shelter populations, practices of animal welfare, and the reasons why animals come into shelters may all have changed, so that what might have been true even a decade ago may be no longer. Relying on analyses that are fifteen or more years old in a rapidly changing landscape of animal welfare does not make much sense for guiding current policy or practice. Further, most of the research on reasons for surrender focuses on people bringing their animals to private, suburban/rural, and/or low-kill shelters.[9] These shelters are typically among lower-intake shelters and thus are not representative of the majority of animals who end up in shelters.[10] California produces the largest number of shelter intakes in the United States, with a per capita intake rate similar to those of the other top-intake states, Texas and Florida. While shelters vary significantly even within Los Angeles, this examination of PAW illuminates processes at work in many high-intake shelters.

The humans in large swaths of PAW's service areas face all kinds of precarity that are often the primary catalysts for dogs entering the shelter, not individual irresponsibility. Precarity means that animal guardians in PAW's service area may abruptly become unable to provide secure housing for companion animals, so that the animals end up at PAW either as strays or as owner surrenders. Marginalized people may not even be aware the shelter exists and thus may simply release a dog, cat, or other animal they can't keep or, as is often the case for animals at PAW, leave the animal(s) in an apartment or backyard after they move out.[11] These animals find their way to PAW when concerned neighbors call to report the abandoned animals or catch them themselves and bring them to the shelter. Guardians grappling with precarity are making problematic choices, but choices routinely made under the duress of sudden eviction or deportation or arrest.

Beso's story is but one of many that illustrate how animals coming into the shelter often are not there because of the deliberate bad acts of their guardians. I routinely encountered owners leaving their dogs or cats at the shelter when I was hanging around at the front of the shelter (something volunteers normally do not do). Women especially often surrendered their animal(s) in tears, as did many men, hardly an indicator of uncaring, indifferent guardianship. Often entire families came for the send-off, and on a few occasions children wrote letters about their dogs to attach to their kennels in the hopes this would increase their chances of adoption.

Overwhelmingly, the guardians I met who left their animals at PAW did so because they had lost their housing: they had been evicted for inability to pay rent, faced eviction because the landlord didn't want the dog on the property, or were functionally unhoused, living either with friends or family on a short-term basis or in their car and unable to have or care for a dog in these conditions.[12] For the car-dwelling homeless—who represent a quarter of unhoused people in the Los Angeles metropolitan area—southern California's often scorching hot weather presents particular problems, as they cannot leave the dog safely in the vehicle while they are at work or trying to access resources to secure housing.[13] Many of these families have complex tales of their downward descent from precarity to homelessness. JoJo, for instance, one of very few women I encountered who appeared to be white and was surrendering an animal, brought her dog to the shelter because her husband, who was the family's primary breadwinner, had had a major stroke. He had to move to a rehabilitation facility. Without his income and with a rapid increase in medical bills, JoJo was unable to pay the bills and was soon evicted from their home. She took her large dog and lived in her car in the parking lot of the care facility. During the day, she and the dog would stay with her husband in his room. However, JoJo needed to find employment, file for a stipend as a family caregiver through Medicaid, and apply for handicapped-accessible, low-income housing, among other tasks. She was unable to do this with an eighty-pound dog, nor could she leave the dog in the car when daytime temperatures routinely exceeded ninety degrees. She saw no choice but to give up her dog and sorrowfully left her at PAW. She checked in with me about the dog regularly for over a month until her cell phone was disconnected (the dog was rescued and later adopted from the rescue).

When Alicia, a Latinx woman in her early thirties, came in with a pair of Chihuahua mixes tucked one under each arm, her eye makeup was already smeared from crying. She explained to me between sobs that she and her family had lost their home and they had been living with the dogs in the car but she couldn't leave them in there when she was working because of the heat. She had even gone so far as to tie them up near her kids' school for several hours with a note on their collars so that no one would call animal control, but she was afraid the dogs would be hurt or stolen if she did that again. So she brought them to PAW in the hopes they would find a permanent home.

Similarly, when Fernando arrived at the shelter with his middle-aged pit bull Oso, he was visibly agitated. He tried to explain to me all of the issues he had with housing over the last year: multiple evictions, couch-surfing, not being able to find a place to rent that would accept a pit bull. After nine months of being unhoused, he had an opportunity to move into his cousin's apartment, but the landlord there wouldn't allow a pit bull either. Fernando tried to find a friend or family member who would take Oso, but without success. Not knowing what else to do and afraid to give up a rare chance at stable, affordable housing, he said goodbye to Oso, kneeling down to squeeze Oso against his chest for several long seconds before turning quickly away from me and the dog.

JoJo, Alicia, and Fernando are among the many people I met who surrendered their dogs to PAW because they were experiencing life crises and felt they had no other options—or even felt that this was the best option for their animal because it would be better for them than living in a car, a tent, or a friend's yard. Contra the discourse of irresponsible owners, they had sought out other options for their animal(s), including reaching out to friends, family, and coworkers to try to rehome their dogs, posting them on online marketplaces and social media, and/or actively seeking housing that would permit their companion animal(s). They faced difficult choices in trying to balance housing crises with the needs of their companion animals.

Veterinary expenses or confusion about how to care for an animal at the end of their life also bring people to the shelter with their companion animals. Staff and volunteers have especially little empathy for guardians who leave their senior companion animals at the shelter because they see this as a betrayal of the relationship between human and animal, particularly since senior animals have lower chances of adoption. Along with the guardians of animals who appear to have been abused or neglected, the guardians who surrender older animals are among the most vilified at PAW. However, when I speak with those surrendering senior animals, they consistently report that they would be happy to care for the animal(s) but are unable to afford veterinary care and believe the shelter can provide care for the animal(s) that they cannot. In one of the first cases of a senior surrender that I observed as a volunteer, three generations of a Latinx family—the youngest a girl of around eight years of age and the oldest a man I believe was her grandfather—brought an aged Cocker Spaniel to the shelter's Impound Window. The dog was unable to walk and seemed to be both blind and deaf. She was twitching as if in some kind of partial seizure and appeared at best semiconscious. The presumed father in the household carried her in a fleece blanket to the Impound Window. A woman who seemed to be his partner and the mother to the two children with them stood beside him, weeping quietly. Bringing up the rear, the man I assume was the kids' grandfather trailed along, his head hung low and his pinched face partially hidden by the wide brim of his cowboy hat. The father explained to me and staff members that the dog was dying and asked us to please help them by putting the dog down. The worker responded in a mix of English and Spanish, letting the family know that PAW could take the dog and she would be evaluated but that family members could not be present for euthanasia and the shelter could decide to extend the dog's life. The adult family members nodded, the mom and kids crying. I assured them I would carry the dog back and stay with her while she went through the impound process. As I held the dog, still wrapped in her fleece blanket, in my arms, the family lined up to say farewell to her. Each one of them kissed the dog's forehead or cheek, whispering words of love and comfort into her unhearing ears. When they had finished, I took her through the side gates and into the shelter. The children were heaving with sobs, and all of the adults were crying too. These were not people indifferent to their dog: they were people who might have been exposed to SCAS's framing of itself as a helping institution or who, even without such exposure, thought of a shelter as a resource for emergency help for an animal in distress and who likely had few other options—and possibly didn't even know about other options. They were not trying to do badly by their dog; they were doing what they thought was best for her within the constraints of their knowledge and resources, both of which were limited by the nexus of their class, status as immigrants, and ethnicity.

THE REALITIES BEHIND THE IMPOUND

PAW tracks why dogs are brought to the shelter when they come in as "owner surrenders": the computer system provides staff with a menu of common reasons, such as "moving" or "too old."[14] Information from this system is not reliable, however, for a number of reasons. Many guardians provide no reason for surrender or have language barriers so they don't effectively select a reason. Staff routinely fail to input information even when it is provided or summarize information in ways the surrendering person would not. The reasons included in the computer system also don't always perfectly capture the actual scenario, since they are from a preset menu. Further, many dogs brought in as strays also are actually guardian surrenders; because surrendering guardians have to pay a $10 relinquishment fee, guardians routinely state that they found the animal as a stray even when it is clear to staff and/or volunteers that the human and the animal know each other well. Since these animals are impounded as strays, staff do not ask for or input background information about why they are being surrendered.

On the basis of my own tracking of guardian surrenders for a one-month period in 2015 using PAW's information on kennel cards, the most common reason for surrendering an animal was no reason at all. The high frequency of nonresponse likely reflects some combination of staff indifference and/or staff error resulting in the person surrendering not being asked to complete the surrender information questionnaire or the questionnaire being misplaced, language barriers (especially for clients speaking Mandarin, Vietnamese, or Tagalog, as the shelter has no staff members who speak these languages, but a significant proportion of the service area population speaks one of these languages as their primary language), literacy issues (since the questionnaire was a form), indifference or emotionality on the part of the person surrendering, and/or concerns about providing information to the shelter because it is a state agency. When a reason was given, the most frequent of PAW's options for why someone left a companion animal included, in order of frequency, "landlord issues," "moving," "unable to care for," "new baby," "owner arrested," and "too old."[15] While I did not capture any such cases during that month, guardians are also sometimes forced to surrender one or more animals if they are in excess of the limit of three dogs or five cats permitted per household in PAW's service area.[16] Most people in excess of the limit have four or five dogs, but the shelter also receives dogs, cats, and rabbits from larger-scale hoarding situations several times each year, when twenty or more animals may come in at the same time from a single home.

Because the computer system limits the explanation, impound staff at PAW must take messy, complicated reasons for why people leave their animals and bureaucratically rationalize them into one neat, simple response. Even when a choice from the computer menu reasonably summarizes the situation, it often hides the complexity of why the animal is coming into the shelter. The reasons the computer system offers for guardian surrender obscure the experiences of inequality that bring so many dogs and other animals to the shelter. Guardians whose reason would be input as "unable to care for" share long stories of not being able to afford food or veterinary care for their companion animals because of un- or underemployment. "Landlord issues" and "moving" hide the lived realities that low-income people often lose their homes and find themselves either homeless or forced to live with friends or family members who won't accept the animal(s).[17] Still other animals come in because their guardians are deported, which is also classified as "moving." These are all circumstances in which surrendering an animal is something other than voluntary. While other options might be possible—such as placing a dog with a family member or friend, or seeking a new home privately—the time lines of precarity and poverty often preclude such efforts.

Dogs regularly come into the shelter because their guardians have been arrested, another category in the shelter computer system that obscures different stories. Many of those arrested are unhoused people whose encampments are raided, or who are picked up by police for quality-of-life crimes, like public drunkenness. Without a permanent address, unhoused guardians are unable to reclaim their dogs; many also do not have the funds to pay the impound fees. In a few cases, a family member reclaims the dog for them, but mostly the dogs belonging to unhoused people stay at the shelter, where their former guardians come to visit them, sitting outside their kennels with their heads leaning up against the kennel bars. These individuals generally have not committed any significant bad act that would justify taking their companion from them. Their dogs are never physically neglected and are often well-socialized and happy animals. When the dogs do have health issues, these are usually just an outcome of the poor living conditions that unhoused humans and animals face. One delightfully cheerful pit bull who belonged to an unhoused man came to the shelter with a weeping rash on her stomach. After she was rescued, a veterinarian established that she had been nesting in fiberglass insulation, material that likely seemed to her and maybe even her guardian scavenged material suitable for a nice dog bed.

Other animal guardians are arrested for crimes that make it impossible for them to reclaim and/or care for their animal(s). If an arrest is expected to be brief, the animal or animals will be held at the shelter until the guardian can reclaim them; more often, the animal begins the process of becoming SCAS's property and is either made available for adoption or put down. Fellow volunteer Suze and I at the same time fostered unrelated young black pit bulls who came to the shelter because their respective guardians were ensnared in the legal system. The former guardian of my foster dog was in jail for drug-related charges; her overwhelmed mother was left to care for five dogs belonging to her daughter and her daughter's boyfriend, who was also imprisoned, and surrendered the two youngest dogs to the shelter. Suze meanwhile named her foster dog Wrangler because his former guardian had dropped the puppy while escaping from mall security officers on a bicycle after stealing a pair of Wrangler jeans. The dog's notes at the shelter advised staff to call the police if anyone identifying themselves as the dog's guardian tried to reclaim him so as to facilitate the shoplifter's arrest. The guardian never materialized, and after several weeks of waiting Suze brought the pup home to foster. Both dogs were adopted into middle-class, white homes outside the shelter's service area. Whether these guardians deserve to be convicted or suspected of criminal activity, I cannot know, and some might argue that losing their companions is a natural consequence of breaking the law. Yet it's critical to note that lower-income people of color living in communities primarily populated by people like them are subject to greater surveillance and less leniency than more affluent and white people.[18] Their companion animals thus are also more likely to be ensnared through surveillance, policing, and punishment.

THE STRUGGLE TO RECLAIM STRAYS

Stray animals constitute the overwhelming majority of animals impounded at PAW. In 2013–14, 70 percent of dogs and 93 percent of cats arrived as strays. The animals who are impounded at PAW as strays often lose their histories entirely, since the circumstances of how they came to the shelter are generally unknown: the shelter staff simply note the location of where an animal was found. The guardians of unclaimed strays are easy for shelter staff and volunteers to imagine as irresponsible owners. Shelter workers and volunteers alike express dismay that dogs are running loose, often without a collar or a microchip, and that their guardians don't seem to care enough about them to come pick them up. These guardians are imagined as completely uncaring and indifferent to the plight of their companion. Cats, in contrast, are rarely conceptualized as having had an individual human guardian; staff and volunteers explain their high numbers in the shelter as the result of *community* failures to spay and neuter cats.

Many volunteers and staff consider the "local people" as a group to be unsuitable guardians to both dogs and cats; while they have no authority to stop animals from going home, volunteers routinely tell other volunteers and sometimes staff that animals should not be returned to their guardians. On many occasions, I have seen staff seeming to make snap judgments about guardians who have come to the shelter to reclaim a lost pet that influence the likelihood of an animal going home. When a white family with middle-class markers came to pick up their Labrador Retriever a few hours after the dog was brought in as a stray, the staff member helping them did everything in her power to expedite the process, even accepting a phone call from a veterinarian's office regarding a rabies vaccine as proof of guardianship, though this is not an accepted form of documenting guardianship at PAW. When a single Latinx man came to try to retrieve his pit bull mix, the staff member required him to show paper copies of veterinary records (which the man had to drive to his veterinarian's office to retrieve) and pictures from his cell phone before they would document the man as the guardian; they then still refused to release the dog to him without a field officer conducting a property check, or a visit to an animal's home to see that whatever condition there had caused the animal to get loose—such as a loose gate or a hole in a fence—had been repaired. People who live in the shelter's service area—especially if they are men of color—are always under suspicion of being irresponsible owners, and the onus lies with them to prove to staff and volunteers that they are not.

In fiscal year 2014–15, only 8 percent of animals impounded at PAW were returned to their guardians, although the number was substantially higher for dogs (17 percent) than for cats (a mere 0.06 percent—only fifty-five cats out of over eight thousand); this is largely in keeping with national trends, although the return-to-guardian rate for cats is much lower at PAW than the also-abysmal national average of 2.5 percent.[19] Because the shelter doesn't collect such data and I have no systematic way to do so, I have no reliably collected data on how many animals' guardians *attempt* to reclaim their companions at PAW, but shelter staff generally state that "about a third" of dogs who come in as strays have someone who attempts to reclaim them—an estimate roughly double the actual rate of return of 17 percent.

Why so few animals return to their original guardians is likely the outcome of a combination of factors. Some guardians may never look for their companion animals at the shelter. I have met several people at the shelter who told me they thought their dog or cat had run away because "he wasn't happy," so they didn't look for the animal, thinking the dog or cat was happier elsewhere. Upon further probing, I found two subtexts to this idea that animals run away: one is a belief that even domesticated animals are somewhat wild and cannot be "owned," and the other is the guardian's feeling of inadequacy in their role as caregiver to animals (e.g., "I work too much," "I didn't walk her enough"). The latter suggests that guardians who lose their companion animals share beliefs about how companion animals should be cared for with responsible owners who do not lose their animals, and that lower-income people internalize negative views of themselves as irresponsible owners. Many guardians who do look for their companions at the shelter look for only a week or so, but the animal may be living on the street or with someone else who found them for weeks or even months before they arrive at the shelter. Cats face the species-specific issue that many people don't seem to have a strong sense of guardianship over cats, or believe that especially cats who run away do so for a reason. Given the abundance of free-roaming cats in PAW's service area, many people who lose one cat often simply wait for another cat to come around. Some guardians flat-out refuse to accept their animals back if they have to be spayed or neutered before leaving the shelter. Other guardians may be wary of visiting a state institution like the shelter because of their immigration status or because of previous interactions with animal control and/or police.

Of those who do find their dogs at PAW, many find it impossible to navigate the process of reclaiming a dog, which can require proof of guardianship, fees and penalties, and one or more visits from field officers to their home. These obstacles likely explain the disparity between staff stating that a third of dogs have someone try to reclaim them, when in actuality only 17 percent of dogs go home with their guardian. The complexities of low-income life—changing work schedules that make coming to the shelter during business hours difficult or impossible, lack of transportation, wages that preclude paying fines or paying for property corrections (like reinforcing a fence), lack of skills navigating often-hostile bureaucrats and complicated bureaucracy, and so on—keep companion animals who come into PAW separated from their guardians and at the mercy of SCAS.

People whose dogs are impounded will find they must advocate for themselves and negotiate a bureaucratic process that also requires them to pay for the mistake of letting their animal get loose: guardians must shell out $18 per day for boarding for dogs, plus the costs of any veterinary care given at the shelter and usually fees related to a field officer conducting a property check. Because the field office is overburdened and understaffed, it can often take two or more weeks for a field officer to be able to complete a property check. So if a guardian finds their lost companion animal on the very first day they go missing but is then required to undergo a property check before the animal will be returned, the guardian can expect a *minimum* cost of $252 to reclaim their dog, and often hundreds more.

Volunteers occasionally raise funds to help guardians pay for these fees, but only if they perceive the guardian to be responsible. I saw supportive efforts only rarely, for example when a gardener accidentally allowed a dog to escape from the yard of a middle-class Asian American family whom volunteers supported because the family visited the dog regularly and hired a lawyer to help get the dog back. Volunteers do not try to help in most situations, deeming the guarding irresponsible. For example, volunteers scoffed when a heavily tattooed, middle-aged Latinx woman with five children in tow asked them to help her get her three dogs back "because the yard feels so empty without them." Even when a national animal welfare organization set up an initiative at PAW to help guardians reclaim their impounded companions by paying portions of their impound fees, the benefit was limited to people whose animal had become stray for the first time. Apparently losing an animal more than once is compelling evidence of irresponsible ownership, and irresponsible owners don't deserve help in getting their companion animals back.

ENCOUNTERING IRRESPONSIBLE OWNERS

Staff and volunteers encounter irresponsible owners many times each day. This is particularly true for staff members assigned to work at the Impound Window because they have the most contact with people surrendering animals; volunteers and other staff members have the ability to avoid guardians bringing in animals if they so choose, but they still interact with people walking the kennels looking for their lost companion animals or seeking companion animals to adopt. Volunteers do sometimes seek out contact with people bringing in their animals, usually in the hopes of learning more about the animal being surrendered so that they can better market them for adoption. Knowing if a dog is accustomed to living with other dogs or with kids is useful information that can help that dog find an appropriate new home. Such information is often not transmitted through the shelter to prospective adopters or rescuers unless volunteers learn the details at impound.

Volunteers are often angry with the people who bring their animals to the shelter. Suze was present when a woman brought in a lactating pit bull and her five puppies. Suze asked the woman about the mother dog's behavior, quickly learning that she did not like other dogs. Knowing that dogs who are not socialized with other dogs—especially pit bulls—have a very low likelihood of exiting the shelter alive, Suze encouraged the woman to bring the dog instead to another open-admission shelter about twenty-five minutes away where the mother dog would have a much better chance of being rehomed because that shelter, located in an affluent area, has a training program and rarely puts dogs down. The woman ignored Suze's advice and left the dog and her puppies at PAW. Frustrated to see the dog being brought back to the area where newly impounded dogs are weighed and tagged, Suze muttered some choice curse words under her breath about the former guardian. As Suze expected, the mother dog was killed at the shelter after her puppies were adopted.

The experience of Phatz, a chunky fawn pit bull, always stays with me because I experienced such frustration interacting with his guardian just before he left him at the shelter. I saw a young Latinx man holding the end of Phatz's leash in the shelter parking lot as two young women fawned over the dog. Phatz was smiling and licking them happily. As I approached, I asked if I could help them, hoping they were at PAW for a dog license and not to surrender the dog—and I wanted to intervene before the dog was surrendered if I could. I noted in my field notes how "it's funny that you can tell already out in the parking lot why someone is at the shelter," an observation that reflects my internalization of the race/class/gender/breed coding of the shelter: a young Latinx man with a pit bull in the parking lot is most likely there to leave his dog behind.

The man, who appeared to be in his early twenties, told me he had lost his housing and could not keep his dog. In response to my questions, I learned Phatz had lived with two other dogs but only outdoors. He was not housebroken or leash trained. I gently told the guardian that PAW was not a good place for dogs like Phatz and asked if he had any alternatives: a friend or relative who could hold on to him while he found a new place to live, or resources to pay for kenneling at a boarding facility (with which I offered to assist if he wanted to pursue this option). The young man said he was out of time and just had to leave the dog. When I suggested taking Phatz to another shelter where Phatz would have a better chance of being adopted, the young man said he did not have time to drive elsewhere and needed to get Phatz out of the house now. No matter what solution I suggested, he responded that Phatz had to go to PAW, immediately. Seeing that the guardian was resolute in leaving Phatz at PAW, I gave him my contact information so he could reach me if he changed his mind.

Like many dogs surrendered by their guardians, Phatz was terrified in the shelter. The moment he moved toward the kennel buildings with their unfamiliar and overwhelming noises and smells, his whole body posture crumpled. The kennel attendant had to coax him into his kennel, where he curled up in a corner, trembling. Phatz was so scared of the kennel attendants that he would urinate and defecate on himself if they approached him in his kennel. Even when I and other volunteers would go to see him, Phatz would cower in his kennel, snarling slightly and always keeping his eyes down and away from us. Phatz shifted from a friendly, affectionate, and goofy companion into a terrified and hostile shelter dog. Phatz was killed by the shelter within a week.

Every volunteer has a similar story, a narrative of desperately trying to persuade a guardian to pursue alternatives before surrendering their dog and failing to change their course of action. Such encounters with guardians contribute to volunteers' and staff members' understanding of people who leave their companion animals at PAW as irresponsible and lacking compassion. I still get a small knot of anger and sadness in my stomach when I think about what happened to Phatz. The reasons guardians provide—moving into a new apartment that doesn't allow dogs, too much barking, having a baby—are, in the view of volunteers and many staff members, remediable situations that responsible adults can negotiate successfully with even just nominal effort. Especially frustrating for volunteers is when guardians surrendering their companions refuse to take the time to drive them to another shelter even though volunteers tell them how much better their animal's chances will be at a different facility. Although the legality and ethics of this are a little fuzzy, there are several low-kill shelters near PAW. A guardian would simply need to stretch the truth and declare that their companion was a stray found somewhere in the other shelter's service area in order to leave an animal there. I do not know if those guardians whom we begged to take their animal elsewhere were indifferent to their companion's situation, in denial about their likely fate at PAW, afraid of being dishonest when surrendering, or in such an emotional state that they could not imagine driving somewhere else to leave their companion. I often felt they had steeled themselves for the moment of surrender and could not delay that moment, even for the twenty minutes it would take to drive to another shelter. Sometimes I sensed they truly did not care whether their companion(s) lived or died.

From the perspective of staff and volunteers, only a limited range of circumstances enable a surrendering guardian to be reclassified in a positive way, usually as a victim of unavoidable circumstance. Even guardians whose companions come to the shelter because the guardians died or became seriously ill are sometimes viewed as irresponsible for not having made arrangements for their dogs. Very little is forgivable, and forgiveness is dependent on the guardian appearing sympathetically to staff and volunteers at the time of impound, usually through a significant emotional display, and having a compelling narrative of why they are unable to keep their companion. Apparent domestic violence cases, for instance, universally garnered sympathy from staff and volunteers. When a Latinx woman brought in her English Bulldog saying her boyfriend told her he would kill her if she did not get rid of her dog, volunteers consoled her, promised to secure rescue for the dog, and tried to offer her referrals. When a Black man arrived at the shelter pushing a poodle mix dog and two cats in a supermarket cart, volunteers fawned over him and shared his story widely with great fanfare: a bus driver several towns away would not let the man bring his pets on the bus, so the man, who had recently lost his home, walked miles with his companions in a shopping cart to bring them to the shelter in the hopes they would receive proper care there and find a new home. Rather than viewing him as an irresponsible owner, shelter volunteers praised his concern for his companions, some of them even tearing up as they told and retold his story. (Thanks in part to the social media frenzy about his story, his companions were rescued together a few days later).

Most staff members and volunteers, like me, encounter surrendering guardians who have a variety of reasons for leaving their companion animal at PAW. Still, the overall narrative about surrendering guardians is their irresponsibility. This occurs for a number of reasons. Staff and volunteers typically do not have extensive contact with people surrendering their animals. This act occurs outside the kennel area, whereas most staff and volunteers are inside or busy working with animals in the kennels. Most volunteers interact with people surrendering animals only as we come into or leave the shelter; I have never observed a staff person seek out contact with someone surrendering an animal, even when they have been standing right near each other.

Volunteers and staff thus mostly work with animals whose history is unknown, and whom volunteers and staff see as improperly cared for by the simple fact that they are in the shelter. Among the large number of animals with unknown histories are always a solid group who arrive at the shelter with signs of physical neglect or even abuse such as severe matting, mange, flea infestation, huge and/or ulcerated tumors, ears destroyed by fly strike, teeth rotting out, emaciation, or extreme obesity. The minority cases of clear physical neglect stand out and reinforce the idea that animals at PAW typically lived with neglectful guardians—even though only a small percentage of animals show any physical signs of neglect. Similarly, while most female dogs who come into the shelter do not appear to have been bred, nor have puppies with them, those dogs who *do* have elongated nipples consistent with a history of breeding or who are pregnant or who arrive with their puppies are the ones who stand out and who buttress the idea that most dogs at the shelter come from the homes of irresponsible owners. Volunteers and staff allow the irresponsible owner narrative to dominate a possible alternative narrative of a sympathetic-appearing surrenderer because they encounter more dogs in the shelter whose previous circumstances of care are unknown to them than they do dogs whose previous circumstances of care are known to them.

Further, the irresponsible owner narrative is a dominant cultural narrative, one that is constantly reinforced by actors outside the shelter. The depiction of low-income people of color as lazy, noncontributing, and freeloading members of society is a dominant representation of the poor in the United States. Dominant American frameworks for making sense of poverty and precarity are both individualistic and cultural, holding that individuals need to take responsibility for meeting their own needs and that certain groups of people, including lower-income Black people and Latinxs, have cultivated cultures of poverty that reinforce the problematic individual behaviors that cause people to be poor.[20]

The cultural narratives about the animal-keeping practices of minority groups who dominate in PAW's service area are also powerful and dovetail with beliefs about irresponsible owners. Latinx Americans and Asian Americans are both groups constructed as having problematic animal practices: cockfighting and other blood sports, eating animals who mainstream white America thinks should not be eaten, slaughtering animals in residential settings, keeping companion animals exclusively outdoors, deliberately breeding animals for income or as trophies (pit bulls and Chihuahuas for Latinxs, Shar-Peis, Pugs, and Shih-Tzus for Chinese Americans, Jindos and Siberian Huskies for Korean Americans). With these cultural narratives about problematic animal practices of lower-income Latinx and Asian people circulating around them, it's not surprising that many staff and volunteers latch on to these ideas and integrate them into their narratives of companion animal homelessness, even if they encounter few cases to support such narratives. These narratives provide relatively easy explanations that blame people—rather than social structures—for the continuous flow of animals into the shelter.

Occasionally, volunteers and the shelter staff do not agree on whether individual cases are cases of irresponsible owners. Disagreements were especially pronounced in two cases involving dogs whom SCAS sought to designate as vicious so that they could be destroyed. One, a white female pit bull named Racha, was at the shelter for about a year while her guardian struggled for her release. Racha was accused of escaping her property and, with other dogs, attacking and killing an unrelated dog near her home. The second was Pretty Girl, a gray female pit bull who, along with her two adult pups, was accused of attacking a man who was caring for them at the request of their guardian while all of them were living in a welfare motel. In both cases, the dog's long-term impoundment attracted the attention of volunteers, who began to feed and talk with the dogs since they could not leave their kennels at all. Neither dog showed any signs of aggression in kennel, which pushed volunteers toward perceiving them as docile and advocating for their release. Further, their guardians came to see them regularly and fought to have them released through SCAS's hearings system. Both Racha and Pretty Girl's guardians paid thousands of dollars in boarding fees while their dogs were held at PAW. In both cases, SCAS was staunchly opposed to the dogs living, and volunteers disagreed with SCAS's assertion of their aggressiveness and with the assertion that their guardians were irresponsible. Volunteers came to see Racha's guardian as someone who made a careless mistake, not as someone who was inherently irresponsible. In Racha's case—I think because her victims were other dogs—SCAS finally released her to a rescue organization, a decision that volunteers celebrated.

Volunteers criticized Pretty Girl's guardian for intentionally breeding Pretty Girl (thereby also creating the puppies who grew up to be aggressive) but otherwise saw both the human and her dogs as the victims of cruel circumstances: poverty, drug use (the victim, Pretty Girl's guardian, and the first person to respond to the attack were all believed to use illegal drugs), and a heartlessly punitive shelter system that assumed guilt unless innocence was proven. The guardian's two other dogs involved in the incident (and who appear to have been the primary perpetrators on the basis of victim statements submitted at the hearing) were killed at PAW after about nine months of impoundment; Pretty Girl's case dragged on for two and a half years, ending in her being killed on January 1, 2020. At a PDD hearing on the case, a representative for SCAS argued that Pretty Girl's guardian, Ms. Gomez, was too irresponsible to keep dogs:

> Ms. Gomez's lifestyle is her business. If she wants to remain a transient or homeless, that is not our concern. What our concern is is public health and safety. Ms. Gomez has shown a pattern of irresponsibility. She pawns her dogs off onto people regardless of their propensity for aggression toward dogs and other people. She's not capable or responsible to control these dogs, and it's [SCAS's] stance. That's why we're asking in the decision that Ms. Gomez not be able to own or possess dogs for a period of up to three years.

Here, the narrative of irresponsible ownership is used to justify SCAS's request to the hearing officer that Pretty Girl's guardian not only have the last of her three dogs killed but also not be allowed to have another dog for three years. Ms. Gomez's homelessness is described as a "lifestyle," which implies it is a choice rather than the outcome of a frayed safety net, some of the highest housing costs in the nation, and Ms. Gomez's status as a poorly educated queer woman of color whom volunteers understood both as being addicted to drugs and as experiencing mental health issues.

Rescuers—or those who take animals from shelters into private nonprofit rescue organizations—often issue the harshest and most public condemnations of people who surrender their companion animals to the shelter, both when at the shelter in person and on social media narratives they craft about the animals they have or are trying to rescue. Many rescuers see the residents of the local service area as so problematic in terms of their animal practices that they mourn when dogs are adopted from PAW locally. Rescuers are also least likely to offer any consideration of extenuating circumstances that brought animals to the shelter in the first place, and they often develop narratives about the animals' histories that obscure the complex realities that led to their being at the shelter. For example, several PAW volunteers interacted with a man who brought his adult pit bull, Juana, to the shelter. He told us about his struggle to keep Juana after losing his home: for months, while she stayed with friends, he had tried to find housing that would allow her to live with him. With no housing prospects for her emerging and feeling out of options, he brought Juana to the shelter, choking back tears as he told us how good and sweet she was.

When Juana was rescued several weeks later, the rescue organization, which was well aware of her back story, posted her picture on their social media accounts, writing below, "Juana was discarded at the shelter like yesterday's newspaper," before going on to reveal her happy ending with a new adoption. Juana's former guardian did not, in fact, discard her "like yesterday's newspaper"—his decision to bring her to the shelter was fraught and emotional for him. He tried to keep her, even making arrangements for someone else to care for her to try to keep her out of the shelter. Alas, the challenge of a rental market hostile to pit bulls and his lower financial resources ultimately brought him to PAW after all. For lower-income animal guardians—and especially for those who rent—sometimes bringing an animal to the shelter is the only viable option that remains.

DEFLECTING RESPONSIBILITY AND SHIFTING BOUNDARIES

Like Juana's former guardian, many people who surrender their animals to PAW do so because they face eviction and lack the financial resources to relocate or to keep the dog elsewhere. Very few guardians are recognized, however, as trying to do right by their dog. Instead, the discourse at PAW emphasizes that community members who bring their dogs in are irresponsible. This in turn helps justify a punitive approach toward both humans and animals. PAW and SCAS must continue to police irresponsible owners by sending out canvassers and field officers to check for expired licenses, homes with more than the permitted number of animals, loose animals, and other violations. Staff and volunteers view guardians who come to the shelter as suspect, so they require guardians to prove the suitability of their home by making repairs, paying fines, and showing up at the shelter, whether to make payments, submit paperwork, talk to shelter staff, beg for more time, follow up because SCAS hasn't responded, or visit their impounded companion animal, before PAW will release their companion animal back to them.

Blaming irresponsible owners also shifts accountability for homelessness among companion animals and their deaths at the shelter *away* from the shelter and its workers and toward the local community. This strategy of blame is highly effective in normalizing conditions and practices at the shelter *and* in maintaining broader social beliefs about low-income people of color as irresponsible. The discourse of irresponsible owners enables the shelter and its workers and volunteers to assume the position of a cleanup crew, taking on responsibility for a mess they didn't make to the best of their ability given limited resources.

Blaming irresponsible owners is especially important for staff, who are directly involved in the work of killing animals. On the few occasions I have observed when members of the public or a volunteer has challenged a staff member about the shelter's practice of killing, the staff members involved in the conversation have consistently deflected responsibility for shelter killing onto former guardians. "Look, I am not the reason that dog was here in the first place!" one manager declared after an upset member of the public accused PAW of "murdering" an impounded dog. This reference back to *why* the dog was at the shelter and *who* was responsible for that redirects attention away from the shelter's practice of killing. When animals die at the shelter, staff revert to holding their former guardians responsible for that outcome, not the shelter's own logic that killing animals is a reasonable response to homelessness among companion animals, and not our society's general anthropocentric justification of violence against animals. PAW is simply carrying out the final step of a process that the former guardian initiated when they lost or surrendered their companion, thus forfeiting the authority to make decisions about their animal and consigning the animal to PAW. By centering the irresponsible owner as the catalyst for the animals' fates, PAW and its staff members are able to avoid confronting the institutional and societal logic of killing, protecting both the shelter and the broader society from facing the reality of shelter killing.

The discourse of irresponsible owners also allows staff and especially volunteers to see themselves as different from—and generally better animal caretakers than—the public served by the shelter. The irresponsible owners don't come from everywhere: they come from what staff and volunteers refer to as "around here," or the neighborhoods that make up the shelter's service area and that are populated primarily by lower-income people of color and many recent immigrants. Volunteers and staff see themselves as different from the public served at the shelter in terms of their animal practices, which in turn are tied to ideas about class and culture. While the community "around here" is filled with irresponsible owners, staff and volunteers see themselves as making the right decisions for their animal companions and offering them a higher level of care.

Particularly during my first few years of fieldwork, I regularly heard both staff and volunteers refer to members of the local community as "uneducated" and "ignorant." Staff, volunteers, and members of the rescue community active at PAW also routinely point to the idea that PAW's service area is populated by recent immigrants, particularly from Mexico and China, who they think do not see companion animals as family members and hold views about animal welfare—most especially resistance to spaying and neutering—that are problematic. The narrative of the irresponsible owner even echoes dominant cultural narratives about immigrants as an invading force with high rates of reproduction as staff and volunteers see immigrants as "flooding" the shelter with their cast-off animals. Staff and volunteers (including those of Mexican descent themselves) complain about how Mexicans and Mexican Americans refuse to spay and neuter because of their "backward" or "superstitious" religious (i.e., Catholic) beliefs and keep their dogs living outside because of cultural norms that are implicitly un-American and low class.[21]

Although I noted only about a dozen instances of this occurring during my fieldwork, a common narrative among staff and volunteers is that many guardians who locate their stray animals at the shelter refuse to take them back upon learning that they must pay to have them spayed or neutered first. One story that circulated widely at the shelter was about an older Latinx woman who decided to adopt an adult cat. Since adult cats are hard to place, volunteers and staff were very happy. Staff scheduled the cat to be spayed before the woman picked her up. During the spay surgery, the shelter veterinarian discovered the cat was in the early stages of pregnancy. The veterinarian terminated the pregnancy, which is standard procedure at PAW. When the adopter came to retrieve the cat, the staff member handling her check out gave her the information that her new cat had undergone a "complex spay" since she was pregnant, and therefore the adopter should be especially watchful for any issues during her recovery. The adopter gasped in shock and announced that her cat was tainted by the sin of abortion and that she could no longer take the cat home. This is a sad story in which a cat paid the price for differences in human views about reproductive politics and animal health (fortunately, word of the situation reached a cat rescuer who took her). The story also became a part of shelter lore, and volunteers especially cited it as evidence of problematic Latinx views regarding the sterilization of companion animals.

Another racialized discourse is that Chinese Americans, particularly first-generation immigrants, adopt large dogs for guarding purposes and small dogs as indoor companions whom they will then neglect. Staff and volunteers complain that Chinese American adopters at the shelter deliberately seek out large dogs, especially German Shepherds, who appear intimidating or reactive in their kennels with the intention of "throwing them in the backyard" as a guard dog rather than as a companion. Both another volunteer and staff members warned me when I started volunteering to "watch out" for Asian men coming to the shelter and kicking the kennel doors. These men, they told me, were looking for German Shepherds who would lunge and bark at them in response and they would try to adopt those dogs as outdoor guard dogs. When I asked if they would also be looking for pit bulls, they responded that Chinese people don't adopt pit bulls because they think those dogs are "Black dogs" (as in belonging to Black people). According to white, middle-class norms of pet keeping, companion animals should be companions, not workers, and keeping a dog for guarding is inappropriate and unfair (these same volunteers routinely celebrate when dogs are adopted to become service animals or, once, a police dog). Those humans who seek out dogs for guarding fail to meet dominant norms about how to treat a dog.

Similarly, staff and other volunteers instructed me to view Asian American women or couples as suspect if they spoke English with an Asian accent—that is, if they carried a marker of first-generation immigration status. These adopters, I was warned, would adopt cute little dogs like Shih-Tzus and Lhasa Apsos but would then not provide veterinary care or grooming for them, so that they would "bounce back" to the shelter in a few years in terrible condition. Asian Americans who spoke English without an accent were largely exempted from these ideas and, if they came to the shelter as a couple or family, were generally assumed to be suitable adopters. Staff and volunteers thus position the animal practices of more recent immigrants as problematic and reify the idea that acculturation to mainstream (i.e., white) animal practices will reduce or eliminate these problematic practices.

While volunteers are assumed to be responsible owners themselves be-cause of their whiteness and/or middle-class status, staff members use the assertion of responsible guardianship as evidence of their upward mobility. Unlike many of the volunteers I worked alongside during my fieldwork, a substantial proportion of staff members live in PAW's service area, and almost all are Latinx and likely working class. Most have completed only high school (although some have associate degrees). A junior kennel atten-dant's typical annual direct compensation is around $40,000, with a ceiling of around $50,000 for more senior kennel staff, which is about 23 percent below the statewide median income for 2015 of $64,500. Midlevel managers typically have earnings in the high $60,000s, and only the shelter manager has a salary approaching $100,000.[22] However, most jobs at PAW include fringe benefits, and some classes of employees are unionized, affording them greater workplace protection than workers in typical nonunionized workplaces. In contrast to other studies of animal shelters, many of PAW's workers—likely because of their lower-income and nonwhite backgrounds—did not seek to work here because they are animal lovers; rather, employment at PAW offers a unionized job with low entry requirements that is preferable to other low-wage jobs for which they might be eligible because of greater job security and compensation.[23]

Staff use their animal practices as a basis of commonality with each other and volunteers, as markers of their upward mobility, and as markers of being "good" employees of an animal shelter. Staff construct themselves as different from the clients whose companion animals are impounded at the shelter: those clients are irresponsible pet owners, while PAW staff are responsible about their management of companion animals. Being a "responsible pet owner" links the staff members to mainstream, middle-class, white America and stands as evidence of their successful upward mobility and their assimilation.

Staff accomplish this by demonstrating their responsible guardianship: they bring their dogs to work (when management permits it, which has not been consistent), place photographs of their companion animals around their desks, and talk about their own companion animals or their desires to have them (many do not have companion animals of their own because they rent or live with their parents, and thus they focus on their future aspirations). Some staff members also take home medically fragile and/or unweaned animals from the shelter to foster. They also routinely express their frustration with people whose animals are in the shelter, using language that differentiates them from such people: "I would never do that!" "These people around here!" "What kind of monsters are these?"

Staff members' efforts to establish their credibility as responsible guardians aligned with mainstream animal-keeping practices are challenged in rare cases when staff themselves engage in the behaviors associated with irresponsible owners. Three times during my fieldwork, I was asked by a staff member to help rehome their personal companion animal. In one such case, the dog was in the shelter, although the dog had been in the care of the staff member's ex-wife since a separation over a year earlier. The staff member's effort to differentiate himself from his ex-wife's animal practices is illustrative: he complained to me and other volunteers that she kept the dog outside and that her "crappy" behavior toward the dog—including bringing the dog to the shelter—was undermining his efforts to raise their child with the animal practices to which he ascribed.

In another case, a staff member adopted a dog from the shelter, kept the dog exclusively outside, and then returned him when he started to show behavior issues typical of "yard dogs." In a third case, the shelter staff member ultimately kept the dog with financial assistance for veterinary care. In the two cases involving the shelter, other staff were quick to criticize their colleagues who didn't adhere to the expectations that companion animals be kept indoors and treated like valued family members.

Staff members who fail to keep animals indoors or who bring them back to the shelter violate the separation between the shelter workers and the local community. Other staff openly condemn their behavior—including around volunteers—freely using negative terms about them, such as "idiot," "jerk," and "ignorant fool." Since those staff members who have companion animals overwhelmingly keep them indoors, those who do not are outsiders, aligned with the problematic public the shelter serves.

The boundary work most staff members and volunteers engage in to contrast themselves with irresponsible owners again shifts responsibility for shelter killing onto animals' original guardians and reduces opportunities for compassionate engagement with the issues that people who are unable to keep their pets may be facing. The discourse of irresponsible owners supports a logic of policing and the practice of taking or keeping animals away from members of the community. I often observed as volunteers in particular used harsh and sometimes demeaning language to appeal to people not to surrender their animals; while staff are prohibited from doing this, their indifferent and more subtly hostile interactions with many members of the public may also stem from frustration with the people they see as irresponsible owners. Judging people who use services at the shelter as irresponsible thus seems to inhibit communicating and collaborating in ways that might help reduce the number of animals in need.

SHIFTING VIEWS OF COMPANION ANIMAL HOMELESSNESS

During my fieldwork, a shift occurred in the animal-sheltering industry in the Los Angeles area. While many public animal shelters continue to see homelessness among companion animals through the lenses of irresponsible owners and public safety, major national animal welfare organizations, including HSUS and the ASPCA, have started to move toward thinking about animal homelessness as at least partially an outcome of human poverty and precarity. At two shelters within thirty miles of PAW, local nonprofit/low-cost organizations started programs to help guardians keep their companion animals. Operating with the mantra "First home, forever home," these programs provide human guardians to companion animals with a range of services and resources, including free or low-cost food and litter, drop-in free training classes, financial assistance with veterinary care, low-cost vaccines and microchips, and assistance in building or repairing fences or gates to contain animals. When guardians still are not able to keep their companion animals with them, these programs work to get the animals straight to rescue organizations so that they bypass the public shelter system altogether.

Recognizing the various challenges guardians in PAW's service area face, the national animal welfare organization I call Humane America began a program at PAW in late 2014 intended to reduce the number of intakes at PAW and increase the number of live releases. Like the programs at other local shelters, this public-private partnership is intended to divert animals from coming into the shelter in the first place but provides a more limited range of services. Staff who work for Humane America, not SCAS or PAW, sit at a table outside the entrance to PAW and speak with those who bring animals in or who express a need for assistance. The program can help guardians with funds for low-cost veterinary care and offers advice for dealing with animal behavior issues and conflicts with neighbors and landlords.[24]

Humane America encourages members of the public who need help with their companion animals to accept assistance through the program without feeling judged for needing help. Still, because Humane America administers the program separately from PAW with their own staff and a tent as an office at the shelter, its approach seems to have done little to shift the discourse of irresponsible ownership *within* the shelter. In some ways, the presence of the program has heightened the discourse of the irresponsible owner because now irresponsible owners are so terrible that they even decline the help Humane America offers them. The trouble is that while Humane America can assist animal guardians with short-term resources like veterinary vouchers, or with suggestions on how to negotiate with a landlord, the program does not tackle the bigger issues that members of the local communities face, like an expensive rental market with virtually no options for pit bulls, high rates of eviction, wages that are inadequate for the cost of living, and tightening immigration enforcement. Short-term material relief can help keep animals and humans together, but it is rarely enough to do so on a longer-term basis in the face of the many challenges faced by low-income people of color in PAW's service area.

4   The Struggle for Shelter Animal Survival

FOR OVER TWO CENTURIES, killing companion animals has been understood as an acceptable solution to the "problem" of homelessness among companion animals in the United States. Although companion animals enjoy a much higher social status and generally a higher quality of life than many other types of animals, such as farmed animals, they are not spared from being killed if they are deemed surplus, unwanted, unhealthy, unsafe, and/or undesirable. Decades after the advent of the no-kill movement, public shelters in the United States, and even many major animal welfare organizations, seem to accept the idea that there is simply no other realistic way for shelters (and society at large) to respond to companion animal homelessness than to end the lives of unwanted animals. PAW and SCAS treat killing animals as an unpleasant, but unavoidable, component of the shelter's work.

Yet shelter death is highly contested in the shelter environment. While staff and volunteers largely agree that irresponsible owners are responsible for why animals—especially dogs—are in the shelter, they disagree on what the shelter's responsibility is to those animals after impound. At PAW, volunteers see impounded animals as sentient individuals with a desire and right to live. They conceptualize impounded animals as animals whom humans have wronged and to whom the shelter should give an opportunity for a new, better relationship with humans. Some staff members share aspects of this view, while many others maintain a stronger commitment to shelter death as an acceptable and appropriate response to companion animal homelessness. Managerial staff tend to treat impounded animals as a population rather than as individuals with specific needs and wants. Both volunteers and staff differentiate between dogs and other types of impounded animals, especially cats, who during the years of my fieldwork faced gradually decreasing, but nonetheless staggering, shelter death rates.

Dying in a shelter is not a random-likelihood event for any given animal but rather a risk that increases or decreases depending first and foremost on the animal's location and then on the animal's species, breed, coloring, age, health status, behavior, and ability to attract the attention of staff and/or volunteers. Some of these characteristics—such as breed and behavior—are in turn linked to broader ideas about race, class, disability, and deservingness. Shelter death risk is thus the outcome of a complex calculation of the value of any given animal, a value that is very much determined through social processes and that reflects human ideas about, and practices of, inequality. Because an animal's value is socially determined, it is also highly negotiable, and staff and volunteers often value animals differently.

In this chapter, I examine how volunteers—who are almost entirely women—resist PAW's practice of defining dogs as unadoptable and therefore as killable. Volunteers' resistance involves rejecting PAW's practice of killing dogs by advocating for individual animals. While this approach appears highly individualistic insofar as it benefits only one animal at a time, the cumulative effect of their advocacy for individual animals is to challenge and destabilize the practice of shelter killing for *all* animals. Although not always successful in saving individual animals, volunteers maintain a consistent challenge to PAW's beliefs about what warrants death as the best solution. Power at PAW thus does not run neatly from top to bottom but rather reflects the intersection of class with situated knowledge in the organizational context of the shelter.[1] Volunteers at PAW use their social capital from outside the shelter to resist the authority of staff within the shelter. In so doing, they reinforce existing social hierarchies of class, race, and gender, while simultaneously challenging PAW's institutional discourse of adoptability, which deems the lives of sick or "stressed" animals as not worth saving. They thus oppose PAW's commitment to upholding anthroparchy vis-à-vis companion animals.

Unlike many volunteer scenarios in which volunteers try to support an organization's work, at PAW volunteers often endeavor to counter or resist the work that the shelter does. Most volunteers see themselves as bound less to the institution than to the animals impounded at the institution. Ultimately, volunteering at PAW is not about helping the state agency that oversees SCAS and, by extension, PAW, or about supporting staff; instead, it is about advocating for animals who volunteers believe otherwise have few or no advocates. Volunteers routinely declare that "it's all about the animals!" When I expressed to another volunteer that I felt bad about not being helpful to staff on a particular occasion, she admonished me: "We aren't here to help the staff, Katja! Your job is to help the animals." Volunteers' focus on helping animals—whom they see primarily as victimized rather than helped by the shelter system— destabilizes idealized images common in US culture of volunteers as supportive of the organizations for which they volunteer and reveals strategies through which volunteers challenge organizational practices.[2]

With their focus on helping animals evade shelter killing, volunteers are often at odds with staff and with PAW and SCAS policies and practices. While not all volunteers at PAW are no-kill advocates, all believe PAW can reduce its death rate substantially by changing routine practices. Volunteers deploy a repertoire of resistance to shelter death that is "a combined result of the interplay between social structures and power relations, as well as [volunteers'] creative experimentation with tactics and experiences of earlier attempts to practice resistance, together with the situational circumstances in which the resistance is played out."[3] Resistance involves negotiation of power relations.[4] In the context of the animal shelter, power includes access to resources and systems of knowledge and control over discourses over animals' bodies.

Volunteers are engaged in everyday acts of resistance that are informal and not organized through any leader or organization. Still, both volunteers and staff recognize volunteers' actions of resistance *as such*. In fact, conflict at the shelter is often quite palpable between volunteers and staff as they negotiate the fates of individual animals and the routine shelter practices that shape those fates. Volunteer resistance is at once spontaneous and routinized, strategic and yet largely reactive.

Examining volunteer resistance shows how resistance must be understood intersectionally. That is, resistance can challenge one system of power even as it reinforces another and can draw on one privileged identity while struggling against another marginalized one.[5] Indeed, volunteers' resistance involves intersections of privilege and marginalization. As self-appointed spokespeople for animals whose voices are not recognized in the shelter, volunteers represent the interests of a marginalized group. Further, women volunteers mobilize for the lives of shelter animals to challenge anthroparchal and patriarchal control over the lives and bodies of both animals and women. However, many volunteers also bring substantial capital into the shelter and occupy positions of privilege outside the shelter relative to the staff members. They overwhelmingly come from outside PAW's service area, often traveling thirty or more miles in Los Angeles' notorious traffic to intervene on behalf on animals who they believe are otherwise forgotten. Volunteers mobilize their social capital to challenge staff assessments of unadoptability and, in so doing, undermine the general shelter logic that shelter death is a reasonable response to caring for animals in a shelter. Their capacity to do so is shaped by their position as women and as mostly white, middle- and upper-class people, so that their engagements with staff are not only about animals and animal welfare but also about race, class, and gender.

NEGOTIATING SHELTER KILLING
AND THE KILLERS AT PAW

Sitting in one of the play areas with fellow volunteer Louise, watching a bouncy Husky run along the fence, our conversation turned to the shelter's internal practices. Because I had been at the shelter for many years, other volunteers often asked me to clarify for them how the shelter worked. That day, Louise was feeling troubled about shelter killing. She didn't understand how animals were selected nor the mechanics of how they were actually killed. As I gently explained to her how the staff would choose animals to die, who completed the task of putting dogs down, and how killing happened, she gasped: "But Bethany [a kennel attendant] is so nice! She puts dogs down?" Her eyes filled with tears. I replied that almost all of the kennel attendants participated in shelter killing as part of their jobs, something Louise could not fathom. To her, it was irreconcilable that a staff member she knew as compassionate and kind toward impounded animals also helped kill them.

I understood some of her feelings: I myself was puzzled that some staff who seemed to invest a lot in their work also managed to kill animals in their care without any signs of obvious trauma or any expressed desire to change shelter practices or to seek alternate employment. While outside critics sometimes refer to those who kill animals in shelters in very negative terms, I never had the sense that any staff member who killed animals as part of their work did so out of malice or with any pleasure. I was also aware that a job at SCAS is quite desirable: for workers with GEDs or high school or community college education, SCAS offers a unionized workplace with better financial incentives and prospects for moving up a career ladder than many other employers hiring this class of workers do. For staff who see themselves as animal lovers and as prosocial, SCAS presents a narrative of helping animals and helping people that justifies those elements of the work that are unpleasant, including the killing of animals. Staff (like volunteers) are able to hold on to happy experiences and stories—the shelter's successes—as a strategy for coping with the problematic aspects of the work. In a society in which animals are killed by the hundreds of millions each year simply as food, it's not that difficult to rationalize the taking of animal life, especially when done in the name of protecting the public or ending animal suffering.

Volunteers are not allowed to observe or participate when animals are killed at PAW, and my own experiences of animals dying are all from outside the shelter, including euthanizing dogs in my care and watching a dog be killed in traffic. Like Louise and many other volunteers, I try to separate my support for ending the human killing of companion (and, in my case, all) animals from my feelings toward shelter staff. When I began volunteering at PAW, I knew that the facility killed a lot of animals and that my volunteering was not likely to change that in any significant way. I wasn't going there to judge anyone or to proselytize no-kill approaches. I also wanted very much to understand *why* SCAS and PAW *did* kill animals in their care. Yet the more I came to understand the logic of killing, the less I thought PAW needed to kill impounded animals.

SCAS and PAW present three core reasons why they kill animals: (1) to maintain public safety; (2) from lack of resources to keep animals in the shelter for prolonged periods of time; and (3) to end animal suffering. Volunteers' experiences at the shelter undermine their acceptance of these reasons. How I came to doubt PAW's reasons for killing animals is quite typical for volunteers, many of whom start volunteering feeling ambivalent about the justifications for shelter killing. Fostering dogs from PAW shifted my thinking to the point that I now believe, as do most other volunteers, that killing can be an appropriate response only in the most dire of veterinary crises. Over a period of four years, my wife and I fostered dozens of dogs with various health issues, especially respiratory infections, pneumonia, and demodex mange, and behavior issues, including crippling fear of humans and/or other dogs, reactivity toward other dogs, and growling and nipping at people—all issues PAW would use as the basis for declaring an animal a public safety threat and killing them—as well as less serious issues like not being housebroken or not knowing how to walk on a leash. My wife and I were able to help each of these dogs be safe and suitable for adoption and · found appropriate placements for all but one of them (whom we kept). Neither of us has any professional or academic background in animal behavior or training—we are simply two dog-savvy adults who have also acquired deeper knowledge of canine behavior through our involvement in fostering. This is not to say that all of these dogs were easy to rehabilitate, and, depending on the definition used for success, we weren't always successful. But all of these dogs could live with people, and we found appropriate adoptive homes for every one of them (in one case, our own). The repeated experience of seeing dogs whom the shelter would have put down move into homes and have happy lives that also enrich the lives of others undermined any doubts I had that shelter death was a reasonable solution to unhoused animals. Fostering eroded any belief I had in the idea that there aren't enough homes for adoptable dogs (even for dogs who don't meet market expectations for adoptability) or that dogs in shelters disproportionately have behavior issues that make them difficult or impossible to place.

Having different dogs pass through my home also contributed to my developing a new level of appreciation for dogs in ways that made it more difficult to justify killing dogs in shelters. I have lived with dogs since the day I was born, excepting a few years in a college dormitory where they were prohibited. I consider myself a dog lover through and through. But in fostering dogs, I came to know dogs differently than I had as a permanent guardian to dogs living in my home. I came to see in each and every dog something special, even in those who annoyed me or were challenging. Trudy the German Shepherd was incredibly difficult to manage on leash and chased our cats mercilessly, but she had the sweetest, kissable face with a mask over her eyes like the Lone Ranger that gave her a perpetual air of mischief. Gladys was terrified of just about everything, but her flapping, awkward footsteps made me laugh. Maple, whose body told the story of pain and suffering, growled at every human she met besides my wife and me, yet she was the most committed companion when I was bedridden for weeks after surgery, lying by my side day after day. When I was too sick to read, I would stroke the contours of her skull bone and run her tattered ears between my fingers while she gazed up at me. Norton was our most magnificent foster, a bicolor pit bull mix with a coat like crushed velvet and yellow eyes immensely expressive and sometimes stern. We rescued him when he developed kennel cough at the shelter and was slated to be killed. At home, he kept us in stitches of laughter with his happy play style and true appreciation for creature comforts—he would throw himself into bed with immense enthusiasm, relishing his new life. Often when he slept, we would rub his thighs or back, causing him to emit deep snores and snorts of pleasure. His thick, sturdy legs ended in massive paws of gold and gray fur, and I liked to kiss his feet. I could not imagine how anyone could slide a needle into Norton's beautiful calf and inject him with poison, for no reason other than a lack of institutional and societal will to keep him alive.

Other volunteers share similar experiences of knowing animals, particularly ones who might be defined as difficult or undesirable as lively commodities because of health or behavior issues. Sharing their homes with animals who have "issues," but whom they nonetheless love deeply, makes them feel that all animals should have a chance. Angie, a volunteer who has adopted and fostered many senior dogs with a range of health issues, asserts:

> Old dogs are the best! People don't want them and so the shelter kills them. . . . People have all these ideas that they are used goods, or sick, or whatever. But no one will love you like an old dog you save from here. So what if they're a little incontinent or need some pills? It's totally worth it.

For Angie, then, old dogs are excellent companions who do not deserve to be killed in a shelter. Alanna cares for two dogs who have significant fear of people but whose trust she has earned and who follow her adoringly. Lien adopted a middle-aged pit bull with the sagging nipples and belly typical of a dog who has had many litters and found her to be a remarkable best friend, helping her shepherd numerous fosters through her home. Almost all of the longer-term volunteers at the shelter have at least one (and often several) animals in their care whom the shelter saw as unlikely to be adopted. The experience of caring for these undesirable animals as their fosters or guardians solidifies their views that all companion animals should be given the opportunity to live out their natural lives.

Volunteers further see ways in which resources at the shelter are not used effectively, which undermines staff claims that SCAS has insufficient resources to keep animals at PAW long enough to be adopted. Most especially, during my fieldwork, volunteers felt that *they* were underutilized as a resource. SCAS and PAW staff generally sought to limit volunteers' access to animals and authority within the shelter; this gatekeeping meant that many initiatives volunteers could have staffed either never came to fruition at all or were far less successful than they could have been. Such initiatives included mobile and on-site adoption events, networking of animals available for adoption through social media and adoption websites, community access to spay/neuter services, and foster programs for puppies, dogs, kittens, and cats. Volunteers offered a significant pool of time and skills to PAW that would have increased the success of these programs, but PAW declined most of their help and made it very difficult for volunteers to maintain those programs that PAW did permit.

GENDER AND RESISTANCE AT PAW

Volunteers' connections to animals, and the ways that volunteers resist the shelter's practices of killing, are deeply gendered. Almost all volunteers at PAW are women, and almost all volunteers engage in resistance to shelter killing. I can count on one hand the total number of regular men volunteers during my eight-year period as a volunteer. In her research on the gender imbalance among animal rights activists, Emily Gaarder finds a number of reasons for why women are more likely than men to engage in this work.[6] My experience at PAW also suggests a high degree of complexity to explain women's overrepresentation among shelter volunteers. Many interconnected structures and pathways lead more women to volunteer at PAW than men. Girls and women are socialized to engage in care work, and, although some of the earliest visible animal advocates in the United States were men, the culture of shelter volunteerism and animal rescue in the United States has skewed heavily toward women for decades.[7] This is particularly true among advocates for companion animals, whom many women see both as family members and as an accessible population in need of care and advocacy. Women's experiences as survivors of violence, including child sexual abuse and domestic violence, seem to make them more connected with animals, whom they connect with as innocent and undeserving victims of mistreatment that no one else will stand up for.[8] At PAW, many women volunteers are open about their experiences of abuse and their belief that helping animals both protects the most vulnerable and contributes to a more compassionate society in general. I also encountered many shelter volunteers who shared with me their feeling that an animal—almost always a dog—had been the first living being to offer them unconditional love or had helped them through a particularly painful period in life, such as a time spent battling addiction or separating from an abusive spouse. Others simply declare that they prefer the company of nonhuman animals to that of human animals.

Volunteering at an animal shelter also provides a socially acceptable way for women to engage in socially celebrated altruistic behavior. Volunteering at PAW generates substantial affirmation from others not involved at the shelter. Although I have participated in many different volunteer projects and efforts at social change, and have numerous accomplishments outside volunteerism, no effort of mine has ever received as much positive feedback from friends and strangers as my volunteerism at a high-kill shelter. People brim over with accolades about my shelter work, calling it "so important" and even "the most important thing you do," often noting that they would be unable to volunteer at a shelter because it would be "too [emotionally] difficult" or because "I would take all of the animals home."[9] The culture of shelter volunteers and the animal rescue community also engages in extensive self-affirmation and celebration; especially coming from an academic environment (where congratulating others occurs far too infrequently), I find the amount of congratulation—including self-congratulation—in this milieu remarkable. For women, whose caregiving labor is typically taken for granted in US society, shelter volunteerism presents an opportunity to be feted and praised for engaging in caregiving work, and even to be routinely cited as a "hero," a social status rarely given to women and instead reserved for men who engage in risky behavior for the benefit of others. Of course, much of the affirmation of shelter volunteers from both inside and outside the shelter community depends on their successful resistance to the shelter: it is by *saving* animals from shelter killing that volunteers become heroes.

Men in turn face barriers to participation in that working with companion animals, especially cats, is feminized in the US.[10] Men are typically not socialized as caregivers, and caring for animals in particular falls outside hegemonic masculinity in the US. The few men who did volunteer at PAW benefited from encouragement because of their gender. I routinely heard women volunteers state in the presence of the men volunteers, "We really need more men around here!" or "It's so great to have a man here today." Men volunteers also experience routine affirmations of their masculinity, as both women volunteers and all staff members ask for their help with more physical tasks and center men's physical strength as important and useful at the shelter. For some men, the attention that their gender brings may be unwelcome; at least one man who stopped volunteering after about six months said he felt other volunteers and the staff had unrealistic expectations for what he could do at the shelter because he was a man. Another who was quite shy simply didn't enjoy the attention showered on him as a man and also left.

In their encounters with volunteers, staff seem to give women more leeway than men as advocates and to expect their involvement in trying to save animals because of the gendered composition of the volunteer body and the gendered composition of animal advocates more broadly. Staff view women asking for more time or for other consideration for impounded animals as normal and nonthreatening, although perhaps as overly emotional; staff members routinely mentioned women's emotionality to make sense of their advocacy work and to forgive any overstepping (e.g., "I know she only asked me that [somewhat inappropriate favor] because she cares so much").

RELATIONAL RESISTANCE

Women volunteers at PAW employ what I call relational resistance, or utilization of interpersonal relationships as a basis for resistance.[11] Women volunteers build two kinds of relationships that are key to their resistance. One set of relationships are those with the impounded animals: volunteers take time to interact with and get to know the animals so that they can subsequently advocate for them. They are uniquely positioned to build these relationships with animals because they can take the time to spend with impounded animals. A second set are relationships with staff members that volunteers can capitalize on by asking staff for consideration of their concerns about specific animals. Volunteers use these relationships with animals and staff in the interest of a superordinate goal—reducing shelter killing and animal suffering—that volunteers and animals cannot accomplish and that staff normally refuse to pursue.

Employing a relational strategy of resistance by capitalizing on relationships with specific animals and/or staff members, volunteers attempt to show to staff members that a dog is adoptable and challenge staff assessments of an impounded animal as less adoptable. Merely expressing an interest in a specific animal to the staff can help that animal be seen by staff as an individual and companion, rather than just as another impounded animal, and volunteers routinely talk to and email staff regarding their observations about an animal's personality and behavior. Volunteers also take dogs out of their kennels and into play yards where staff may see them. Volunteers place the impounded animals in front of staff in roles like help-seeking innocent or future family pet. When a large dog has a characteristic that would reduce their adoptability—such as being older or black in color—volunteers identify other characteristics that would make them *more* adoptable, such as getting along well with other dogs or having obedience skills, and make those characteristics known to staff.[12] "Look at what a good boy he is!" they declare to staff. These efforts at positioning a dog as deserving and adoptable help that dog secure more time at the shelter to find an adopter or rescue, thereby making it more likely that the dog will be released alive.

Volunteer Maria told me about her practice of spending time with dogs whom the staff have identified as difficult: "When I come across a dog I know the staff are going to claim is difficult—maybe they hide under their bed in their cage or snarl—I take them out and help them warm up . . . and then I take them into the office so they [staff members] all see that the dog is okay and can be adopted." Volunteer Charlene emailed the shelter staff notes from her experiences with dogs she spent time with during her weekly session volunteering at the shelter. Still another volunteer conveyed, "I just always drive home what's good about a dog to the staff, and what makes them stand out—like a dog who catches balls out of the air, or a pittie who just won't stop rolling over for belly rubs. I think then they start thinking about them as someone's pet, not just one of a million dogs they see come through the shelter."

Volunteers often build relationships with the staff so that they can subsequently ask them for favors, including giving specific animals more time at the shelter. Occasionally, a genuine friendship emerged between a staff member and a volunteer. Even when, more commonly, these relationships remained situational acquaintanceships, they often involved some level of care, such as offering support during familial crises outside the shelter. So while these relationships were transactional, they also involved caring.

Volunteers are quite open about how they try to build relationships with staff so that staff will extend them favors. Bringing food for the staff is a common practice: one volunteer baked for the staff each time she came in so that she could, in her words, keep staff "wrapped around my finger." Most volunteers give key staff holiday gifts and regularly bring food like doughnuts, muffins, and cakes. This practice of payola helps encourage staff to have positive feelings toward specific volunteers and thus be willing to take the time to talk and email with these volunteers about animals and, when necessary, extend the "due-out" date, or the first date for which an animal will be evaluated as a candidate to be killed, of dogs those volunteers like.

Other volunteers skip the gifting and just focus on being very friendly and cheerful with staff; Maria said, "The managers here always seem kind of grumpy and down, so I just smile and laugh a lot and try to make small talk with them. . . . I kind of butter them up so that they will help me out when I need it." Another noted that she always comes to the shelter's celebratory events, like the annual Christmas Eve lunch and occasional other seasonal events, as a way to foster personal connections with staff members. One couple who were longtime volunteers even hosted catered staff parties at their home in Beverly Hills as a way to show appreciation and foster goodwill.

Staff, in turn, will ask specific volunteers for help in securing rescues for dogs of whom they are especially fond. On many occasions, I received personal appeals from the shelter staff I had built relationships with, imploring me to "work my magic" and find a rescue for an animal the staff liked. These relationships between staff and volunteers are thus often about respective back-scratching—and often felt to me very much about tit-for-tat exchanges: if a staff member helped me help a dog, I could then expect they would ask me for help. These interactions are one set of moments in which volunteers and staff both feel they need each other and draw on a shared sense of intent and goals.

VOLUNTEERS' REPERTOIRE OF RESISTANCE
IN STRUGGLES OVER ADOPTABILITY

Killing at PAW organizes routine activity and interactions. The threat of it looms constantly: from the moment an animal enters the shelter, volunteers worry about the animal's fate. This fear is particularly acute for dogs, even though cats are much more likely to be killed at the shelter. The high rate of deaths for cats is explained at least partially by PAW's fixed policy that cats identified as feral are unadoptable and will be put down. While volunteers could organize to advocate for a change in this policy, they have not done so, and the fact that staff can point to a policy to justify the killing closes off the kind of space for negotiation that exists with dogs.

Direct discussion of shelter death is a taboo at PAW; from each volunteer's first orientation meeting for new volunteers, shelter administrators advise us that we may not talk with staff about shelter death—which is always referred to as euthanasia in official PAW documents—and the volunteer manual specifically instructs volunteers not to ask staff members about shelter practices of euthanasia. Through the creation of this taboo, the shelter management exerts power over volunteers. This gag order, however, breaks down in reference to specific animals: volunteers and staff routinely engage in conflicts about the risk of shelter death for *specific* animals, as well as for categories of animals. The most common way in which this occurs is through volunteers asking staff to extend an animal's due-out date.

Ultimately, negotiation around the due-out date and other factors that can affect an animal's chance of live release means that the risk of shelter death for any particular impounded animal is established, not through objective criteria, but rather through social meanings and social interactions. These in turn reflect dynamics of power, resistance, and different resources and forms of capital available to staff and volunteers. Volunteers and staff at PAW have different forms of capital and unique relationships to the shelter, the impounded animals, and the social world outside the shelter. Most staff are at the shelter forty or more hours per week working shifts that can run at any time during the day or night, seven days per week. Volunteers have much less contact with the shelter environment than staff. Although two volunteers during the research period were at the shelter almost daily, most are at the shelter one or two days per week, and some as little as once per month, and generally only when the shelter is open to the public. Volunteers have much greater autonomy than staff: volunteers have no clear supervisor, no set tasks, and no measures of efficacy.

Because they can control what they do (within the limits PAW managers set) and when they do it at the shelter, and because they volunteer primarily to have contact with impounded animals, volunteers generally spend more time getting to know the impounded animals than staff are able to, which is critical for their advocacy. Volunteers focus on socializing with impounded animals and helping adopters. Even those volunteers who assist staff with activities that involve less contact with impounded animals, such as cleaning kennels, will do the work at a slower pace than the staff do so that they can interact with the animals.

Volunteers also differ from staff in terms of their demographic backgrounds. During my fieldwork, volunteers were typically middle- and high-income whites and Asian Americans.[13] With the exception of a handful of high school and college students, most of the volunteers were women between the ages of thirty and sixty-five and typically held professional, college, and/or graduate degrees.[14] Like me, many other volunteers were employed full time outside the shelter in white-collar occupations, often in positions that afforded them a degree of flexibility in terms of their work hours or that rendered them part of the so-called creative class.[15] Relative to staff, then, volunteers generally occupied positions of greater privilege, with stable incomes in white-collar occupations and, among many, flexible work schedules. They volunteered at PAW because they were fond of companion animals and wanted to help animals in need. They also held values about animals consistent with white middle-class norms of animal keeping in which companion animals are considered family and treated accordingly.

Managerial-level staff have the authority to make decisions about which animals will be killed and when, and they are therefore seemingly the most powerful actors at PAW. However, volunteers work to undermine this power and especially to challenge shelter killing as a practice. Volunteers resist both what the shelter has established as risk factors for shelter death *and* the shelter's discourse of shelter death as a necessary but regrettable outcome.

Volunteers assert that the vast majority of companion animals are adoptable and should not be put down, and they use knowledge systems about companion animals from *outside* the shelter to resist companion animal death within the shelter.

The core site of contestation is in defining companion animals, especially dogs, as "highly adoptable," a coveted category that lowers their risk of death to almost nothing (cats, whose chances at live release are so much lower than dogs', are not generally discussed as frequently in these terms, other than in the differentiation of feral or community cats from those who have been socialized with people). The language of adoptability is part of the hegemonic shelter discourse created and maintained by the shelter bureaucracy. Volunteers use this framework to highlight how more impounded animals than not are adoptable and to emphasize that shelter death is avoidable.

Shelter management gives dogs whom they consider "highly adoptable" more time at the shelter to find an adopter or rescue by extending their due-out date. Highly adoptable animals may be eligible for transports to no-kill shelters. In the shelter environment, situated in a broader social context where companion animals have come to be seen as a type of consumer product, "highly adoptable" dogs include those with one or more of the following characteristics: small dogs, puppies, white dogs, fluffy dogs, and purebred dogs of popular breeds. Dogs become less adoptable as they mature, or if they are over thirty pounds, black or brindle in color, showing signs of any type of health or behavioral issue, a mixed breed, a pit bull, a Chihuahua, or a mixed breed that includes either pit bull or Chihuahua characteristics.[16] The risk of death varies depending on the specific constellation of characteristics from each of these lists. For example, a blind, twelve-year-old white miniature Poodle typically is seen as more adoptable than a ten-month-old, black-and-white pit bull, even though the former is sick and old and the latter is healthy and young.[17]

Except for animals who are deemed unsafe for adoption, PAW does not formally classify impounded animals into categories of adoptability, nor does the shelter track the attributes of adopted animals to determine criteria for adoptability. Rather, shelter managers define adoptability on the basis of their perceptions of which types of animals are most often adopted or rescued.[18] Staff often invest their energy into these animals because they see them as the most deserving and as having the highest likelihood of success.

Those animals the staff favor get their due-out dates extended and receive more staff effort to promote their adoption or rescue, so that they are more likely to be live releases, in turn reinforcing the staff's beliefs that these types of animals are more likely to be adopted or rescued.

In chapter 6, I elaborate on the challenges pit bulls face in animal shelters like PAW because of their racialization. Their low status is tied to beliefs about race, class, gender, and safety, but their adoptability—as with other dogs—is also a reflection of the commodification of companion animals. Many guardians expect companion animals to meet their personal needs, whether for personal protection, emotional support, or particular forms of companionship. Adopters who come to PAW always have a list of criteria for the companion they are seeking: size, personality, training level, appearance, and other characteristics may be part of their wish list for an ideal companion. While ultimately some adopters select a companion on the basis of a so-called love connection, few experience such connections with animals who don't already meet their idea of a good pet.[19] No one comes to the shelter looking for a small, fluffy dog and leaves with a pit bull.

What kind of animal an adopter and the staff see as desirable is itself the outcome of social processes. Many animal guardians are constrained by rental agreements that allow only certain types and/or sizes and/or species of companion animals, reflecting social beliefs about what types of dogs are appropriate to live where. Companion animal fads propel some types of animals into the mainstream. During the period of fieldwork, Siberian Huskies and Alaskan Malamutes (who are always available for adoption at PAW) experienced a surge in popularity due to the role of wolves in the successful television series *Game of Thrones*. Los Angeles was ground zero for the rise in popularity of so-called purse pets, or dogs small enough to be easily carried in a handbag, when celebrities like Paris Hilton began toting them around in bags in the early 2000s (although Hilton reportedly paid $8,000 for her "micro-Chihuahua"). Staff view animals who are young, purebred, and/or small as most adoptable but also will sometimes develop a soft spot for an underdog, such as a less adoptable animal with a particularly sad origin story or an especially charismatic personality.

Volunteers struggle to position animals in the "highly adoptable" category so that staff will extend their time at the shelter and possibly give them other consideration, like specialized veterinary care or a new behavior evaluation. Volunteers use one or more of the following relational strategies in their repertoire of resistance, each of which I discuss in turn, to challenge shelter determinations of adoptability and reduce the risk of shelter death: (1) educational; (2) health based; (3) moral; (4) reputational; and (5) legal.

Educational Strategies of Resistance

Part of establishing a dog as adoptable is distancing that dog from the "unadoptable" category. Employing an educational strategy, which reflects volunteers' specific forms of knowledge about dogs and canine behavior outside the shelter and in the context of middle-class homes that see dogs as "furkids" and family members, many volunteers challenge staff representations of specific animals or groups of animals as less adoptable or unadoptable. Pit bulls are one category of dog that the shelter staff classify as less adoptable. Volunteers routinely engage in strategies for challenging staff assumptions about, and practices around, pit bulls, using rhetoric from the pit bull advocacy movement outside the shelter to bolster claims that these dogs should not be treated differently than others. Volunteers show staff photographs or videos on cell phones of pit bulls engaged in silly or friendly behavior in an effort to destigmatize these types of dogs.[20] They bring the impounded pit bulls into contact with staff, cooing over them, petting them, and making the dogs visible in the role of companion. Volunteers Alana and Suze tell staff about living with pit bulls in apartments, thereby undermining the institutional practice of trying to place pit bulls only in single-family homes with fenced yards, a limitation that volunteers see as unnecessarily restrictive. More assertive strategies include telling staff they are misinformed about these dogs; sometimes volunteers do this in a friendly, casual way, as when they tease staff with whom they have rapport about being scared of pit bulls, and at other times they express greater seriousness, as when they implore staff to stop "singling out" pit bulls to be put down and to move away from "breed discrimination," sometimes using the mantra common among pit bull advocates to "judge the deed, not the breed." Through these various strategies, volunteers work to distance pit bulls from their social position within the shelter as undesirable and even dangerous dogs and to instead associate them with being potential family members within "good" (i.e., middle-class, non-Black/Latinx) homes, as I discuss in greater detail in chapter 6.

Educational strategies also involve volunteer challenges to the shelter practice of designating certain animals as available only to rescue groups that are partnered with PAW. Dogs who are categorized as "rescue only" have a health or behavioral issue, as assessed by shelter staff, that makes them unsafe or unsuitable for placement with an adopter, and they are much less likely to exit PAW alive. With regard to "rescue only" dogs, volunteers mobilize their knowledge of dogs outside the shelter to challenge practices within the shelter. They bring in rhetoric from dog trainers and behaviorists—a category of experts absent in the shelter environment but prevalent in American companion animal culture—pointing to "shelter stress" as a reason why some dogs exhibit undesirable behaviors in the shelter environment. Drawing on their experiences with former shelter dogs outside the shelter, volunteers show staff pictures or videos of dogs flagged as aggressive at PAW interacting sociably with humans and/or other dogs out of the shelter. When a dog is deemed unadoptable because of alleged aggression, volunteers invoke the stories of other dogs who shared this designation but turned out to be loving and happy companions. Because dogs who are deemed aggressive at PAW can very often be well-adjusted companions outside the shelter, and because volunteers have occasionally been allowed to bring in outside trainers to evaluate dogs, volunteers have a body of evidence to support their claims that negative behavioral evaluations in the shelter should not doom a dog to the "unadoptable" category.

Staff and volunteers bring two different forms of knowledge to their negotiations about adoptability. Staff uphold the shelter's policing perspective toward human-animal relationships, while volunteers emphasize helping. Volunteers capitalize on their experiences with dogs outside the shelter to remind staff that ultimately dogs will live outside PAW and that judgments of their behavior at PAW are not predictive of their later behavior, a claim that has been widely supported by major animal welfare organizations and by research in the field of animal behavior.[21]

Health-Based Strategies of Resistance

Shelter animals are put down—at PAW, as at many American shelters, given a lethal injection of sodium bicarbonate—with the justification that death ends their suffering. Unlike animals whose bodies are used for meat or other products, minimizing suffering is a key frame for discussing the death of companion animals, whether in a shelter or in a private home. Euthanasia is a widely accepted tool used to end the apparent suffering of companion animals.[22]

The institutional logic at PAW holds that some animals are too sick to be saved or that their illnesses pose too great a threat to the functioning of the shelter—including the well-being of other impounded animals. Widely contested among and between staff and volunteers, PAW's practices of establishing animal health rely on three sets of interlocking logics. The first draws on medicalization, identifying some types of illnesses and symptoms as atypical, undesirable, or incurable. Staff at PAW view animals with those illnesses and symptoms as unadoptable. A second stresses the safety of the community of humans and other animals over the rights of individual dogs. Following this logic, animals who have contagious diseases pose a risk to other impounded animals; during my fieldwork, PAW put down dogs with kennel cough to reduce contagion and especially aggressively culled cats who had the feline virus panleukopenia or who even had been possibly exposed to it. Finally, a third logic draws on the widespread discourse that animals' lives should be ended to alleviate suffering and stresses that certain types or degrees of animal suffering are unbearable for the afflicted and for the caregivers and witnesses to the afflicted. That is, not only is an animal's expression of pain or suffering a reason to end their lives, but when a sick animal causes human emotional distress or significant human effort, the animal's life should also be ended.

Volunteers engage in routine efforts to resist PAW's designation of particular animals as unadoptable for reasons of physical or mental health that rely on these logics. Key to their struggles is the assertion that an animal is well enough—physically and psychologically—to be adopted out to members of the public, or at least to be kept alive to be given that opportunity. The most common ailment to afflict dogs and cats at PAW is upper respiratory infection (URI), also often referred to as kennel cough. Symptoms of URI including nasal discharge, coughing, sneezing, lethargy, and loss of appetite. Just as for humans who get colds that blossom into bronchitis or pneumonia, in a small subset of cases, URI in dogs and cats can turn into something more serious like pneumonia. This is especially likely to occur among very young or very old animals. The other most common category of ailment is skin conditions. Many animals at the shelter suffer from alopecia caused by flea allergy, from demodectic or sarcoptic mange, from tick infestations, and from skin irritation or hair loss for unknown reasons. Of course, digestive issues—particularly diarrhea—are also prevalent, although these are less likely to be seen as serious symptoms unless chronic or occurring in young animals. PAW also receives many dogs with masses; in female dogs, these are often mammary growths in dogs who appear to have been used for breeding. In some cases, the masses are gigantic: one fifty-pound dog had a mass easily the size of a basketball protruding from his side, and another dog of similar size had a mass the size of a large grapefruit hanging from her neck. Shelter veterinary staff are also called upon to deal with a good number of orthopedic injuries, including broken bones and soft tissue injuries.

In their resistance, volunteers mobilize their knowledge of veterinary care and animal behavior to challenge shelter practices of putting down animals classified as sick or behaviorally challenged. They also more broadly push back against the idea that physical or mental health conditions they see as treatable are reasonable justifications to end the life of an impounded dog. Because the shelter cannot conduct blood tests or take X-rays, volunteers have an opening to challenge veterinary claims using the only veterinary information both staff and volunteers have available: symptoms. Kennel cough is highly disputed as a basis for determining death risk. In a normal home environment, dogs will generally recover from kennel cough without any treatment; even in the shelter, most dogs will recover with antibiotics. However, shelter staff often claim dogs "are not responding to treatment" or are "developing pneumonia" and thus should be put down. Volunteers counter with observations about symptoms—a dog is still eating, their nasal passages are clear, they aren't coughing, et cetera—as a way to negotiate more time for an animal.

The effectiveness of volunteers in challenging veterinary and behavioral designations at PAW is facilitated by the workplace structure and resources there. The shelter lacks the resources of a normal animal hospital, which throws the validity of diagnoses into question. Further, in contrast to organizations using volunteer labor that rely on professionalized staff with specialized training, such as social workers, teachers, or tradespeople, nonveterinary staff at PAW rarely begin the job with relevant educational or professional experience and instead learn by doing. Thus staff functionally have the same on-the-job training as volunteers. Volunteers who keep companion animals or who are involved in rescue often see themselves as having *greater* knowledge about companion animals than do staff members.

While veterinary staff at PAW do have specialized training and associated degrees, volunteers often see the RVTs as unreliable in their assessments of animals' physical and mental health and thus routinely challenge the RVTs' claims about impounded animals. Part of this has to do with lack of resources: veterinary examinations at PAW include, at most, an evaluation of physical symptoms presented and possibly a temperature reading, a skin scrape, a black light exam, or listening through a stethoscope. Ultimately, the lack of diagnostic resources and the low level of education required for RVTs mean that volunteers see themselves as equally or more capable of interpreting symptoms than the RVTs are. Further, many volunteers see the RVTs' role at the shelter as being one of justifying and normalizing killing: volunteers identify RVTs as agents of the shelter who facilitate the continuation of the shelter's practices of killing and who play a critical role in making such killing appear "humane" and therefore forgivable.[23]

My interaction with an RVT regarding a goofy, middle-aged pit bull named Gorda is typical of the back-and-forth that can occur in disputes about health between staff and volunteers and also demonstrates that such resistance is not always successful. I brought the dog to the RVT to show her how lively she was and to ask the RVT if she could give Gorda an antibiotic injection to accelerate her recovery so that she might attract attention from prospective adopters. The RVT replied that it was "too late for that" because Gorda was already showing signs of developing pneumonia and would probably need to be put down if not rescued promptly. When I pointed out that Gorda, who was enthusiastically snorting as I rubbed her belly while talking to the RVT, was alert, active, and eating and breathing well, the vet tech shot back, "But if you look into her nostrils, you can see her mucous is thickening. Around here, that almost always means pneumonia is setting in." The RVT rejected my effort to assert evidence of Gorda's health by showing her a happy, belly-rub-seeking dog and instead affirmed a prognostic framework based on her experience with disease progression at the shelter. Her knowledge trumped mine because of her status as a veterinary technician and her specific reference to her experience with this disease in the shelter, which exceeded mine. Her response may also have been influenced by Gorda's status as a middle-aged brown pit bull. While I saw Gorda as experiencing a temporary health issue, the RVT maintained that she was on a path of serious decline.

A few days later, a rescue volunteer and I were able to find a rescue for Gorda. She had ear infections in both ears and localized mange (neither condition was diagnosed or treated at the shelter), but her kennel cough was just that: kennel cough, not pneumonia. For me and other volunteers, she became another example of the unreliability of veterinary knowledge at PAW, and I made a point to tell the RVT in question about Gorda's diagnosis and prognosis. In this way, I undermined the RVT's veterinary knowledge and challenged her understanding of what type of dog was savable/adoptable. My experience of a dog after she left the shelter thus presented me with an opportunity to assert the correctness of my knowledge claim over the RVT's.

One important differentiation in the logic of shelter staff and volunteers is that staff state that they see animals suffering from respiratory infections as a threat to the well-being of other animals. Staff have a stated goal of controlling the spread of disease within the shelter through practices of the veterinary subfield of shelter medicine.[24] The staff are facing an uphill battle because the kennels themselves are sixty years old and are not designed per contemporary standards for maintaining ideal hygiene. The enclosures for cats don't meet any recommended standard for shelter cat cages other than that the cats are secure: they have nowhere to hide, have no space to stretch out or play, and are subject to high levels of noise—including the distressing sound of barking dogs—during most of daylight hours.[25] Dog kennels are small and lined up next to each other with inadequate ventilation to slow or stop the spread of respiratory illnesses. Small dogs are often packed four or five to a kennel, so if one dog in a shared kennel becomes ill, the chance of transmission to kennel mates is very high. The shelter has almost no capacity to quarantine sick or injured animals, particularly dogs over fifteen pounds.[26]

Shelter staff claim that they use information about the spread of disease to minimize the risk of contagion to other animals, but the challenges of the shelter's facilities seem to make achieving a disease-free environment impossible. Upper respiratory infections run rampant among both dogs and cats year-round. The shelter cannot treat many diseases, and the response is generally to kill any animal who has shown signs of disease, tested positive for the disease, or even been exposed to the disease.[27]

Staff members use health issues as a justification to restrict volunteers' and sometimes even adopters' access to certain animals. While staff assert that such practices reduce the contagion, volunteers counter that the shelter has so many other, more serious mechanisms of transmission that these efforts are really not about protecting animals but about controlling volunteers and animals in ways that reduce animals' chances of live release. Little dogs are especially likely to be brought up when volunteers discuss the issue of staff-imposed restrictions on handling dogs with kennel cough: it is a common occurrence that volunteers are forbidden from taking out a particular little dog because the dog is sick, but the dog is not isolated in a kennel and instead remains cohoused with healthy kennel mates (who, almost invariably, become sick a few days later). From volunteers' point of view, the cohousing poses a far greater threat to the health of other dogs than volunteers' contact with sick dogs does.

The shelter's use of health claims to control volunteer access to impounded animals, and to make determinations about which animals should be put down, exemplifies a type of biopower. PAW asserts control over the lives and bodies of impounded animals by determining which animals are healthy enough to live, be touched and cared for, or die. Volunteers resist these assertions routinely, through challenges to both diagnoses and prognoses. Rather than accepting the shelter staff's knowledge as expert knowledge, volunteers see their own knowledge as guardians to companion animals at home and often as longtime volunteers to be equal or even superior to that of staff. This enables them, as educated, affluent, white women from outside the shelter, to reinscribe hierarchies of power and status within the shelter.

Moral Strategies of Resistance

The volunteers' repertoire of resistance to shelter death also involves a moral strategy through which volunteers assert moral reasons for rethinking the boundaries of adoptability. In interactions involving moral frameworks, volunteers typically hold the upper hand because their appeals resonate with dominant norms of animal sheltering in the region and the nation— namely, the idea that shelters should provide adoptable animals with as much time as is possible to find a home and not put animals down because of curable illnesses. Thus the most frequent moral framework volunteers invoke is fairness. In order to be fair, volunteers assert that staff cannot discriminate against impounded animals on the basis of color, age, breed, or health status or put down animals when the shelter has available space to house them. These appeals to morality may be especially compelling to staff because PAW practices what no-kill advocates refer to as "convenience killing," or putting animals down even when kennel space is available in order to reduce staffing needs/costs. Volunteers routinely use space as a basis for moral claims; the overwhelming majority of appeals I heard for extensions of a due-out date made by volunteers included mention that the shelter had open kennels available. Shelter death when the shelter has room for more animals is particularly unfair and morally repugnant to volunteers.

To demand fairness, volunteers implore staff to "give the dog a chance," even if a particular animal does not fit within the normal parameters for adoptability. "Giving a chance" often stands in opposition to management's framing of the shelter as a short-term stop for dogs, not as a place to wait indefinitely for adoption. Managers remind volunteers that PAW "cannot be warehousing dogs" and present the morally based argument that "warehousing" stresses the dogs, increases their problem behaviors, makes them less adoptable, and leads to outbreaks of communicable illnesses. Volunteers counter with an alternate morally based argument that time is essential for animals to have a fair chance at being adopted.

Alanna's advocacy for a sick dog involved morally based resistance. Although the shelter doesn't have the necessary equipment to diagnose pneumonia, staff can use shelter resources to send sick or injured animals to contracted private veterinary clinics in emergency cases. Volunteers routinely intervene on behalf of sick or hurt animals to urge the staff to send an animal to a private veterinarian, in part because animals who receive this investment of SCAS resources are rarely killed when they return to the shelter. When volunteer Alanna heard that a young adult pit bull was going to be put down because he was not responding to antibiotic therapy for kennel cough, she appealed to the shelter management to send him to an outside vet, asserting that the dog was a "good" and "adoptable" dog who "deserves a chance." Alanna argued that it would be "tragic" and "an injustice" to end an animal's life over such a minor illness. Her resistance to the shelter's intent to put the dog down thus used moral language rather than a health-based argument. She emphasized that the dog should have the opportunity for adoption and appealed to a moral sense that putting a dog down for a minor illness would be unfair and wrong.

Moral claims of fairness resonate with discourses outside the shelter that position dogs as companions to be cherished and cared for, not put down for treatable illnesses. Claims about fairness and appropriate care also echo aspects of the discourse of irresponsible owners. Volunteers routinely implore staff to "do better" by impounded animals than their previous guardians did. In negotiating with a staff member about a sick cat, volunteer Jenny argued, "If we don't get her to a vet, we're no better than the people who left her here." If failing to give an animal a chance at adoption or denying them veterinary care, PAW itself would assume the morally problematic position of the irresponsible owner.

Reputational Strategies of Resistance

Dovetailing with moral strategies, volunteers sometimes threaten the reputation of the shelter and its employees, specifically capitalizing on social norms dominant outside the shelter to put pressure on shelter staff to keep animals alive and using their social capital to threaten exposure of moral violations at the shelter. In democratic societies, the state continually needs to (re)assert its legitimacy to its citizens.[28] Changes in the scope and pace of media have produced legitimacy crises that in turn have pushed the state to become more transparent and publicly accountable. Volunteers at PAW occupy positions as potential watchdogs who sometimes assert power over staff by threatening broader public, media, or policy maker attention to shelter practices around death.

In contrast to private slaughterhouses that animal rights activists must carefully infiltrate, public shelters offer an open door for volunteers to observe and speak out about institutional practices. Many volunteers have large (1,000+) social media followings, and several are also linked to rescue organizations, celebrities, and/or other online influencers who may have tens or even hundreds of thousands of followers. Volunteers thus have the capacity to draw negative attention to shelter practices and will do so if they feel the shelter staff are treating a particular animal unfairly.

Volunteers believe that when confronted with shelter killing, the public generally empathizes with impounded companion animals. Media attention, including attention through online social media such as Facebook,

Instagram, and Twitter, can have negative consequences for the shelter. For example, volunteer Chris photographed Jesse, a healthy German Shepherd impounded at PAW, lying listlessly with his face near fecal matter in an obviously dirty kennel, causing him to appear distressed and neglected. The image attracted attention on social media, resulting in innumerable angry calls from the public to the shelter that staff perceived as unfair and overwhelming. It also resulted in the dog being rescued and the director of SCAS issuing a press release about conditions at the shelter and implementing new measures to keep kennels at PAW cleaner—so the photograph, even if somewhat misleading, had an immediate effect on the animal in the image and on the shelter.

Staff quickly recognized that a volunteer was the spark behind the fury around Jesse, and they are aware that many volunteers have social media presences large enough to mobilize a wave of calls on behalf of an animal. In fact, staff regularly implored Chris, a volunteer who had an especially large social media presence, "not to post anything on Facebook" about certain animals in need when they feared the cases could attract negative attention. (After the conclusion of this fieldwork, SCAS even introduced a controversial media policy that limited what information volunteers might post about SCAS animals on their personal social media.)

By threatening public scrutiny, volunteers remind the shelter staff that the public does not support inhumane treatment of animals, including shelter killing, and that some members of the public will express their concern to PAW and SCAS directly, as well as to local political leaders responsible for funding these agencies. PAW and SCAS seek positive public attention focused on happy-ending stories about homeless animals and resent negative attention. Staff report that negative attention is emotionally injurious to them as individuals and undermines the organization's mission by casting the shelter in a negative light that could deter people from seeking services there, including adoption. Staff also fear discipline from superiors, which can be an outcome of volunteers drawing public attention to a bad act. SCAS's director is notorious for implementing a type of discipline staff call "freeway therapy," which involves transferring workers from PAW to another SCAS shelter, creating one-way commutes of up to one hundred miles.

Some volunteers, for their part, are afraid of retaliation by staff at PAW and specifically fear that animals they like will be hurt if they draw attention to what they see as problems at the shelter. Two volunteers who met with a journalist from the *Los Angeles Times*, for example, derailed the journalists' interest in an exposé on conditions at PAW because they refused to speak on the record for fear of losing their volunteer status. Even as volunteers assert the power of their social networks to resist shelter death, they recognize the power of the shelter staff to terminate them as volunteers and are careful not to overstep in their challenges to shelter practices.

Legal Strategies of Resistance

Legal strategies invoke legal frameworks to challenge shelter designations of dogs as unadoptable because of illness. California law validates killing as a management tool for animal control agencies but also creates openings for resistance to shelter killing. Under California law, although impounded animals have a mandatory hold period to give owners a chance to locate lost companions, animals can be put down during their hold period if they are "irremediably suffering." The California legislature and courts have never clearly defined what constitutes irremediable suffering, thus leaving shelter management with leeway to define it. Volunteers routinely invoke the term *irremediably suffering* to refer to their knowledge of this law. In so doing, they remind the shelter of its legal obligations and volunteers' capacity to mount legal challenges. California law also requires that shelters provide appropriate veterinary care, so volunteers again can invoke the law as a resource to force staff to approve of an animal being sent to an outside veterinarian.

Invoking the law may be especially effective at PAW because about five years before I began fieldwork a California judge issued a stipulated order to SCAS in response to a lawsuit brought by volunteers and rescuers asserting that SCAS was engaging in unlawfully inhumane treatment of impounded animals. Most managerial staff at PAW worked for SCAS at that time and thus are familiar with this case and its outcome, which involved a good deal of negative publicity for SCAS. Because of this case, staff recognize that volunteers and rescuers have the resources and know-how to mount a legal challenge if needed, and staff seek to avert such an outcome. California law thus allows the shelter to put animals down while also giving volunteers the power to challenge practices around shelter killing.

Still, of the strategies I have identified for resisting shelter killing, legal strategies are the least commonly used, particularly in isolation; they are most often used in combination with another strategy. Reference to legal issues typically occurs only when a particular case has escalated over a period of many hours or even days and involves multiple volunteers. Thus threatening legal action appears to be a tool of last resort for volunteers. The response by a rescuer and former volunteer to the shelter's threat to put down Cara exemplifies a combination of challenges to shelter practices that ultimately ended in a legal strategy. The shelter contacted volunteers after Cara developed kennel cough, advising that she was very sick and needed to be rescued within two hours or she would be put down. The rescuer responded via email:

> I was informed that [a shelter manager] would not extend the dog past 12pm and she would be euthanized if I could not make it there in the next two hours. As the [attached] video taken on Saturday indicates—the dog is healthy and happy and has no indications of illness. Though I realize dogs quickly contract diseases in the shelter environment, I find it hard to believe she has become an "emergency" medical case in a mere three days. It is unreasonable to expect a rescue can drop everything and pull a dog with two hours' notice. The dog has guaranteed rescue in place; I am merely working to find someone that can go there ASAP and get her to our vet. If you decide to euthanize the dog prior to that, you have my personal guarantee that this story will go viral and [PAW] will have to answer to the public for the death of Cara. Therefore, I would appreciate if you give us through the afternoon to rescue her from the shelter.[29]

The rescuer's e-mail thus uses multiple strategies from volunteers' repertoire of resistance to challenge the shelter staff's intention to put the dog down at noon. First, the rescuer/former volunteer makes a health-based challenge when she questions that a dog could go from healthy to life-threateningly ill within less than three days. Second, she uses a moral strategy by asserting that it is unfair to the rescuer and to the dog to provide only two hours for the dog to be saved. Third, she threatens to expose PAW if staff puts the dog down, thus mobilizing a reputational strategy by reminding staff that the shelter is publicly accountable for its treatment of impounded animals. Each of these strategies reflects her possession of social capital outside the shelter. Subsequently, the rescuer had an attorney send a second email that invoked California law, threatening to take legal action against the shelter if PAW killed Cara. This reveals the social capital that empowers volunteers and rescuers and that they use to intimidate staff. Cara was given until the end of the day to be rescued and, as it turned out, did not require veterinary treatment beyond a course of antibiotics. Unsurprisingly, Cara went on to become another case volunteers used as an example in future challenges of dogs designated as veterinary emergencies.

VOLUNTEER POWER AND RESISTANCE

At PAW, the killing of impounded animals is a contested practice that places institutional actors with different positions inside and outside the shelter into conflict. Volunteers use relational strategies that involve everything from begging to demanding in order to promote what they understand as the interests of impounded animals to live.[30] Working with the people who put animals down as part of their job and who are their superiors in the institutional hierarchy, volunteers employ a repertoire of resistance that includes educational, health-based, moral, reputational, and legal strategies to challenge institutional thinking about, and practices of, shelter death. Rejecting institutional ideology and instead incorporating key aspects of the no-kill movement, volunteers construct shelter killing as problematic and as an unacceptable way to manage homelessness among companion animals.

Volunteers' repertoire of resistance reflects social processes at work both inside and outside PAW. Ultimately, power and resistance do not operate through clear organizational hierarchies but rather are complicated by differences in the social capital of staff and volunteers. Volunteers can and do challenge staff authority, introducing competing frameworks about organizational mission and goals. Even in an organizational structure with a clear hierarchy that places volunteers at the bottom of the ladder of authority, volunteers' class position and whiteness and the attendant resources, coupled with their extensive experience working with dogs within the framework of white middle-class norms of animal keeping, are sources of power volunteers use in their resistance to shelter practices around killing animals.

Animal practices in the context of a high-kill public animal shelter become a site for conflict as predominantly middle-class, white women volunteers and their norms and understandings of companion animals come into contact with predominantly lower-class, Latinx mixed-gender staff whose workplace culture expects them to see impounded animals through the lenses of public safety, animal health, and population management and to kill animals they deem unsafe, unhealthy, and/or unwanted.[31] Although staff are in a position of power over volunteers and impounded animals, volunteers use their various forms of capital to resist staff and PAW's animal practices. They see their cause as morally right and employ any available relational approach to work toward saving animals. Staff in turn often respond with a heavy hand, using the authority of SCAS as a shield from volunteer appeals and even as a weapon against volunteers whom they perceive as making trouble or asking too much of staff.[32]

While institutional logics ultimately determine which animals survive, and while individual staff, following SCAS procedures, decide which animals will die, volunteers are not deploying so-called weapons of the weak.[33] Rather, volunteers bring into the shelter both their middle-class practices of human-animal relationships and their attendant social capital—including veterinary knowledge, familiarity with animal welfare law, connections to the media and attorneys (or the social standing to make credible threats about having and being able to use such connections)—and these serve as sources of power. Structures of inequality outside PAW enable volunteers to legitimate their repertoire of resistance, a process that involves them asserting the dominance of the largely white middle-class volunteers over the lower-class and substantially nonwhite staff as they seek to enhance animals' rights.[34] Contra most scholarship on workplace resistance, which involves those with overall lower status resisting efforts by those with overall higher status, volunteerism—not just at PAW, but likely elsewhere—creates situations where volunteers have higher status outside the volunteer context than staff do. This complicates power dynamics, resulting in volunteers helping to maintain existing social inequalities between humans even as they seek to help animals impounded at the shelter.

5   The Transformative Power of Grief

CHRIS STOOD AT THE EDGE of the long corridor of kennels, angling her digital camera between the bars of a cage in an effort to get a clear shot of a nervous pit bull who cowered in the corner opposite her, unwilling to approach her even as Chris enticed the dog with clucking noises and the offer of a treat. For over six years, Chris walked purposefully up and down the four buildings full of kennels at PAW a few times each month, taking a photograph of each large-breed dog and many small dogs as well. She would also photograph the information posted on their kennel card by the shelter about them. Once at home, she would upload the images and create an album of posts on the social media site Facebook in the hopes that prospective adopters or rescuers would see the pictures and come to PAW to rescue or adopt an animal. She would regularly check the impound numbers of the dogs included in her album on SCAS's website to see who was still available at the shelter. For each dog no longer showing on the website, she would call SCAS's customer service number to find out what had happened to them, after which she would sort the images of those dogs with one of two designations, one she titled "Happy Tails" and one called "Final Walk."

During my period of fieldwork, Chris's images were central to making dogs at PAW visible. Her online albums of dogs currently at the shelter worked to individuate each animal, providing a close-up look at their face and sometimes their body so that their eyes, markings, and body language were clearly visible. Once the dogs left the shelter or died there, her albums became sites of celebration and mourning, respectively. When she posted an update that a dog had been rescued or adopted, other Facebook users following her would soon comment with enthusiastic expressions like "Happy dance!" or "Thank God!" When she posted an update that a dog had been put down at the shelter, collective mourning—and often rage—would ensue. Sometimes the responses were angry at the shelter ("Monsters!" "Murderers!") or at the former owner ("Asshole owner!"), and they often reflected sadness: "RIP" and emoticons of faces streaming tears. Chris's albums of dogs form a site for collective celebration, mourning, and memory. Volunteers and others revisit the dogs whose images are included in her online albums, providing opportunity for reflection, grieving, and remembrance.

Volunteers at PAW are engaged in constant negotiation with shelter death. In chapter 4, I examined how volunteers resist PAW's practices of killing animals by trying to save particular animals from being killed. Here I focus instead on how volunteers engage in grieving and remembrance, which form another type of resistance, one that takes place after the animals are dead. Drawing on a growing literature that examines the killing of animals, I analyze the rituals shelter volunteers use to mark the deaths of shelter animals as losses and to transform these otherwise anoynmous lives and deaths into socially recognized and openly mourned lives and deaths.[1]

Public or visible mourning is often feminized emotion work, and at PAW women are the nearly sole participants in the display of grief for animals whom PAW has killed. Their deaths present an opportunity for women volunteers to express their love for animals with whom they have developed intimacies in the multispecies contact zone that is the shelter. Volunteers participate in affective relationships with impounded animals and each other, relationships that, for volunteers, are based in a sense of what Haraway calls "response-ability"—or an ethical way of reacting that breaks down barriers across and between minds and bodies.[2] By creating a culture among volunteers that integrates their grief for these animals, volunteers also demand acknowledgment of their relationships with shelter animals. Volunteers create a community of caring in which they mourn and remember together, offering one another solace over shared losses. Further, the killing of shelter animals opens up a space for women volunteers to express their rage at a masculinist bureaucracy that kills animals, seemingly without regret.

Mourning is stitched to questions of what and who count as grievable. Volunteers' insistence on grieving shelter animals challenges deeply entrenched anthroparchal views that the lives of shelter animals (and of almost all but the most exceptional animals) don't matter. By embracing animal lives as grievable lives, volunteers contest the societal judgment that shelter animals are unimportant and insist instead that they be seen and grieved. As Peter Redmalm notes in his analysis of pet owners' grief for deceased companions, "Grieving an individual non-human animal challenges non-human animals' general status as material resources, non-social objects and replaceable members of a species or of the very vague category of 'animals.'"[3] Through their acts of mourning, volunteers make shelter killing visible and create a space for discourse around it. Their mourning critiques the killing of companion animals and demands that those who observe their mourning reconsider how humans relate to companion animals.

Through their practices of remembrance, volunteers assert that the lives of shelter animals are grievable, yet they treat the deaths of animals *outside* the shelter as worthy of more grief than the deaths of animals *inside* the shelter. In this way, volunteers perpetuate anthrocentrism by valuing animals who have a readily identifiable relationship with a single human (i.e., a guardian or "owner") more than those who do not. Further, grieving is unequal for different types of dogs: pit bulls and cats in particular are less grievable because of their high rates of death and volunteer bias.

GRIEVING IN A HIGH-KILL ANIMAL SHELTER

Volunteers at PAW experience grief in an institutional context that does not recognize grief as an appropriate response to the death of impounded animals and that offers no socially acceptable rituals for grieving the lives of animals who have died. While this may seem unimportant, social rituals around death are central social activities that clue us into whose lives matter. The animals who are killed at PAW are understood as living what Judith Butler terms ungrievable lives, or lives "that cannot be lost, and cannot be destroyed, because they already inhabit a lost and destroyed zone."[4]

Those who live ungrievable lives are denied social intelligibility. This in turn reduces the social intelligibility of those who would want to mourn for the ungrievable dead. When denied the opportunity to grieve for someone whose life is ungrievable, survivors lose their own social intelligibility.

James Stanescu's summation of the cascading effects of marking some lives as ungrievable draws attention to many dynamics apparent at PAW:

> Disavowing the life of another (and being unable to mourn always disavows the life as such) does not just cede the one whom you care for into social unintelligibility, but also cedes part of yourself into social unintelligibility. A part of you becomes unreal and ghostly. The connections we make with others are what give us livable lives; denying those connections renders our lives less livable. Mourning is a way of making connections, of establishing kinship, and of recognizing the vulnerability and finitude of the other. The protocols that refuse to recognize our mourning refuse all sorts of tangible, social intelligibility.[5]

For shelter volunteers, the denial of the significance of the death of a shelter animal is also a denial of their own selves. Volunteers knew and cared about the deceased animal: denying volunteers' loss and their right to mourn renders them less intelligible and denies the significance of the animals they care for and the relationships they form with those animals.

PAW marks deceased animals as ungrievable: they are simply "outcomes" in the computer system. Staff euphemistically refer to animals who have been killed as "no longer with us," or, less commonly, "PTS" (or "put to sleep"—but staff rarely use the full phrase, as if to create distance from the act of putting to sleep). Presumably as a way to help staff detach from the killed animals for whom they have cared, the dead animals' lives are unacknowledged and not memorialized. In my years of fieldwork, I never saw a staff member display emotion about the death of an animal. On the few occasions I have seen staff handling dead animals, they have done so with indifference. On one occasion, a midlevel worker barked orders at a subordinate staff member while pushing a dead dog's body in a wheelbarrow. On another, I was working a few feet away while two staff members laughed about something unrelated as they lifted the body of a dead dog together into an oil drum. They were careful with the body, and the nervous tinge in their laughter suggested a self-consciousness about laughing while in the midst of the task, particularly with me working within earshot. The benefit of treating these animals' lives as ungrievable is that no one is responsible for an ungrievable death. If the deceased is ungrievable, that death is less of a death, and not a death that should be cause for concern for the shelter, the community, or the broader society.

Volunteers, however, very much see the dead animals as grievable and their deaths as problematic. In addition to trying to stop shelter killing before it happens, volunteers engage in mourning as an act of resistance to PAW's refusal to mourn, as a true emotional response to the loss of someone they knew and cared about and had hopes for, as a basis of solidarity with one another, and as an act of resistance against the killing of shelter animals. Volunteers develop their own practices of grief and remembrance because the lives—and therefore the deaths—of shelter animals are invisible in society and lack any preexisting rituals. The constraints of the institutional setting mean that volunteers are not able to engage in the rituals afforded companion animals in homes, such as being present at the end of an animal's life, getting a clay imprint of the animal's paw, or spreading cremains. Volunteers "draw creatively from a variety of old and new practices and symbolic materializations to produce new forms of mourning" for the animals who are killed at PAW.[6]

The sense of loss that volunteers experience begins with the type of relationships they have with impounded animals while they are alive. Volunteers deliberately and specifically seek to witness the animals for whom they care, an opportunity generally not afforded to overburdened staff, who are pressured to view impounded animals more as a population than as individuals. Witnessing goes beyond simply looking at a nonhuman animal.[7] Instead, it involves seeking out a moment of recognition of, and emotional and embodied engagement with, a nonhuman animal. While nonhuman animals are most often treated as if they have no voices and cannot communicate their interests to humans—what Sunaura Taylor calls the preferably unheard, since she identifies that humans generally *choose* not to hear or understand nonhuman animals—those who seek to witness nonhuman animals actively listen to animals by learning how they communicate.[8]

Witnessing is an embodied experience, one that is attached to emotional and sensory experiences. In the context of an animal shelter, witnessing is especially intimate, as volunteers interact with impounded animals physically: they stroke and massage animals, carry them and even tuck them inside their clothing if they are scared or cold, clean the saliva and gound from their faces, accept their kisses, dodge their attempts at leaps, nips, and scratches, seek to restrain animal bodies, feel animal bodies close against their human bodies. Volunteers get to know the bodies of animals and experience both pleasure and pain from their interactions with animal bodies at PAW. For volunteers at PAW, feeling animal bodies is central to witnessing and is one of many ways in which volunteers come to know impounded animals.[9]

Witnessing is something many volunteers at PAW see as central to their volunteerism. Volunteers recognize the individuality of different animals and respond to their needs accordingly. If a dog is very fearful, shaking in their kennel, a volunteer might sit outside the kennel in a nonthreatening position, such as with their back to the dog, and wait for the dog to approach. Pieces of doughnut, hot dogs, or other treats may facilitate the effort. Some volunteers will sit like this for an hour or longer attempting to build a relationship with a scared dog. Similarly, if a dog is excitable or even reactive, volunteers will assume nonthreatening, calm postures, and reward calm behavior, until they are able to approach the animal. Volunteers take dogs out of their kennels into the play areas, where they build intimacy with the dog: they pet them, rub their bellies, look into their eyes, let the dog kiss their face and neck, pick up the dog's feces, and sometimes even roll around on the ground with them. Dogs quickly come to recognize volunteers they have befriended and wag their tails and approach their human friends with loose, wiggly bodies or happily tapping feet. The dogs learn the sounds of volunteers' voices, the pacing of their footsteps, the smells of their bodies, what makes them laugh, and what makes them sternly tell the dog, "No."

In these many ways, volunteers and impounded dogs become intimates, moving into a type of kinship bond. They shape each other's identities and ways of being, what Harlan Weaver identifies as "becoming in kind," or the process of "jointly crafted ways of being and unexpected kinships within the identity categories of larger social worlds" that "provide the conditions of possibility for specific experiences of race, gender, class, sexuality, species, and breed."[10] Volunteers' identities as "pit bull ladies" or "medical dog helpers" emerge in interaction with animals, whose own identities in turn shift because of their relationships with volunteers: volunteers help establish some dogs as "good" dogs, or as "special dogs" who need extra attention, or as part of a group of dogs a particular volunteer is working to help. Most importantly, being noticed by a volunteer is often the only opportunity impounded animals have to be recognized as agentic individuals, as volunteers initiate interaction with dogs by recognizing and wanting to know them as individuals.

Volunteers don't necessarily seek out a connection with all impounded animals. Rather, most volunteers have a "type"—a species or group or set of characteristics—that appeals to them. While I started volunteering without a type, I soon came to connect with pit bulls and large mixed-breed dogs because I saw that these two categories of dogs were most likely to be overlooked by staff, prospective adopters, and rescuers. Some volunteers deliberately steer away from animals who are less likely to leave alive so as to avoid the pain of mourning; others—most especially volunteers who work with cats—learn to negotiate the constant killing while still witnessing individual animals.

Volunteers attempt to reduce the suffering that animals experience while impounded at PAW. For volunteers in the cat building, distributing wet cat food, cat treats, and catnip can make the period of impound more tolerable for the cats. For volunteers working with large dogs, taking dogs out to the shelter's small dog runs so the animals have some brief freedom of movement, or providing them with products that they can safely chew on in their kennels, are efforts at improving quality of life. Sometimes witnessing an animal leads to recognition that an animal wants mainly to be left alone and that creating a mechanism for privacy for them is the best way to honor their wishes. This might involve hanging a towel or blanket over their cage, providing something new in their cage for an animal to hide in or under, or simply leaving an animal alone.

Witnessing in the context of the animal shelter can also have instrumental purposes that ultimately result in witnessing becoming part of the commodification of companion animals. Volunteers recognize that one of their best tools for attracting the attention of prospective adopters or rescue organizations toward a specific animal is by individuating the animal. This means showing members of the public that an impounded animal has distinct and singular characteristics, behaviors, and desires. While anyone curious to learn about an impounded animal can identify what about them might appeal to prospective adopters, volunteers who witness have a deeper connection with an animal that also ups the pressure on the volunteer to find a way out of the shelter for that animal. Witnessing strengthens advocacy, even as it also increases the emotional risk for volunteers.

The political economy of contemporary pethood in the United States focuses on dogs and cats (as well as other companion animals) as products whose social and economic value (just like that of humans) is determined by appearance, color, age, size, and ability. In a throwaway society in which capitalist ideologies encourage us to buy, consume, dispose, and buy again in an endless cycle, companion animals are both commodities and supports that help humans negotiate the strains of capitalism. Donna Haraway and Heidi J. Nast, for example, have theorized the contemporary preoccupation with pet love as reflective of the postindustrial context, in which humans, increasingly mobile and disconnected from one another, see companion animals (or "pets") as ideal love objects because they are relatively portable and can be shaped into whatever a human guardian wants them to be.[11] In an era of increased transience and aloneness, companion animals offer humans an opportunity for a love bond with a childlike being who is easier to manage and control, travel with, and dispose of than an actual human child.[12] Companion animals are expected to meet the needs of their human guardians. As I observed time and time again, prospective adopters approach the adoption process with a list of "wants" for their future companion animal and are typically quite rigid in their commitment to that list.[13] Animal adoption websites like PetFinder and AdoptAPet help adopters identify animals who meet the adopters' desires.

Humans choose companion animals from shelters, breeders, or pet stores *to buy*, in the process often breaking animals' social and familial bonds in pursuit of human interests.[14] Typically, pure-bred animals and "designer" animals (including exotic cats and deliberately mixed-breed dogs like the Labrador Retriever-and-Poodle crosses known as Labradoodles) have greater value to humans, in terms of both what they cost (usually at least $1,000 and often much, much more) and the pride humans take in them, than animals from shelters. However, shelter animals constitute a significant proportion of companion animals in the United States, and in many communities in Los Angeles, people who purchase animals from breeders or pet stores are stigmatized for making that choice.[15]

Companion animals are further commodified with the support of the animal services industry. The instability of postindustrial life has helped catalyze massive growth in the industries focused on services and care for companion animals, which have skyrocketed since the 1980s. Spending on companion animal care has outpaced GDP growth; spending on veterinary care for companion animals, for example, grew three times faster than the GDP between 1991 and 2015.[16] Contemporary guardians to companion animals "spoil" their animals with toys, food, and paid services and increasingly provide their animals with specialized veterinary care such as orthopedic surgery and oncological treatment. These services are sometimes provided through large corporations like Mars, Inc., which, in owning multiple food brands such as Royal Canin, Pedigree, and Whiskas, *and* veterinary chains, including Banfield Pet Hospitals and VCA, has stakes in various aspects of animals' lives.

In a cultural context in which companion animals are commodified family members—especially among the middle and upper classes where volunteers hope the animals will end up—a core task for volunteers is to show potential adopters how a specific companion animal could fit into *their* lives and meet their needs—that is, how the animal is a desirable product for them. Volunteers struggle to give impounded animals value as lively commodities, or as commodities that have value precisely because they are alive.[17] Volunteers work to show that these animals have value as givers of affection, attention, and companionship and that they have desirable traits that shelter workers and prospective adopters might overlook. They are actively refashioning impounded animals from unwanted throwaways into valuable lively commodities who offer prized qualities like loyalty, affection, cuteness, and soft fur—so trying to make shelter dogs as or more appealing than puppies from breeders.

This process requires individualizing the animals. When visitors come to PAW, which at busy times of year holds up to 350 dogs and 100 cats at a time, they often report feeling overwhelmed by so many animals and the accompanying noises and smells. Many prospective adopters over the years have told me they cannot come to a shelter at all because they are unable to process the sheer number of animals; they experience the shelter environment as a sensory and emotional overload.

Volunteers help reduce these feelings by providing adopters and rescue organizations with more information about impounded animals—ideally *before* a prospective adopter or rescue even comes to the shelter—so that that adopter or rescuer sees a specific animal as an individual on whom they can focus. Taking photographs and videos of the dogs to post on animal adoption websites and social media is a key part of this, or what volunteers and rescuers refer to as networking shelter animals. The images are meant to capture the individuality and features of the animal. Narration in the videos focuses on the animal's personality, with particular emphasis on how an animal is loving and eager to be a best friend. A nonprofit organization partnered with PAW also coordinates a well-organized networking program at PAW that brings highly skilled amateur and professional photographers into the shelter two times each month to take photographs and videos of a subset of impounded dogs and cats (and sometimes also other types of animals). The images and information are posted on over a dozen companion animal adoption websites such as Petfinder.com and AdoptAPet.com and draw attention to the positive features of the impounded animals. All of these efforts work to present shelter animals as desirable and to show people who might be interested in them that they are individuals with specific attributes and qualities.

Volunteers also use improvised strategies to show off the animals to adopters who are already at the shelter. Large dogs are usually housed alone, and sometimes pit bulls will occupy an entire row of kennels. Small dogs routinely share kennels with three or four other little dogs. The number of dogs and the crowding of them often makes it difficult for visitors to differentiate between them. The simple black-and-white kennel cards attached to each kennel contain only the most basic information about the animal(s) in that kennel and no information about personality or behavior. Volunteers add handwritten notes to these cards, often with hearts or smiley faces, to highlight what they have observed about the dog. Because of the limited space, the notes are usually brief, but many volunteers believe they help adopters home in on a specific animal rather than become overwhelmed by the large population of animals at the shelter. A number of volunteers also know the animals *as individuals* and offer to assist prospective adopters in finding an animal who would be a good fit for their household. A particularly loyal volunteer who works with the cats almost daily has a reputation as a cat matchmaker, while several volunteers have expertise in different types of dogs, like pit bulls or small dogs.

Volunteers' involvement in witnessing facilitates both the commodification of the animals and volunteers' ability to mourn the animals once they are dead. They work to establish that these animals are grievable, using a wide array of tools—including grieving with each other—to remember animals whose lives end at the shelter. When an animal is killed at the shelter, the volunteers who have witnessed that animal—and also many who have not—experience grief and engage in acts of remembrance. They may look at photographs or videos of the deceased animal, either close to the time of the death or weeks or even months later. Remembrance is shared among volunteers, who see each other in person and who may also exchange emails, text messages, phone calls, or direct messages on social media to share the sad news of an animal's death and to express their distress about the death and their thoughts about the deceased animal. They remark on specific characteristics the dog or cat had or express how they felt about the animal when the animal was alive. For example, in the wake of the death of a young female pit bull, volunteers observed that she was "so sweet," "unbelievably cute," and "my absolute favorite right now." In grieving, volunteers remember an animal's physical characteristics and personality, acknowledging the loss of a physical body. "She had such a gentle face," "I loved his little smooshed nose," "His fur was like velvet—I loved petting him," and "She had the most beautiful markings" are comments that draw attention to the deceased animal's unique physical being. "She made me laugh so much," "She was over the moon whenever I went to see her," and "He was so shy, but so sweet," instead focus on the animal's personality. Comments about an animal's physicality and personality routinely lead to assertions that an animal "did not deserve this" outcome. Volunteers also lay claim to the importance of remembering by frequently noting, "I will remember him" or "Her memory will stay with me."

Even those volunteers who have not met a particular animal, or don't know that animal well, will participate in the grieving process in a form of vicarious grief, or grief for those one does not know personally. Empathy and deep emotional connection between some human and nonhuman animals can exist even in the absence of extensive direct contact and knowing.[18] For instance, although some human witnesses might see a cattle transport truck passing by on the highway without any particular empathy or concern, an animal rescuer or animal rights activist sees the caging and distress the transported cattle are experiencing and knows that these animals are destined for continued suffering and slaughter. At the same time they feel helpless to stop the truck or to save those particular animals from their fate as farmed animals. Thus an encounter like this can be a moment of grief and trauma.[19] In the context of an animal shelter, vicarious grief is even several steps closer, as volunteers are emotionally and personally invested in the full population of impounded animals. As much as they emphasize marketing animals as individuals, they ultimately do not want any adoptable animal to be killed at the shelter. Further, by participating in the social act of mourning, they validate that the deceased animal's life warrants mourning, and in this way both support those volunteers who did know the animal personally and/or well and resist the shelter's insistence that the animals are ungrievable.

"The act of witnessing animals' predicaments, and then sharing their stories, is a political act that resists the erasure of individual animal lives, suffering, and deaths."[20] Chris's online photo albums are a site of protest and emotional expression, as are the communications between volunteers as they convey their sadness and frustration about what the shelter has done in killing a specific animal. They challenge the commodification of companion animals by asserting that they *all* have value. Almost always, the expressions of grief segue into a conversation of what volunteers can *do* to force the shelter to behave differently. In many instances, volunteers contest the staff's decision to put down a specific dog, sometimes sending emails or letters to managers at SCAS and, in at least one instance, involving a local elected official in a complaint. The trouble is that no response can ever satisfy, and even on the very rare occasions when a manager is contrite or acknowledges an error, the animal cannot be brought back to life.

Beyond their collective rituals of grief and rage, volunteers also engage in private mourning. Sometimes volunteers create their own memorials at home. Some light candles or incense at their home to remember a dog who was special to them. Chris has a custom painting of a dog of whom she was particularly fond hanging in her home (she received the painting as a gift from someone who admires her shelter photography). Although I do not consider myself a religious or spiritual person, on several occasions in my first eighteen months of volunteering I would take a short moment of quiet to remember a dog or dogs who had been killed that day, and I often shared my feelings of grief with my partner in part because her acknowledgment meant that someone outside PAW saw and recognized the life that had been lost. Many volunteers reported to me that they routinely cry over dogs who have been killed, in the bathroom or in their car in the parking lot.

For volunteers, who generally recognize impounded animals as individuals who deserve to live, PAW's practice of shelter death is difficult and emotional. Volunteers routinely talk about the distress that shelter death causes them, and many volunteers have taken breaks from volunteering to try to manage their feelings of loss and anger. One of my saddest memories as a volunteer at PAW was when I had to tell a friend and fellow volunteer that a dog she had planned to rescue had been put down accidentally a few hours before she arrived to pick up the dog. I watched as her face crumpled before me and she slumped into a sob. That dog's life had mattered to her. He was a friend, and someone for whom she envisioned a future better than his present. She remembered him, and she remembers him still.

MAKING SENSE OF SHELTER KILLING

Gemma entered PAW as an owner surrender at a relatively quiet time of year. A fawn pit bull with tightly cropped ears, she seemed to have been someone's beloved companion: she was a little chubby, appeared to be housebroken, knew how to walk on leash and how to sit and give paw on request, and came into the shelter both spayed and with a microchip. Although she was scratching at middle age, other volunteers and I thought she was an excellent candidate for adoption, especially after she passed her shelter-administered temperament test with excellent scores. Chris took a photograph of Gemma in her kennel in which Gemma looked beseechingly up at the Chris, her stance soft and her expression worried and pleading.

A few weeks after Gemma's arrival at PAW, the shelter participated in a large off-site adoption event that volunteers knew from previous experience usually ended with all dogs and most cats being adopted. We took for granted that the shelter would send Gemma to the event, since she met all of PAW's criteria to go to an outside event.

The day before the adoption event, Gemma disappeared from the shelter's online listing of available animals. I called the shelter to find out if she had been adopted or rescued. My stomach dropped when the worker who took my call told me Gemma had been neither adopted nor rescued; rather, she had been killed. Within minutes, I was texting with other volunteers, sharing news of this injustice. We could not understand why the manager had approved her to be killed when she was just days away from near-certain adoption.

In the days that followed, volunteers continued to express their anger about Gemma's killing, which we saw as cruel and unnecessary. She was healthy and highly adoptable and should have gone to the adoption event. Her death became a referent among volunteers for managerial indifference, incompetence, and callousness; for at least nine months after her death, when other dogs were killed that volunteers thought could have been easily saved, they would invoke Gemma. For example, when a young pit bull who volunteers believed was highly adoptable was killed several months later, volunteers mentioned Gemma. One volunteer summed up a sentiment I heard time and again: "Who knows why they [shelter staff who decide which animals are to be killed] do what they do? Just remember what happened to poor Gemma."

Volunteers hold PAW and SCAS responsible for shelter killing while simultaneously negotiating relationships with shelter staff who authorize or are involved in killing. Volunteers find themselves occupying a social space that binds them to shelter staff even as they identify as animal advocates who want to see PAW and SCAS significantly change how they relate to animals and to humans, especially to stop killing animals. They often experience rage at PAW—particularly at managers—when an animal is killed. Volunteers may use curses ("Fuck them!") and insults ("Cold-hearted bitch!") as they condemn shelter managers for instructing staff to put down a particular animal. This especially occurs if there is a perception of injustice, such as putting a dog down because they have mild kennel cough (which volunteers see as an excuse to "target" a dog), killing an animal before their mandatory hold period is up, or killing an animal when prospective adopters tried to interact with the animal but were turned away because the dog had not yet completed a temperament test.

In spite of their anger at PAW and SCAS about shelter death, volunteers typically defend shelter workers from allegations of being murderers made by outsiders, including those who post on social media and prospective adopters, rescuers, and members of the public who come to the shelter. Overwhelmingly, volunteers see the staff who carry out the actual kill-ing process—RVTs and kennel attendants—as workers simply doing their jobs. While volunteers recognize that the shelter managers and the overall culture at PAW are too focused on death as a solution to companion ani-mal homelessness, many volunteers also conceptualize the staff as working within an institutional structure that gives them few options for creativity or innovation and has indoctrinated workers to believe that killing animals is a humane solution to homelessness among companion animals.

Staff who shared their feelings with me regarding shelter killing told me it was generally difficult for them, especially when putting down dogs (as opposed to cats or other animals). One staff member told me that it was the "hardest part of the job for sure" but also that "animals are better off euthanized than living on the streets." One RVT insisted that she refused to help put down healthy animals and noted that she had had many conflicts with managers about this. On several occasions, I heard staff members defending themselves from members of the public and/or from rescuers, asking, "Do you think we *want* to euthanize animals? We wish all animals had homes!" No doubt there is variation among how different staff mem-bers relate to the shelter's practice of killing—variation that can likely be explained by how long they have worked for SCAS, as longer-term staff seem to be most comfortable with killing and newer staff less so; if and how often they are involved in any part of the process of selecting animals to die or the actual killing; possibly gender, age, and ethnicity. But the general attitude among staff at PAW during my research was that this was an unpleasant but necessary part of their job and part of their service to the community to manage the size of the population of unwanted animals and to maintain public safety.

Volunteers have their own understandings of how staff relate to the prac-tice of shelter killing. Volunteers are especially likely to describe managers as "old school," which means that they spent most of their careers working in shelters before the shift toward a no-kill model began infiltrating the animal-sheltering industry. In talking about shelter death with a group of volunteers, one volunteer noted that one manager, who appeared to be in his early or midforties, "has been working in animal welfare since he was eigh-teen. Of course he doesn't think like us! Those were the Dark Ages—imagine how much things have changed since then." The "Dark Ages" this volunteer refers to are the period before reducing shelter killing became a priority for many animal shelters and when, according to longtime staff, upwards of 90 percent of incoming animals lost their lives at the shelter.[21] Volunteers thus attribute managerial attitudes toward shelter death as at least partially the outcome of professional socialization in a different era of animal sheltering. They hardly see this as an excuse, however, and routinely express to one another and even to some staff members that managers need to "get with it" by working harder to reduce shelter killing.

JUSTIFIABLE DEATHS

For me, as for other volunteers, there were times when we believed putting a dog down at PAW or outside PAW was the morally right decision. One morning when I arrived at PAW quite early before the shelter opened, I ended up in conversation with an RVT who was assessing a senior German Shepherd who had come in as an owner surrender. He was unable to stand and could not control his bowels or bladder. His skin hung on his thin frame and his hips narrowed to a fraction of what they would have been when he was a young dog. He shivered uncontrollably and was nonresponsive to human contact. The RVT was distressed about how to proceed, clearly aware that the dog was suffering but also, I thought, seeking reassurance that she was initiating a fair request by asking the supervisor on duty to authorize immediate euthanasia. I supported her effort to seek approval from the supervisor to put him down. Even if the old dog were approved to be sent to an outside veterinarian for further treatment, the arduous journey in an SCAS truck and the seeming improbability that he could meaningfully recover led her and me to support euthanasia. He was dead within an hour.

While I of course felt sad for the dog, moving quickly to end his suffering seemed to me the best course of action. Some volunteers were upset that the dog wasn't given the opportunity to be rescued so that he could have been put down outside the shelter, a death they considered more dignified. However, there was general agreement that the dog was suffering and should be "released" from his pain. Volunteers define irremediable suffering differently than staff, but when they accept a case as such, they support ending the animal's life.

Many volunteers also believe that there are "fates worse than death" outside the shelter. These fates include being adopted into homes where animals experience abuse or neglect, or being rescued into situations where the dogs are abused or neglected. Volunteers are mixed in their views about the desirability of "yard dogs," or dogs who live entirely outdoors. Some see this as an acceptable, if undesirable, life for a dog, and a reasonable alternative to dying at the shelter, while others think a dog is better off dead than living this way, devoid of significant contact with humans and usually understimulated, as such dogs are unlikely to be walked. Similarly, some volunteers endorse sending dogs to so-called sanctuaries, or rescue organizations that keep dogs until they die—usually in outdoor accommodations with shelter in the form of a doghouse—rather than placing them with adopters. Dogs who are sent to sanctuaries are usually senior animals or animals with behavioral issues that make them unsafe or nearly impossible to place. Some rescues that purport to place dogs functionally operate as sanctuaries. It is not unheard of for a dog to wait five or seven years in a rescue facility, often living in a fenced dog run with a shade tarp and a plastic Igloo doghouse to protect them from the elements, with very little human interaction. This type of rescue, according to critics, fails to help the dogs become more adoptable: the dogs do not receive training, socialization, or behavior modification and after extensive kenneling may struggle to transition into a home environment.

At least four times during the period of fieldwork, local rescues that had rescued dogs from PAW engaged in hoarding or abuse. The circumstances of such cases varied considerably. One such situation involved a rescuer I met on several occasions and with whom I shared overlapping social networks. A schoolteacher who lived alone in a modest, but comfortable, private home, she violated local ordinances limiting households to three pets per household; at the time Animal Control impounded her animals, she had eighteen dogs and several cats in her home. Because of the number of animals she was living with, she had trouble controlling fleas, and SCAS officials alleged that her animals were infested with fleas and that some were suffering from significant hair loss due to their flea infestation. Animal control officers told the local news media that the house stank of urine and feces. The rescuer herself reportedly told a mutual friend that she slept in her living room because she couldn't get the fleas out of her bedroom. Her animals were impounded and rehomed with the assistance of the various rescue groups with which she worked.

Hers was a case of relatively benign neglect. The animals in her care were healthy, except for the fleas. They were well fed and socialized with people and other animals; had access to food, water, and shelter; and received attention and stimulation from her. All of the animals were deemed healthy enough to be adopted out by SCAS. While eighteen sounds like a very high number of dogs for any one individual to have, she was operating as a rescuer and identified only five of the dogs as being her personal companions. The others were to be placed in adoptive homes as soon as possible, and at least one of the dogs actually belonged to another rescue that had asked her to care for the dog until adopted. Her case seemed less one of long-term hoarding than of an inability to turn away from animals in need whom she felt she could rehome within a few months.

In another case that volunteers found more troubling, a rescuer was found to have shot and killed several dogs she had rescued, burying them on her rural property. A dog from PAW had been in her care but fortunately had already been adopted at the time she starting shooting her dogs. In another case, which garnered the most attention from volunteers and staff, a foster for several rescue groups was discovered to have dozens of (mostly small) dogs in her care in deplorable conditions. Some of the dogs were emaciated and had medical needs ignored, and they were euthanized by the local animal control agency (not SCAS) after being confiscated. Her case attracted a good deal of attention both because of the severity of the neglect and because two well-known and generally respected rescues had dogs in her care. Neither rescue had sent representatives to check on their dogs, which could have helped avoid the emergence of such a dire situation. She was criminally prosecuted and pled guilty to ten counts of felony animal cruelty.

These stories of hoarding and abuse create anxiety among shelter volunteers, who want PAW's animals to end up in safe, clean, and caring home environments. For volunteers, cases of neglect and abuse raise questions about whether getting out of the shelter alive is always the best thing for a dog, since some of the destinations where dogs end up cause them great suffering. Abuse in rescues also serves to justify the shelter's practice of killing. Shelter staff—particularly managers—routinely point out that not all rescuers provide good places for animals and that so-called no-kill facilities

in particular are efforts at justifying hoarding; SCAS's system-wide volunteer coordinator has even sent out emails to volunteers with purported
news stories about hoarding that take an anti-no-kill angle. Ultimately,
volunteers sometimes waver in their commitment to no-kill because they
fear these fates they see as worse than death. When new rescue organizations appear, as they do with some frequency, volunteers tend to approach
them with great skepticism, concerned about the possibility of hoarding or
abuse, or even about extensive kenneling, inadequate resources to support
the dog, or what they see as poor rescue practices. Fortunately, hoarding
and other problematic incidents involving rescues seem to be extremely
rare, and volunteers generally support animals going to rescues over being
killed at the shelter.

DEATH AND DANGEROUS DOGS

PAW identifies some dogs as "too dangerous" to be adopted. Overwhelmingly, volunteers believe this judgment should be made by a rescue organization, not by shelter staff. Volunteers see rescuers as doing more to have
dogs properly evaluated by veterinarians, trainers, and/or behaviorists,
whereas many see shelter staff as looking for behavioral reasons to justify
putting dogs down. SCAS's level of tolerance for bites is so low that SCAS
shelters typically put down any dog who enters their shelters with even the
claim of a bite history. In most cases, these claims are not investigated, and
the circumstances and severity of the bite are never clarified. That is, SCAS
does not need to substantiate a bite report to put down a dog for aggression,
nor do they differentiate between a dog who snapped at someone who stuck
his hand in a food bowl while the dog was eating and a dog who seriously
injured a neighbor by climbing over a fence to attack her. A bite is a bite,
and in SCAS shelters it's an acceptable reason to kill a dog.

A separate category of dog encompasses those who are accused of having
bitten someone and whose guardians refuse to relinquish them to SCAS.
These dogs are designated as PDDs and also have very little chance of live
release. They are assumed guilty until proven innocent, and their guardians must go through a series of hearings within SCAS in order to have the
dogs returned to them, an outcome that I observed only once. Most often,
guardians of PDDs agree to surrender their dog(s) because the shelter staff
convince them that this will be easier for them and reduce their liability. In

one high-profile case involving a dog at another SCAS shelter, a dog accused of biting a child was ultimately released to an animal sanctuary where the dog lives with limited human contact and no possibility of adoption.

Among animal rescuers, responses to bites are sometimes controversial. Dog bites with clear triggers—such as food aggression—were considered remediable, or at least manageable, by many rescuers I came to know. But for many rescuers and shelter volunteers, biting humans without provocation is seen as a legitimate reason for putting a dog down, partially out of concern for public safety and partially out of concern about legal liability. There remains a vocal contingent of dog rescuers who externalize responsibility for all dog behavior onto humans: these people argue that no dog should be put down for aggression. In their view, dogs' behavior is managed by humans, and humans create circumstances that place dogs under stress and result in aggression. However, among rescuers with whom I had regular contact, every single one of them has put down at least one dog because of aggression toward people or even other animals (rescuers will not generally put down a dog because of dog aggression, but in these cases they considered dogs in question as nearly impossible to contain and as highly motivated to find and injure other animals).

Some of the willingness on the part of rescuers to put down animals whom they have saved from shelters but who later demonstrate aggression is about protecting public safety. Many rescuers have "no tolerance" policies for dogs who bite humans because they are not willing to place any human at risk for the sake of a dog. Here, then, animal rescuers reinforce anthroparchal ideas about whose lives matter most: a dog who poses a threat of injury to humans is unacceptable. If a dog has a history of biting only a specific *kind* of person—for example, young children—rescuers often consider placing that dog in a specialized home without that type of person present. However, a pattern of biting will inevitably result in a dog's being put down. "I am not willing to put people's safety at risk—some dogs *are* dangerous," one rescuer told me.

Just as important as concerns about safety, however, are concerns about legal liability and about the financial health of the rescue: keeping a dog with a major behavior issue could result in a lawsuit and almost always involves paying for a dog to be in costly training programs or secure boarding. While I am aware of only one case in which an adopter sued a rescue because the adopted dog injured a person, the specter of legal liability looms large. A rescue can easily spend tens of thousands of dollars on housing a single difficult-to-adopt dog. In the Los Angeles area, trainers typically charge a minimum of $50 per day for secure boarding with training; the least expensive boarding facilities at the periphery of the metropolitan area charge closer to $20, but without training or even regular contact with humans. A month with a trainer in boarding will cost at least $1,400 (and often much more, as trainers offer only a few spaces to rescues, so that rescues often have to turn to more expensive trainers who have space or have to pay nondiscounted fees), a substantial expense for small rescue organizations, which typically have annual budgets of around $50,000. Even larger rescues—which have budgets in the hundreds of thousands—often resent difficult-to-place dogs whose boarding costs siphon resources from the rescue that could be used for other dogs or for other projects, like spay/neuter clinics. Rescuers thus generally avoid rescuing difficult-to-place dogs and may resort to killing such dogs.

When rescuers put down animals who are deemed unsafe for placement, they behave like the shelter staff at PAW: the animal's remains are left with the veterinarian for mass disposal, there are no acts of remembrance, and there is usually no public acknowledgment of the death at all. These animals end up being the most forgotten: they die in the company of strangers with usually only one or two people (if any) besides the rescuer and the veterinary staff knowing their life has ended. There is no memorialization because acknowledging their deaths would bring scrutiny to the rescue caring for them. They simply disappear.

THE SOCIAL VALUE OF HUMAN TIES

Rescuers' willingness to kill dogs they have identified as difficult and to leave their deaths unacknowledged without any effort at remembrance stands in stark contrast to how they and shelter volunteers respond to the deaths of dogs who have been rescued from PAW but are not yet adopted at the time they die for health reasons. These dogs receive extensive memorialization—more so than those who die at the shelter—and the people caring for them are celebrated as heroes. Alex, a middle-class white woman, was a newer volunteer at the shelter when she decided to take home a senior dog, Kali, as a foster. When she first told me about her decision a few weeks after she had taken the dog home, she still seemed surprised by her own impulsivity. "I never planned to foster at all," she told me, "let alone just come here and leave with a foster dog." Kali, a pretty, pure-bred Shetland Sheepdog, had arrived at the shelter in reasonably decent condition but seemed to be at least thirteen or fourteen years old. Hard yellow tartar crusted her teeth, and some teeth appeared nearly completely rotted through. Her eyes were cloudy and she teetered a bit when she walked, but she responded with a wagging tail when people petted her or talked to her.

About a month after Alex brought Kali home, her health began to deteriorate markedly. First, Kali woke up one morning unable to stand without tipping over. Alex rushed Kali to her veterinarian and soon found herself taking Kali to a specialist to check for possible neurological conditions. At one point, Kali appeared to have some kind of neurological event and was hospitalized for two days until well enough to come back home, still without a clear diagnosis. As she moved through the layers of veterinary testing, Kali's health continued to decline. About ten days after she first awoke unable to stay standing, Kali was dead in her dog bed in the morning. Alex had spent over $5,000 on veterinary testing and care for Kali in the two weeks leading up to her death. Had Kali remained in the shelter, she would have received little or no additional veterinary care.

Like many companion animals adopted from a shelter, Kali underwent a rapid transformation from being an impounded dog with limited, if any, social value and in whom only basic survival-level resources would be invested to a companion who was seen as a valuable and important individual who deserved excellent veterinary care. When Kali died, Alex received her ashes back from the crematorium and set up a memorial for her. Other volunteers offered her an outpouring of support, including condolence cards and emails. Even more than a year after her death, Alex still talked about Kali periodically, a topic that always resulted in other volunteers commenting on what a "sweet dog" she had been and how Alex was her "guardian angel."

Even though Kali never made it to the point of adoption, already as a rescued foster dog her status skyrocketed above that of dogs in the shelter. As soon as an animal crosses the threshhold *out* of the shelter and becomes a companion to a person, that animal's social value increases substantially. Ultimately, the social value of companion animals is human-centric: shelter animals have less value as long as they are in a shelter and not attached to a person. When they become attached to a human animal outside the shelter, their social value increases. Two cases of dogs who died within a few months of each other exemplify this. One was a female pit bull mix, Jessie, who was a favorite of volunteer Suze. Because she met the adopters during their adoption process and could see how ill-equipped they were to integrate Jessie with another dog in the home, Suze went to their home to help them work on building a relationship between the dogs. The adopters ignored her advice, and the dogs got into a fight. The adopters brought Jessie back to the shelter. Suze then signed on to foster Jessie, but a staff member failed to make the appropriate note in her record and Jessie was killed on the day Suze was slated to pick her up. Suze was angry and sad about what happened. I and a few other volunteers who work with pit bulls reached out to her to offer support, but Jessie's death was generally unacknowledged within the larger community of volunteers.

When, a few weeks later, another volunteer rescued a senior dog whom the shelter wanted to put down because of his health condition and whom the volunteer's veterinarian put down within hours of being rescued, the outpouring of condolences was substantial. There is little evidence to suggest that Suze was any more or less connected to Jessie than the other volunteer was to the senior dog who died outside the shelter. In fact, an argument could be made that Jessie had *greater* value because she was young and healthy whereas the other dog was known to be old and sick. However, only one of these dogs had left the shelter and been welcomed as a foster animal. The senior dog's status shifted markedly upward the moment the gate at the side of the shelter clinked shut behind them and they left behind their identity as a homeless dog and became a companion animal again.

Other pieces in the puzzle help explain the differential reaction to the deaths of these two dogs: some volunteers showed a pervasive favoritism toward smaller dogs and bias against pit bulls, and some were too angry about Jessie's death to approach her death from the perspective of mourning or of offering support to Suze. Still, the comparison illustrates a general pattern: when a dog or cat (or any other animal) leaves PAW with a foster or adopter, that animal becomes a companion, and that, in and of itself, warrants greater social recognition of both their life and their death. Becoming a foster animal or an adopted animal renders the animal socially intelligible in a way that being a shelter dog or even a rescued animal living in a boarding facility does not. This intelligibility means that they have a grievable life. Shelter animals occupy a liminal space as companion animals with no one to be a companion to. Absent their clear relationship with a human guardian, their lives are of less value in the human world and their grievability is diminished. While still members of the same species, their status on the species hierarchy drops when they become animals without a human guardian: shelter animals don't have the same status or value as "owned" animals.

ACHIEVING A DIGNIFIED DEATH

Just as shelter animals are denied social intelligibility, so too are they denied what volunteers and rescuers refer to as a "good" or dignified death. For volunteers, this means being in a loving environment at the time of passing and, after death, having their body handled respectfully and laid to rest. Since the mid-1990s, a growing number of animal welfare and animal service organizations have adopted a stated commitment to the so-called five freedoms to which nonhuman animals held in human confinement are entitled: (1) freedom from hunger and thirst; (2) freedom from pain, injury, and disease; (3) freedom from discomfort; (4) freedom to express normal behavior; and (5) freedom from fear and distress. Some advocates have promoted a sixth freedom: freedom to die a good death.[22]

Shelter volunteers do not see being killed at the shelter as a dignified death. Several features of shelter death make it undignified. First, it occurs with people who do not know the animal well (and who many volunteers think do not care about the animal) rather than with familiar people, such as a guardian. Second, shelter death is not dignified because it is unjust and unnecessary. With the exception of severe medical cases, volunteers do not see that the death of a healthy, adoptable animal can be dignified. Third, the handling of the body is undignified: a staff member places the body in a rusty oil drum with the bodies of other deceased animals for storage until the rendering plant sends a truck to take the drums, rather than storing the body separately from other bodies and cremating the remains, as is done for companion animals in homes. Fourth, the animal is never properly laid to rest and in fact is even reused; while many human guardians choose to cremate the bodies of deceased companion animals and have some ritual for handling the cremains (such as burial or ash spreading), the remains of shelter animals are sent to a rendering plant.

Most volunteers avoid thinking about the animals' remains once their body leave the shelter. I instead visited the rendering plant to see what happens there.[23] Located about twenty miles from PAW in an area devoted entirely to industry—much of it focused on the transportation and disposal of waste—the rendering plant is made up of a set of ramshackle buildings along an eerily quiet four-lane road. Marked with flimsy "No trespassing" signs, the gates to the plant stood open when I arrived; a few men had gathered by their cars at one side of the lot, speaking in Spanish. The stench from the facility was powerful, and my stomach tumbled while I adjusted to the odor. Seagulls loitered on nearby lamp and fence posts, preening their feathers with an attentive eye steeled on the goings-on at the plant, scanning for offal or other edibles.

When I visited, the plant was not actively rendering: the rendering process is conducted only when a certain volume of input is available. The rendering plant receives animal material from a range of sources, so rendered animals include roadkill animals, shelter animals, and pieces of unused animal from slaughterhouses (some of which are in the immediate vicinity). I have seen videos of piles of dead animals heaped outside the rendering plant, and am grateful not to have witnessed that personally when I went. A cluster of oil drums like the ones used to store bodies at the shelter stood along one wall of the main building facility; the offices are located in a separate small building close enough to be seeped in the stench.

Not unlike any meat-processing plant, the plant is composed of a series of chutes, vats, and conveyers along which the bodies of dead animals are moved and transformed into tallow or protein meal. What struck me most about the facility was how unsophisticated it looked. Before visiting the rendering facility, I had envisioned an innocuous cement building with shiny, bright steel cauldrons inside filled with bubbling fat. Instead, the facility was almost entirely open to the outdoors and the equipment looked as if it would struggle to grind to life. I could hardly imagine the limp machinery in motion. Perhaps death pervades the space, making the plant seem lifeless too. As I stood there, grateful for the wind that enabled me to breathe in spite of the stench, I thought about Monster, Gemma, Jessie, and so many other dogs I had known and cared for whose bodies ended up here. Although society decided they had no value, the rendering plant found another way to commodify them, by turning their fat and bone into tallow and protein meal. Animals' service to humans never ends.

Some rescuers want only for animals (particularly dogs) to die else-where—not at the shelter—with someone whom the rescuers see as caring about the dog, and where they will not be rendered (private veterinarians overwhelmingly send animal remains to crematoriums, even if the guardian does not want the cremains back). Take this social media post written by a rescuer who had saved a stray animal that then died:

> I have been crying for . . . hours. We gave him a name. We gave him love, cuddles and morphine. The vet determined this blind and deaf and very neglected boy was in severe pain and distress. At his age there was nothing that could remedy that. We let him go peacefully. Not on the streets. Not in traffic. Not in the back room of a kill shelter. Not at the hands of uncar-ing people. This boy spent his final hours loved, doted on, warm, cared for, and held. This is what I must focus on so I don't feel I failed him.

This animal rescuer's post emphasizes that the dog was recognized as an individual: he was given a name. He was also given attention, affection, and pain management. His death was peaceful and took place in the presence of someone who cared about him. Even though the rescuer had hoped for a different outcome—namely, that the prognosis was more promising and the dog could be treated and made available for adoption—they saw this outcome of private euthanasia as far more desirable than a death at the shelter itself.

Many volunteers at PAW helped provide what they see as dignified deaths to shelter animals by taking animals who they believed could not be saved out of the shelter and to local veterinarians, where they accompanied them through the euthanasia process. This act generates substantial support from other volunteers and from rescuers and those engaged with the rescue com-munity on social media. When Alanna pulled out of the shelter a very old Labrador Retriever who could not stand and brought her to a local veteri-narian for euthanasia, the rescue she worked with posted an image of the dog's paw in her hand. The picture garnered hundreds of online comments from people praising Alanna and the rescue for their compassion and for making sure the dog did not experience the indignity of death inside the shelter. Similarly, when Rose took home an ancient-looking Chihuahua who had blood in his urine, she was hailed as a hero for taking the time and money to do a full diagnostic workup before her veterinarian advised her that same day that the best course of action was euthanasia.

Volunteers' and rescuers' ideas about dignified death are often anthro-centric in that volunteers impose human ideas about death and dying on animals that animals may not share. In dealing with sick shelter animals, it's sometimes difficult to tell if an effort to get a sick dog out of the shelter for the sole purpose of a dignified death is really about the animal's experience of the death or about human comfort and social status. For the dog, being euthanized in a private veterinary clinic in the company of a volunteer who has seen the dog for the first time just hours before may not be any different or better than being euthanized by shelter workers at PAW. What *is* different is that the rescue and the volunteers involved in providing dignified deaths to shelter animals can position themselves as altruistic, compassionate, and even heroic for "saving" this dog from the indignity of shelter death.

GRIEF AS TRANSFORMATIVE POLITICS

Volunteers' grief operates as a form of resistance to shelter death and as a transformative political act. By mourning the lives of shelter animals, volun-teers mark these lives as grievable, thereby restoring social intelligibility and ultimately transforming animals who are otherwise unseen, unrecognized, and unappreciated into animals who have social value. Simultaneously, they assert the value of their own work with these animals by demanding rec-ognition of their ties to shelter animals as meaningful and important. They also draw attention to the problematic practice of shelter killing by witness-ing the lives of animals who are killed, making such killing visible, and cre-ating a space for discourse around it. This space exists both offline and on social media and is itself transformative in its insistence on the legitimacy of grieving shelter animals and on the imperative to stop shelter killing.

Volunteers' acts of mourning move from the individual dogs and cats to the social structures that have contributed to their deaths. The personal becomes political as volunteers criticize PAW and SCAS and often implicate "irresponsible owners" and, in the case of pit bulls, breed prejudice in their social media posts and interpersonal conversations about shelter killing. On one volunteer-managed social media site promoting the adoption of pit bulls from PAW (of which I am an administrator), the standard language to announce a dog has been killed refers to the deceased dog as "yet another victim of the deeply dysfunctional and breed-biased SCAS system, and of irresponsible owners and breed prejudice." These death announcements also routinely include information on how to spay/neuter pets or on how to support local low-cost spay/neuter programs, and occasionally they implore followers to email SCAS managers to protest particular policies and practices, such as convenience killing. Volunteers thus make grief covertly and overtly political, demanding institutional and societal change regarding how shelter animals live and die.

Importantly, then, through their acts of grief, PAW volunteers draw attention to the structural conditions shelter animals face. While the memories they express about any particular animal are individual—that is, specific to that animal—their challenge extends to the shelter and to society at large. Their mourning critiques the killing of animals and demands that those who see their social media posts about an animal killed at the shelter consider how humans relate to companion animals and even all animals. They often implicate former guardians, the shelter system, and anthroparchy in their remembrances. For them, honoring the life of the animal who has died means trying to prevent another animal from being killed at a shelter: each death should be a lesson, a reminder of the need for change, and a push for action against human violence against animals.

Animal shelter and rescue volunteerism is typically depicted in society and in scholarship as individualistic work carried out by emotional women who focus on saving individual animals.[24] Yet how volunteers grieve at PAW reveals a different dynamic in which volunteers both recognize and celebrate individual animals while extending that recognition and celebration to demand different, better treatment for all animals of the class of shelter animals, and often for other types of animals as well. Their mourning falls outside the bounds of what the shelter expects or wants of them as volunteers but ultimately is one of the most important mechanisms for engaging in resistance that problematizes shelter killing both within PAW and SCAS and for a broader audience as the unjustified killing of individuals who deserve to live.

6 The Peculiar Problem of Pit Bulls

WHEN MONSTER ENTERED PAW, his life chances were much lower than those of other dogs for one reason alone: the staff member who impounded him classified him as a pit bull, the most maligned type of dog at PAW and in the United States more broadly. His breed designation had many implications for his stay at PAW. These included that volunteers could not take him out of his kennel until after he had undergone a temperament test that would purportedly assess how safe he would be for adoptive placement. Adopters walking through the kennels would be less likely to stop and ask about him as a dog they might want to adopt. If they did stop at all to look through the cage bars at him, it might be instead to comment on his muscularity or scariness, or to try to antagonize him by banging on the kennel bars. PAW would give him less time to be rescued or adopted than other dogs; in fact, if an interested adopter or rescue did not request that staff perform a temperament test on him, he would be killed before he was ever even evaluated as a prospect for adoption. If he was tested and passed, he might have a few additional weeks to find a home or rescue; if he failed, he could be killed as soon as the next day. Had Monster been a Boxer or a German Shepherd, he would not have been subject to these same restrictions: as long as he didn't display any problematic behaviors at intake like snapping or growling, he would have been able to join volunteers in the play areas right away and to enjoy extra time to be adopted. Yet no matter how gentle or friendly the pit bull Monster behaved at intake, his temperament would necessitate assessment because he was part of a group of dogs understood as being at risk for violence against people and other animals.

PAW and SCAS see pit bulls as different and problematic compared to other dogs, and they are hardly alone in their approach toward pit bulls.[1] Arguably one of the most well-known "breeds" or types of dogs in the US, if not globally, pit bulls are widely depicted as fearsome animals who share the social worlds of equally fearsome people.[2] Pit bulls are understood as part of depraved, impoverished, and criminal communities and are themselves seen as depraved, impoverished, and criminal.

Pit bulls present a rich case for interrogating how inequalities of race, class, and gender among and between people and animals are bound up together precisely because pit bulls occupy a racialized, classed, and gendered space in American culture.[3] Like the people who are believed to be their guardians—poor Black men—pit bulls are viewed as savage, not fully companionable, and thus not truly assimilable in the same way as other dogs associated with nonwhite groups, such as Chinese- and Japanese-origin breeds like Pugs, Pekingese, and Akitas.[4] While all dogs, because of their long history of domestication, sit at the boundary of culture and nature—the divide humans see between themselves and animals—pit bulls are more tied to nature than any other type of domesticated dog. Their presumed violence and physicality—both markers of Blackness and masculinity—render them more animal and less suitable for human companionship.

The relationship between Black people and pit bulls is not simply guilt by association; it is one recent expression of centuries of white Western construction of nonwhites as animal. Blackness and animality have served for centuries as counterpoints to the (white) human in Western thought.[5] White supremacy has successfully constructed Black people as Other by tying Blackness to animality, which necessitates consideration of how Blackness and animality are interconnected.[6] Black people have been consistently constructed as not-human, tied instead to nonhuman primates, to working animals (mules, oxen), and, more recently, to pit bulls.[7] Both groups—Black men and pit bulls—are constructed as like each other but unlike whites and deeply frightening to them because they are purportedly violent, impulsive, difficult to control, physically powerful, and reproductively prolific. Arguing,

as I do here, that pit bulls and Blackness are co-constituted draws attention
to the interconnectedness of human and nonhuman animals and to the processes that operate to shape all of our existences.

The perceived role of pit bulls as companion animals to the Black underclass since the latter decades of the twentieth century is a starkly different
social location from the one pit bulls occupied through much of American
history. Pit bulls and dogs with similar physical characteristics, particularly
Mastiffs, have been tied up with white supremacy since before Emancipation,
when slave "trainers" were responsible for walking their white owners' dogs
for miles each day so that those dogs, which included hounds (especially
Bloodhounds), pit bulls, and other types of dogs, could be used for hunting
and terrorizing escaped slaves.[8] English and later Irish immigrants were the
first to import pit bulls to the United States and to breed them in larger numbers in the mid-eighteenth century, and the dogs remained firmly constructed
as an animal belonging to white people through the late nineteenth century,
serving as an iconic family pet popular among frontier families, who relied
on them to help with farmwork and deter wild animals and trespassers. Their
television debut came in the form of the lovable Petey in the early television
show *The Little Rascals* (aka *Our Gang*).[9]

Yet by the late twentieth century pit bulls had become synonymous
with Black masculinity. During and after the civil rights era, as white violence against Black people raged on, these dogs became protectors of Black
homes, and in poor urban communities they afforded security and status to
men who feared violence from both police and peers, and who sometimes
also sought guards for cash or drugs.[10] As Nast notes, "The dogs served as
important income generators in their own right and as security devices
in a world of precarity."[11] The dogs thus served a significant role in Black
communities facing rising unemployment, economic precarity, and the es-
calation of mass incarceration.[12] Shifts in domestic and international politics
contributed to the coupling of Black men and pit bulls: Rachel Levine and
Justyna Poray-Wybranowska assert that "when the War on Drugs replaced
foreign military operations as the greatest source of fear for the American
people, and drug-involved Black Americans replaced foreign nations as
'public enemy number one,' so too did the homebred pit bull replace the
German breeds as the most feared type of dog."[13]

This link between Black masculinity and pit bulls was and still is cap-
tured and reinforced through the image of pit bulls as companions to Black

male "thugs" depicted in hip-hop and rap media and in the mainstream media, and of pit bulls as part of illegal dogfighting operations involving Black men in both poor urban neighborhoods and the rural South.[14] The mainstream media reported on the purported violence of the dogs, stoking fears.[15] Once trusted guardians of white children and whites' property, in the late twentieth century pit bulls instead came to be seen as fearsome menaces, an extension of the racist specter of the dangerous, criminal Black man.[16]

Dogfighting is central to the image of Black men with pit bulls, even though organized fighting of bulldogs and pit bulls originated in Britain and was popular among white men, especially of British and Irish descent, in the United States from at least the early 1800s through the early part of the twentieth century (as was cockfighting, another animal practice that today falls outside the animal practices of the white mainstream). When Black people first began to organize dogfights, whites maintained that they were too unskilled and feeble-minded to work with the dogs.[17] Through the latter part of the twentieth century, the growing strength of humane advocacy among whites contributed to a new racial boundary, this time one in which whites—especially from the middle and upper classes—separated themselves from Black and poor people by not engaging in and instead condemning dogfighting as cruel and barbaric.[18]

The use of pit bulls in dogfighting is powerfully linked to human beliefs about their breeding. Human animals have long understood dog breeds as distinctive categories of dogs that purportedly differ in appearance and behavior.[19] Echoing key aspects of claims about race among humans, and especially scientific racism, breeders, kennel clubs, and owners alike assert that the genetic selection of dog breeds for certain traits results in dog breeds of differing behavior, intelligence, health, and fitness for various tasks. While only a small number of pit bulls have been bred or used for fighting, contemporary understandings of pit bulls hold that *all* dogs with pit bull heritage possess a genetic predisposition for aggression toward animals and people. This belief in the biological basis of pit bull aggression stands in contradiction to the fact that pit bulls are not even a breed of dog but rather an ill-defined category.[20]

Ultimately, pit bulls are now "raced Black,"[21] and, like Black men, they are consequently subjected to discriminatory policies and practices based on fear of the risk they purportedly pose to whites, to public safety, and to the social order. Pit bulls are the targets of state interventions, including violence, intended to regulate, contain, and, often, destroy them.[22] Breed-specific legislation (BSL) and insurance industry practices function to limit where these dogs can live.[23] In 1980, Hollywood, Florida, became the first municipality in the United States to place restrictions on pit bulls; by 2017, BSL prohibited pit bulls in communities across the US. BSL supporters point to the purported dangerousness of pit bulls and sometimes a limited set of other types of dogs (e.g., Rottweilers, Doberman Pinschers), arguing that banning such dogs will reduce dog bites.[24]

While municipal BSL affects only a small slice of US residents, restrictions placed on these dogs by insurance companies, landlords, and public agencies (such as foster care systems and public housing agencies) further limit where a pit bull dog may live.[25] Proponents of restrictions on pit bulls maintain that the dogs have been bred to be aggressive and pose a greater risk to the public than other types of dogs—so they are dogs who are inherently more dangerous than other types of dogs. BSL is often justified specifically through narratives focused on ensuring public safety and reducing legal and financial liability: while the relationship between breed and bite risk remains an open question, and research on the effects of BSL has shown no significant reduction in dog bites after the introduction of BSL, banning or restricting certain types of dogs—often only pit bulls, but sometimes also other breeds—allows communities to feel they can exclude undesirable animals, as well as the (Black/criminal/unwanted) people who live with them.[26] Insurance companies and, by extension, landlords and housing associations believe prohibiting the dogs reduces the risk of lawsuits stemming from dog bites.[27]

BSL doesn't seem to have diminished the popularity of the dogs. As many as eighteen million pit bulls may live in the United States (out of about ninety million domestic dogs total), and pit bulls are among the top three most popular dog breeds in twenty-eight states.[28] They are overrepresented in shelters and are the least likely to be adopted from them, in part because they are targets of the restrictions identified here, so that it is more difficult for their human guardians to care for them for the duration of their lives than for most other types of dogs.[29] Pit bulls thus face a peculiar problem: they are the dogs most in need of new homes but are less likely to get them than any other type of dog.[30] That they are homeless and that they are often difficult to rehome are, in different ways, outcomes of contemporary expressions of racism, classism, and gender stereotyping.

Several scholars have examined the intersection of race and breed in the case of pit bulls, often focusing specifically on the high-profile case of National Football League player Michael Vick's central involvement in fighting pit bulls or on other dogfighting cases.[31] These analyses have revealed the centrality of race to the Vick case, despite animal advocates' claims that they were acting and reacting in racially neutral or race-blind ways. Animal advocates' reactions to the Vick case especially reflect and reinforce racial ideologies that construct Black men as violent criminals with little regard for others' lives who are deserving of the most extreme carceral and corporeal punishments available.[32]

In the first part of this chapter, I move away from focusing on large-scale seizures of pit bulls who have allegedly been used for dogfighting to examine instead the *routine* mechanisms that make pit bulls the most killed dogs in America. Pit bulls are not being killed in large numbers directly because so many are used for dogfighting;[33] rather, the high rate of killing of pit bulls in shelters is the outcome of shelter policies and practices that treat all pit bulls as higher risk and more dangerous than most other types of dogs. PAW and SCAS, which embrace breed-specific shelter practices and policies, justify their actions through a discourse of public safety that appears race-neutral but relies on racial beliefs about criminality, danger, Blackness, and pit bulls. In the second part of the chapter, I turn to the efforts of the white women who dominate as volunteers and rescuers of pit bulls at PAW. These rescuers participate in remaking pit bulls so that the dogs start to shed their identities as companions to Black and poor Latinx men and become suitable members of white middle-class households that embrace corresponding norms of domesticity. In this pursuit of helping individual dogs, rescuers assert the primacy of white animal practices that ignore the structural conditions that bring the dogs into the shelter in such high numbers in the first place.

THE RACIALIZATION OF PIT BULLS
AND THEIR GUARDIANS AT PAW

Pit bulls' connections with human inequalities are intersectional:[34] in Los Angeles pit bulls are locally understood as part of low-income urban Black and Latinx communities and are especially associated with men guardians. From a class perspective, wealthy people are believed to be too "civilized" to engage in barbaric activities like dogfighting, and it's no coincidence that the only affluent person who has been publicly shamed for dogfighting in the US, Michael Vick, is Black, newly wealthy after growing up in poverty, and a man.[35] Pit bulls are associated specifically with Black masculinity, and with masculinity more generally: dogfighting is a man's activity, and pit bulls, as dogs associated with fighting who can be physically powerful, are dogs who belong with men.[36]

At PAW, the racial dynamics of pit bulls operate differently than in some other parts of the country. Specifically, Black people are underrepresented in PAW's service area (compared to Los Angeles as a whole, the state of California, and the nation).[37] Instead, the largest proportion of people who live with pit bulls in PAW's service area are Latinx. When shelter staff and volunteers interact with the guardians of pit bulls at PAW, they are almost always interacting with someone who is Latinx, not someone who is Black. That most of PAW's public is Latinx doesn't eliminate the linkages between Blackness and pit bulls, but it does open them up in different ways. Blackness operates as an absent referent at PAW. The dogs remain dangerous because of the broader cultural association between Black men and, locally, lower-income Latinx men of color—men who are believed to belong to gangs and/or to participate in criminal activity or, at best, to be "low class" and therefore problematic in their animal practices.

Latinx people occupy a different racial positioning than Black people historically and in the contemporary period. Mexican Americans figure especially large in California history, and they have encountered various barriers to full economic, educational, and political participation in the state and in the nation. An extensive literature documents historical forms of discrimination, the continued experience of discrimination especially against darker-skinned Latinx people, and gaps in educational and economic equality that persist even after multiple generations in the United States.[38]

The racial divide in the United States was originally understood as a divide of Black and white. Following increases in the proportion of non-white, non-Black immigrants in the latter half of the twentieth century, many conceptualizations of the color line shifted to white and nonwhite. The rising status of some nonwhite groups in the United States propelled a reconsideration of the American racial divide to recognize three groups or classes in the racial hierarchy, with whites at the top, followed by assimilated and light-skinned Latinos, Middle Easterners, Chinese, Indian, Korean, and

Japanese Americans in a category of honorary whites, and, at the bottom, Black people, dark-skinned and unassimilated Latinos, and newer and poorer Asian immigrants as the collective Black.[39] From an Afropessimist perspective, the distinct legacy of slavery means that Black Americans will always occupy a unique (and probably the lowest) position on the racial hierarchy, distinct from others classified as the collective Black in this typology.[40]

Importantly, contemporary understandings of the US racial structure acknowledge that some people and groups of people—on the basis of their color, their racial group, their education, and other factors—can move up or down the racial hierarchy. Even if never in it, Latinx people can move *closer to* the category of white or of Black depending on their class position, education, family background, color, self-presentation, and other factors.[41]

For a Latinx man, *having a pit bull* serves as a mark of elevated risk of criminality (such as involvement in gangs, the drug trade, or dogfighting). Even the many Latinx men who have no other markers of risk—such as the many older (fifty-plus) men I met whose style was aligned with Mexican ranchero rather than with urban "gangsta"—became suspect at PAW when they had a pit bull in their care. The pit bull points to the absent referent—urban low-income Black people, who, while present in other parts of Los Angeles, are not in fact present in PAW's own service area. Pit bulls have become an agent of racial contagion for nonwhites and poor whites: consequently, by keeping an animal tied to Black men, Latinx men become implicated in Blackness and its troubled meanings in contemporary America. That is, pit bulls are dangerous and problematic because of the ways in which they have been co-constituted with Blackness, whereas Latinx men become dangerous and problematic in part because of their association with pit bulls. As Erin Tarver asserts, pit bulls become "the carriers of the contagion of criminality."[42]

PERSECUTING PIT BULLS THROUGH
THE DISCOURSE OF PUBLIC SAFETY

Pit bulls are the victims of a type of mass incarceration in American animal shelters, and the advent of their overrepresentation at large public shelters like PAW coincides with Black men's overrepresentation in prisons.[43] The United States is home to a substantial shelter industry, composed of somewhere between 3,500 and 5,000 sheltering facilities and an estimated total of ten to twelve thousand organizations without facilities offering animals for adoption.[44] While it is notoriously difficult either to establish *which* dogs are pit bulls or to acquire reliable nationwide data about them, shelters consider pit bulls to constitute *at least* 25 to 30 percent of dogs impounded in US animal shelters each year, and much more in many urban centers.[45] At PAW, at least a third of impounded dogs at any given time are classified as pit bulls, and often at least half are. They are disproportionately policed in the community and are more likely than other types of dogs to be brought into the shelter as PDDs, usually because of incidents involving other animals; in fact, virtually all PDD cases at PAW during my fieldwork involved pit bulls. This overrepresentation probably reflects that people from the community are more likely to call SCAS about an issue with a pit bull than with other types of dogs because of their own breed bias and that SCAS officers are more likely to impound a pit bull than other types of dogs after an incident. Small dogs, for instance, are notorious for biting, and we have had many smaller dogs at PAW who bite, yet I don't have a single note about a dog under forty pounds coming into PAW as a PDD case. Even those who were surrendered for biting were not labeled in this way.

PAW and SCAS use a traditional animal control framework of public safety to position pit bulls as particularly risky for the community and therefore as requiring targeted surveillance and interventions. The public safety frame is effective and efficient for PAW and SCAS: focusing on public safety shifts the frame away from why so many pit bulls are killed at PAW to why so many pit bulls are unsafe dogs—which is, of course, in PAW's institutional logic, because of their irresponsible owners, who breed aggressive dogs, fail to socialize their animals, and don't properly manage their dogs' behavior. This narrative about public safety and bad dogs operates with eerie similarity to dominant narratives about Black male incarceration: Black men are in jail in high numbers to protect the (white) public because Black people are inherently criminal and part of a culture of poverty that encourages the reproduction of criminality.

Importantly, the perception of pit bulls as threats, within SCAS and among individual staff members, has a genealogy. The State of California banned dogfighting in 1975, resulting in a push for police and animal control enforcement. Many SCAS managers began their careers in the 1990s, when the so-called pit bull panic was just starting to wane. They likely encountered significant numbers of pit bulls who were undersocialized and/or neglected, and probably some who were used for fighting; they certainly would have been inundated with warnings about such dogs from the animal-sheltering industry and popular culture, and within their training and the operational culture at SCAS. Many staff still see pit bulls as the dogs most likely to come from "bad" or "gamey" (i.e., fighting) lines, to *be* "bad" (i.e., prone to aggression, physically difficult to manage, not for everyone), *and* as the dogs least likely to be appropriately trained and contained, and thus most hazardous to the public because they might bite another dog or a person. Staff see the dogs as physically more powerful than other types of dogs, but with instincts (which many staff concede have been "bred into them" by humans) that are *too* animal. They possess the strength and capacity to injure and lack the moral compass, training, and/or breeding to manage that strength.[46]

Public opinion about pit bulls seemed to start to shift toward a less unfavorable view only in the early 2000s. Bay Area Doglovers Responsible About Pit Bulls (BAD RAP), an Oakland-based advocacy group for pit bulls, was founded in 1999; Angel City Pit Bulls in Los Angeles followed just over a decade later. Both actively promote "responsible" ownership of pit bulls and seek to present the dogs positively to the public, showing off so-called breed ambassadors, or pit bulls who are particularly happy and docile, at private and public events and in the media.[47] Ironically, the horrors of the Michael Vick animal abuse case, in which Vick and his associates were shown to have engaged in gruesome violence against dogs they used for fighting, helped reposition pit bulls as victims rather than as offenders; the so-called Vicktory Dogs became the subjects of a best-selling book and a documentary film.[48] Even just since I started volunteering at PAW in 2012 until I finished fieldwork in 2017, I have observed a sea change in public views toward these dogs. Far more adopters who are thinking about a large dog will at least consider a pit bull, even if they do not end up adopting one. Pit bulls have been featured positively in major national news magazines and major newspapers.[49] National animal welfare organizations like the ASPCA and HSUS have stood up against BSL and advocate for the dogs as part of their programs.

These changes have been slower to observe in SCAS's policies and PAW's practices, where staff have continued to label some dogs as pit bulls and have subsequently engaged with them differently from other types of dogs and continued to view pit bulls primarily as threats to public safety. PAW classifies dogs as pit bulls using a one-attribute rule: having even one physical characteristic that is like a pit bull, such as a stocky build, a smooth coat, or a blocky head, will earn a dog designation as a pit bull, even though they could easily be a mix of other dog breeds and appear with this phenotypic presentation. Previous research has established that identification of pit bulls, or what Weaver calls "pit bull profiling," is highly inaccurate,[50] and a recent trend in animal sheltering called the no-label movement is pushing to *not* designate any breed for dogs available for adoption in shelters, which may increase adoption rates as it reduces prospective adopters' breed bias.[51]

Yet volunteer challenges to breed designation as a pit bull at PAW have a failure rate of close to 100 percent: I know of only one instance in which a volunteer's appeal to staff to change a dog's breed from pit bull was successful. I made countless visits to the manager's office to ask for breed changes; each time, they would look at the dog's impound photo on their computer screen—usually a dim image of the dog in the Impound Room, their face turned to the side and their body invisible—and say, "That looks like a pit bull to me, Katja!" One longtime shelter volunteer, Irene, offered to purchase DNA tests for all of the dogs at PAW, but PAW and SCAS managers declined, claiming it would be too difficult to implement DNA testing. Irene was baffled by SCAS's response and continued to push the higher-level managers within SCAS to consider her offer but gave up after they continued to reject the idea.

I asked one manager why he was so committed to keeping the pit bull designation on a dog whose origins, the manager conceded, seemed quite unlikely to be pit bull. He replied, "Because the public needs to know what they might be getting. . . . They need to know the risks." A pit bull is, according to SCAS, a dog associated with particular biological and social risks, and to deny that a dog *is* a pit bull is to obscure these risks in ways that could place humans in harm's way. Categorization—whether by breed or race—cues into broader discourses of desirability and risk. Refusing to relabel specific dogs so that they are no longer classified as pit bulls reflects SCAS's commitment to identify animals who SCAS believes pose a risk to public safety, a commitment that in turn reflects anthroparchal, breedist ideologies. In an anthroparchy, the assertion of human interests can always be easily used to justify and explain away decisions that harm animals.

A dog's breed classification determines their quality of life while impounded and their chances of survival—so the category has serious implications for the dog. Returning to PAW's operations as a carceral institution, pit bulls are the high-security inmates at the shelter. Not just any kennel attendant or volunteer may handle them, nor may they enjoy the same privileges of using the exercise areas with volunteers. Who may access these dogs is significantly restricted, which in turn means that their freedoms are more limited than those of other animals at the shelter. The outcome is that during my years of fieldwork, a majority of pit bulls were killed without ever having been to the exercise area at the shelter or having received any kind of individual attention, other than through contact with the veterinary staff.

SCAS policies that prioritize public safety, label some types of animals as pit bulls and therefore as high risk, and force those animals and the people attached to them to meet different standards help explain why pit bulls represent the overwhelming majority of dogs killed at the shelter. The rules set by SCAS and how those rules are put into practice at PAW make it more difficult for people already committed to adopting a pit bull to do so. These policies also mark pit bulls as different, problematic, and undesirable, thereby reducing the likelihood that an adopter who might consider a pit bull will proceed with that choice and conveying a broader negative message to the adopting public.

PAW has a set of practices that function as obstacles to even making pit bulls available for adoption and that make it more difficult for people to adopt pit bulls. These practices capture SCAS's interest in public safety, or the protection of the (white) (human) general public from possible threats. In the context of PAW and SCAS, maintaining public safety means preventing animals who may threaten or injure humans from having the opportunity to do so: risk must be identified and either contained or exterminated.

When I began volunteering at PAW, special adoption requirements were already in place for so-called dominant-breed dogs, including pit bulls and about a dozen other breeds that SCAS classifies as such.[52] That other dogs are included in these procedures reduces the appearance that pit bulls are being specifically targeted; however, these other breed types rarely come into the shelter at all, and when they do, breed-specific rescues are quick to rescue them. The policies thus have a disproportionate impact on pit bulls, and so-called dominant-breed policies are ultimately pit bull policies that result in the high rate of killing of dogs so identified.

For a pit bull to be adopted, the dogs, the shelter, and the humans hoping to adopt must complete a number of requirements. The first requirement dogs have to satisfy is successful completion of a temperament test. The test is used in SCAS shelters like PAW mainly to designate some dogs as unsafe for placement altogether. As administered at PAW, it has six primary components, including resource guarding (assessed by placing a plastic human hand in the dog's food bowl while the dog is eating) and dog aggression (assessed by walking past another dog on leash). A staff member scores the dog in each of the areas and assigns an overall letter grade of A to F; PAW makes those who score D or lower on any section of the test unavailable to the public for adoption and instead usually available to rescue organizations only, sometimes with the requirement that the rescue's director sign an additional liability waiver, a simple document with only a few custom fields that nonetheless routinely takes staff one to three weeks to prepare, during which time the dog waits at the shelter.

The temperament tests are contentious because most volunteers and rescuers (and even some staff members) do not see the tests as accurate or reliable assessments of how any particular dog is behaving in the shelter or of how they will behave outside the shelter environment. The ASPCA, which originally helped propagate the temperament testing method known as the Safety Assessment for Evaluating Rehoming (SAFER) protocol, has even distanced itself from this assessment method after years of aggressive promotion. The predictive value of the test is highly contested: research examining if a dog's performance on a shelter evaluation like SAFER predicts their behavior outside a shelter is mixed and generally shows limited or no predictive value.[53] At least one pair of researchers describe such tests as no more reliable than "flipping a coin" in terms of identifying problematic behavior.[54]

Further, SCAS violates the SAFER guidelines for how to administer the test. Test administrators are supposed to undergo a rigorous training and certification program, but in SCAS shelters the training consists of simply shadowing current evaluators. I am not aware of a single staff member at PAW or within SCAS who completed the official SAFER training to administer these tests. Although SAFER dictates environmental and timing conditions for the test, SCAS does not follow these procedures. To draw an analogy with a test with which many humans are familiar, the in-vehicle portion of a typical driving test required to receive a driver's license, the scope of violations in how temperament tests are administered at PAW might be similar to making you take the driver's test with no food or sleep for a day and surrounded by aggressive drivers veering their vehicles toward you and honking loudly.

The inconsistencies in the temperament test, and very likely the content and procedure of the test itself, make it an unreliable method for evaluating how dogs behave outside the shelter. Volunteers and rescuers who work with dogs inside and outside the shelter consistently see that dogs who scored poorly on the test are happy, easygoing dogs once in a typical home environment, while some dogs who earn top scores on their tests in the shelter turn out to have aggression issues toward other dogs or sometimes even people once they are out of the shelter. On several occasions, volunteers petitioned to have a dog who failed their test be reevaluated, and these reevaluations by a different staff member resulted in dogs jumping from grades of F to B or even A, supporting volunteers' contentions about serious problems with interrater reliability. Volunteers also found that some dogs who had passed their tests were not safe to take out of their kennels, and most of the bites by pit bulls involved dogs who had already passed their tests and been cleared for adoption. In spite of research findings and the experiences of SCAS's own staff, volunteers, and rescue partners, the temperament test was used as the basis for judging the temperament of individual animals throughout the research period and served as the basis for condemning to death those pit bulls whose character was deemed unsafe.

Failing the test is almost always a death sentence because very few rescues are willing to take the gamble on a possibly dangerous pit bull—even though rescuers also widely agree that the tests are unreliable. Dogs who fail the test are also caught in a terrible catch-22: PAW makes them available to rescue organizations only (not adopters), but representatives from those organizations may not take the dogs out of their kennels to conduct their own assessment because PAW has already deemed them unsafe to take out.

Dogs who pass the evaluation are made available to the public for adoption, although typically for far less time than any other type of dog. Through at least 2017, pit bulls who earned high scores on their temperament evaluations might be granted two weeks beyond the completion of their test to be adopted or rescued. If a shelter staff member was particularly fond of a specific dog, that dog would likely have more time. One of my favorite dogs, a copper pit bull named Elsie, survived at the shelter for over six weeks in 2016 before being adopted because one of the field officers both advocated for her and made it a habit of buying and then feeding her tacos each day from the taco truck that parked outside the shelter at lunch time. His tender concern for her and his satisfaction of her love for tacos drew the attention of managers, who repeatedly pushed her to the bottom of the evaluation list used to determine which dogs to kill each day.[55]

When members of the public want to adopt pit bulls, PAW requires them to complete a short application and an interview prior to adoption. While this process sounds simple enough (and even desirable to some—many volunteers believe it should be required of all adopters), it in fact can be quite drawn out and thus deters adoption. Adopters may not interact with a dominant-breed dog until the dog has passed their temperament test. If an adopter applies for a dog who hasn't been tested, it can take a few days to a few weeks for the shelter to test the dog; during periods of staffing shortages or management changes, completion of the tests has taken over a month. By then, most adopters have gone to other shelters to adopt other dogs or have given up altogether. In a number of cases, dogs waiting for tests contracted kennel cough and then were deemed too sick to test, or even to place; they were then killed.

Once the test is done, the shelter still may take days or even a week to coordinate an interview with a prospective adopter. Finally, if an application does make it to the interview stage, staff have immense discretion to turn people away. They may reject the application if they see a pit bull acting enthusiastically around a small child in the potential new home. They may decline the application if they sense that a prospective adopter has stretched the truth on their application in any way. If they are concerned that the resident dog finds the potential new dog too overwhelming—even if not showing any signs of aggression—they can turn the applicant away. Staff will justify their decision about placement using the language of public safety. Since staff, not volunteers or members of the public, hold the monopoly on knowledge claims about public safety as state agents responsible for maintaining public safety vis-à-vis companion animals, volunteers and adopters who are trying to move the process along or who contest an adoption decision have limited leverage.

The framework of public safety extends to those who work and volunteer at the shelter and who, like the public, must be protected from these potentially vicious animals. Just a few months before I began volunteering at PAW and a few years before I began my fieldwork, a pair of Presa Canarios, a dog breed included on SCAS's list of dominant-breed dogs, mauled one of the few men volunteers then at the shelter. The dogs had already passed their temperament tests and apparently showed no obvious signs of aggression when the volunteer greeted them from outside their shared kennel. However, the dogs lunged at him almost as soon as he opened the door to their kennel. According to other volunteers present at the time, only the swift intervention of two staff members prevented the attack from being much worse, even fatal. The volunteer had extensive bite wounds. Not long thereafter, a Boxer—not a breed that SCAS identifies as a dominant breed—bit a prospective adopter at another SCAS shelter in a much less serious, but nonetheless injurious, incident.

Apparently in response to these incidents, SCAS began rolling out new restrictions on if and how volunteers and the public could interact with dogs. SCAS management informed volunteers that they could take dominant-breed dogs out of their kennels only after they had passed their temperament tests. This meant that the dogs would not spend any time in the small play areas—hardly meaningful exercise for generally active dogs, but at least a change of scenery from their kennels—until after they passed the test. Volunteers found this grossly unfair because of the delays in getting dogs tested. Volunteers interpreted this new policy, not as a safety enhancement, but as a strategy by the shelter management to further restrict volunteer access to dominant-breed dogs and to reduce the dogs' chances of live release. As one longtime volunteer complained to me, "This isn't about safety. It's about protecting their own asses from lawsuits and making sure we don't get these dogs out of the shelter."

This new policy became a site of everyday resistance for volunteers, many of whom (myself included) continued to take out dominant-breed dogs, even knowing they had not been temperament tested. "I just play dumb," said Grace, a long-term volunteer who continued to take out untested pit bulls for months after the policy change. "Some of the staff just don't say anything, and, if they do, I just act dumb—who reads all of the policies?"

The new policy also created challenges for volunteers because PAW had no system in place for identifying which dogs had passed their temperament tests. For over two years, I and other volunteers struggled with the shelter management to find a way to communicate with volunteers about which dogs had passed their temperament tests and could be taken out to the play areas. Since volunteers can't access PAW's computer system, they are dependent on staff members to tell them which dogs have passed their tests. The only way for volunteers to know is to take each dog's impound number and either find a staff member willing to look up the dog's test status right away or wait in the often interminably long front office line to pose this question to the front office staff. These conditions mean that volunteers are only rarely taking out even dominant-breed dogs who *have* passed their temperament tests because volunteers are unable to identify those dogs, given that staff keep no lists of who has or has not passed the test. In 2016, the shelter further restricted access to temperament-tested dogs by telling volunteers that they could no longer interact with dogs who had earned a grade of C or lower on their temperament tests. Dogs with scores of C are available to the public for adoption, so volunteers were confused and upset that they could no longer help prospective adopters with these dogs. Ultimately, PAW's practices meant that the dogs who were among the most athletic and energetic at the shelter rarely or never left their kennels, creating conditions that increased the risk of in-kennel behaviors staff saw as problematic (barking repetitively at the front of the kennel, circling, jumping, etc.) and that would result in a dog being flagged to be killed.

Staff members, especially managers, frequently remind volunteers that SCAS's measures are "for your own safety" and are intended to protect volunteers, as well as staff and the public. Managers are especially vocal in telling volunteers that "staff are out there in the field every day, and we see dog bites and how bad they can be. We just want to keep everyone safe." (It's curious that managers consistently make these claims, since they are *not* out in the field, and generally haven't been for at least a decade.)

The institutional narrative at PAW to explain these various decisions, and the wide range of policies and practices that make it extremely difficult for pit bulls to leave the shelter alive, rest on PAW's assertion that public safety depends on restricting access to these dogs. While the discourse of public safety appears race- and class-neutral, it is a discourse thick with raced, classed, and gendered meanings. Public safety is not simply about the dogs as dogs but also about dogs as attached to humans: who owned them previously and who might own them in the future. That pit bulls are so strongly associated with lower-class Black masculinity means that they are dogs associated with violence and criminality.[56] The dogs, like the people associated with them, are seen as animals who are at elevated risk for exhibiting deviance and aggression. As Bénédicte Boisseron notes, "Today the black man is the one responsible for making the dog seem un-kind. . . . The perception of canine aggressiveness has metonymically shifted from a zoonotic to a racial context."[57] Emphasizing a discourse of public safety allows staff at PAW and SCAS to mobilize a social good that conceals a racialized social problem. For the dogs tied up with Blackness, as for Black men themselves, the discourse of public safety provides a powerful justification for differential treatment and incarceration.

VOLUNTEER RESISTANCE TO BREED DISCRIMINATION

Volunteers resist PAW's emphasis on public safety as a justification for restricting access to pit bulls through three strategies. First, they counter the idea that pit bulls are any more likely to cause serious injury than other types of dogs, especially large-breed dogs. Volunteers eagerly point out that most of their bites in the context of volunteering are from Chihuahuas and small terriers, not from any type of large-breed dog; this is also true for staff members. Neither of the two most injurious attacks by dogs on humans at PAW were perpetrated by pit bulls. The attack by the Presa Canarios was the most dramatic and frightening, whereas the bite that proved closest to fatal for a volunteer came from a Chihuahua, who bit a long-term volunteer in the hand, seeding an infection that put her in the hospital for days and placed her at serious risk of amputation of her arm. Volunteers also note that research on the relationship between breeds and biting does not support the idea that pit bulls are more likely to bite or more likely to cause serious injury.[58]

Second, volunteers insist that they, too, want to minimize the risks they see of interacting with dogs who are likely to be stressed and anxious in the shelter environment. While they rarely, if ever, invoke the concept of "public safety," they assert their own interest in not being injured as volunteers—that is, they don't want to place themselves at risk. Volunteers maintain that they always exercise caution with any unfamiliar dog until they have had time to get to know the dog. In asserting a freedom to make decisions for themselves and to be assumed competent, volunteers challenge the staff's legitimacy and authority as arbiters of public safety, as well as misogynist views of women as helpless and too emotional to make wise decisions about how to interact with impounded animals and as unsuitable companions to strong, large dogs.

Third, volunteers challenge the reliability of the shelter's assessments of the risks pit bulls pose. Volunteers make these appeals both on a case-by-case basis and for the whole class of dogs. For instance, when a managerial staff member, whose first name is Beth but whom volunteers refer to as Officer Death because they feel she is "kill happy," reported that Junebug, a brindle pit bull mix, was lunging at her through the kennel bars and thus was not safe for adoptive placement, volunteers mobilized to implore the shelter's top manager to reevaluate the dog. Another volunteer and I took videos of Junebug in her kennel meeting people she had never seen before and sent them to the manager to document how she was not aggressive to strangers. Along with the videos, we asked for Junebug to have "a fair chance at adoption" by being given a full evaluation. (The manager rejected our appeal, but we secured a rescue for Junebug, and she lives very happily—and with no acts of aggression—in her new home.) When the same staff member designated a particularly gentle and sweet pit bull, April, as aggressive, staff gave volunteers only one day to secure rescue for her. We did so, and the dog was featured a few weeks later in an article in a major national newspaper about animal rescue, showing her happy and calm in her rescue. Of course, volunteers sent the news story to staff members as a way to not-so-subtly tell them that they had made a mistake about the dog. I could fill dozens of pages of this book with examples of pit bulls who PAW insisted were dangerous and who went on to live out their lives as companions without ever hurting another person or animal. I could also fill a page or two with stories of dogs of various breeds who the shelter said were safe for public adoption and who ended up hurting another dog or biting a person. My experience is typical for volunteers: all of us see that the assessment system does not predict how dogs behave once out of the shelter.

Through these challenges, volunteers ask PAW not to conceptualize pit bulls as a problematic or risky breed. This necessitates severing the dogs from their former guardians; in fact, volunteers routinely blame former guardians for any undesirable behaviors a pit bull might have, and suggest that with the "right" kind of guardian the dog will thrive. The project, then, is to rehabilitate the image of shelter pit bulls by separating them from Black and Latinx masculinity.

Volunteers also organize together to appeal for the whole class of dogs in meetings with upper-level PAW and SCAS managers.[59] During these meetings, a small group of volunteers who work mostly with pit bulls have asked the management to explain their policy choices and to consider changing them in the interest of giving pit bulls an equal chance at adoption and to make their kenneling more humane by giving the dogs opportunities for enrichment, like time with volunteers in PAW's small play areas. During my fieldwork these meetings never resulted in any concrete changes, although managers often promised that changes would be coming (and some changes did occur after I finished fieldwork). Rebuffing volunteers' appeals to fairness and justice, managers consistently responded by emphasizing public safety. In my field notes, I recorded this interaction between me, Alanna, two SCAS managers, and a PAW manager:

Alanna and I went to see [managers] Jorge and Shondra at SCAS's main office. . . . [Manager] Pam from PAW was also there. . . . The meeting struck me like all of the others: us appealing our case for more progressive and fair approaches to pit bulls, and the managers shooting down everything we said. Alanna stated several times that she feels the shelter is unfair to pit bulls as a breed and that most of them don't get a fair chance at adoption because of the on-going problems with how long the temp[erament] tests take. . . . We asked if it wouldn't be possible for us to take out pit bulls [from their cages for exercise] who hadn't been temp[erament] tested yet—as we had in the past—if we [volunteers] now worked in pairs. That would reduce the risk to us that the shelter seems so worried about, but also would give the poor dogs a chance at some exercise and one-on-one time. . . . Without actually saying no to our request, Pam responded that we should appreciate SCAS' concern for our safety. "You wouldn't believe what I've seen out there," she said. "I've seen some really bad bites. We just don't want that to happen to any of you." Shondra jumped right in, "We see all of these attacks. These dogs can be really dangerous. . . . We trust you, we just don't want you to get hurt.". . . . Afterwards, when we were alone, Alanna looked at me in frustration and asked when the heck Shondra [who has only had a desk job at SCAS] ever would have seen a pit bull attack.

Our meeting highlights volunteers' use of claims about fairness as a strategy to try to persuade SCAS and PAW managers to allow pit bulls more freedoms at the shelter. The managers present, however, quashed our effort by invoking their concerns about volunteers being bit, claiming that volunteers didn't even understand the full range of risk to them from working with pit bulls. This infantilization likely reflects the preponderance of white women volunteers, whom staff may see as particularly unfamiliar with—and therefore naive about—pit bulls. Their gender, race (mostly white or Asian), and class meant that the PAW volunteers who worked with pit bulls didn't fit any expectation of who normally is familiar with these dogs, nor of who has the physical strength SCAS sees as necessary to control the dogs.

The discourse of public safety that dominates PAW's practices vis-à-vis pit bulls and the discourse of equal opportunity, fairness, and humane care that volunteers embrace are laden with scripts and meanings about race, class, gender, safety, knowledge, and power. While PAW relies on a dominant narrative centered on policing, risk, and protection—which itself reflects a dominant social script about pit bulls as the companions of poor Black men—and asserts its expertise about dangerous animals, volunteers implore the shelter to consider pit bulls as individuals and to give them the same chance at stimulation and adoption as any other type of dog. They push for moving away from categorization and breed-specific practices in the hopes of saving these dogs from disproportionately high rates of shelter death.

TAKING THE DOG OUT OF THE GHETTO

In addition to the resistance volunteers engage in to advocate for pit bulls, a substantial pit bull advocacy community exists that seeks to "rescue" these dogs by taking them from shelters like PAW, rehabilitating them if needed, and placing them in adoptive homes.[60] These advocates—who include many shelter volunteers—work to counter negative stereotypes about pit bulls and to show them as happy and loving companion animals. From the perspective of these advocates, solving the so-called pit bull problem is central to reducing the problem of homelessness among companion animals as a whole since pit bulls make up such a large proportion of shelter dogs.

Pit bull advocates vocally oppose what they see as breed discrimination. These advocates, who include shelter volunteers, rescuers, and even celebrities, work both to help individual pit bulls and to advance the reputation of the breed by repositioning the dogs as lovable, loyal family companions. Pit bull advocates do this in the face of racialized, classed, and gendered meanings ascribed to the dogs without challenging these meanings or their contributions to maintaining structural inequality.

At PAW and in Los Angeles, the pit bull rescue community is composed primarily of white, educated, middle- and upper-class women, some of whom volunteer in shelters but most of whom are involved with a rescue organization outside the shelter environment. Lower-middle-class and working-class women are also involved in the project of pit bull rescue, as are nonwhite women (particularly Asian Americans), but they are a small minority. Men are rarely involved in rescue beyond being paid by rescuers to help train dogs, reflecting a typical gendered division of labor: women provide routinized care for the dogs while men provide specialized care in the form of training. Rescuers themselves are mostly unpaid, although some larger and better-funded organizations do have paid staff and/or compensate foster homes in some way for their care work. Ultimately, in the Los Angeles rescue community, it is primarily white women's work to remake pit bulls from dogs associated with the Black underclass to dogs that will be welcome in affluent white homes. These are the people who are best positioned to help redeem pit bulls, as their white femininity stands in opposition to the Black masculinity that has resulted in pit bulls being understood as violent and dangerous.

At PAW, I worked closely with pit bull rescuers as they selected dogs to rescue and then took them from the shelter. I became part of a network of other people who foster pit bulls for rescue organizations and participated in the activities of rescues. As a foster parent of pit bulls for an all-breed rescue organization, which involves providing a temporary home to a dog until adopted, I learned firsthand how rescuers think about how to make a dog more adoptable, or appealing to prospective adopters, and what kinds of homes are seen as desirable for the dogs.

Pit bull rescuers acknowledge and challenge discrimination against pit bulls through their mantra "Judge the deed, not the breed." The mantra reflects a breed-blind logic analogous to a color-blind approach. In focusing on the behaviors of each specific dog and asking others to do the same, pit bull rescuers take an individualistic approach to interacting with dogs rather than one that sees pit bulls as members of a category. They resist the idea that the dogs' behaviors are predominantly the outcome of biology/ genetics/breeding and routinely assert that pit bulls' personalities are instead the outcomes of how they are treated. Rescuers further deny that the dogs' behavior has to be irrevocably shaped by their former home and claim instead that it is severable from their past and can reflect their current living situation. In this way, a dog is constructed as upwardly mobile, unlike the low-income Black people and Latinxs who presumably were the animal's previous guardians and who will remain behind while their companion animals move up in the class and race hierarchy.

In her discussion of race and pit bulls, Boisseron states that "contact with a specific human race and gender will determine whether the [pit bull] dog is perceived as a threat or as a loving companion to humans."[61] Similarly, Weaver discusses how his presence as a white person minimizes the negative stereotypes that strangers hold about the pit bull of whom he is guardian.[62] However, placing a pit bull next to a white person is not enough to distance them from the dominant image of them as the companions of poor Black men; a more complete process of redemption must dissociate pit bulls from the dangerousness of Black masculinity that makes the dogs undesirable and must bring pit bulls closer to the middle-class, white mainstream. Pit bull rescuers and volunteers do this work by maneuvering within the framework of racialized, classed, and gendered meanings ascribed to the dogs, as well as within shelter systems whose politics of death often first places pit bulls into a zone of social death and ultimately literally kills many of them.

The core task pit bull rescuers have set for themselves is to help pit bulls find permanent homes by removing them from what they see as undesirable circumstances as current or former property of lower-income people of color and moving them into mostly white, middle- and upper-class homes. They accomplish this, first, by removing the dogs from their previous living situation, whether taking them out of public shelters or, less commonly, rescuing stray or abandoned animals from the street or from backyards or lots where their former guardians have confined them (so-called junkyard dogs constitute a small but visible proportion of the rescue work of Los Angeles–area pit bull rescues, as do dogs who live under freeway overpasses or with unhoused humans).

From there, pit bull rescuers initiate a series of practices to bring the dogs closer to whiteness. As Melissa Weiner notes, "Contemporary discourses and ideologies of whiteness, rooted in the colonial encounter, use cultural racism frames to posit white people as civilized, clean, orderly, rational, punctual, intellectual and organized, while blackness appears as dirty, chaotic, tribal, irrational, emotional, sexual, exotic, lazy, athletic or criminal."[63] I add to these lists that ideologies of whiteness privilege the animal practices of whites as humane and compassionate and disavow those of most people of color as instrumental (often to the point of being inhumane) and unfeeling. I approach whiteness "as a multiplicity of identities that are historically grounded, class specific, politically manipulated and gendered social locations."[64] Analyzing the culture of whiteness as it pertains to animals, particularly pit bulls, contributes to expanding our knowledge of how animals—whose lives are central to so much human activity, whether as food, companions, symbols, or threats—are caught up in human inequalities in ways that can obscure and reproduce those inequalities.

Pit bull rescuers are well aware that many people see the dogs they are trying to help as undesirable, as belonging in low-income communities of color, and as animals who should be feared. Rescuers consistently complained to me that it's harder to find homes for pit bulls than for any other types of dogs because prospective adopters find them "scary," believing they have been bred for purposes of guarding and/or fighting. Rescuers also noted that people are afraid of adopting pit bulls who have come out of the shelter system because they might have been bred for fighting or "raised badly," a concern that also implicitly ties the dogs to criminality and lower-income communities of color, since it is in such communities that dogfighting and neglectful dog guardianship in general are believed to take place.

In their efforts to redeem pit bulls, rescuers ask shelter workers, prospective adopters, and donors, among others, to set aside their beliefs about the dogs' pasts and their behavior and to view them as individuals seeking the equal opportunity offered by the American dream. As one rescue volunteer said in a moment of frustration about problems she was having placing a pit bull she had rescued, "Really, what are we trying to do but give them the same chance everyone is supposed to have in America?. . . . We're just trying to take the dog out of the ghetto and the ghetto out of the dog!" This kind of positioning makes pit bulls part of the American narrative of upward mobility, specifically one in which being given a fair chance makes it possible to move out of the racialized and lower-income "ghetto" and into a more affluent, whiter setting. Further, her comment highlights an idea of racial and class purification: a rescuer can excise the "ghetto" from a dog by separating the dog from its guardians and moving the dog into an environment in which the animal can be cleansed of its origins through veterinary care, training, representation (especially on social media), and life in a middle- or upper-class foster home.

Even as pit bull rescuers argue against breed discrimination and BSL, they reify existing ideas about race, class, and animal practices in echoing culture-of-poverty perspectives through their emphasis on the deficiencies of people they see as irresponsible owners. Rescuers understand the overrepresentation of pit bulls in shelters as the outcome of a pattern of problematic animal practices in lower-income communities of color. Rescuers particularly problematize that Black and Latinx men are unwilling to neuter their male dogs for fear of emasculating them and won't spay their females because they see the dogs' reproductive capacity as central to their social value and biological destiny. Rescuers further critique urban Black and Latinx communities for not seeing companion animals as sufficiently part of the family and instead seeing them as resources, whether protective (as in guarding) or financial (as in breeding or possibly fighting).

In meeting a female pit bull with sagging belly skin, elongated nipples, and enlarged genitalia, all indicators that a female dog has been bred, one rescuer remarked, "Ugh, this poor baby machine. She's probably been sitting in some Mexican guy's backyard just spitting out puppies for him to sell." This comment captures several ideas about the original guardian of this pit bull. First, the guardian is Mexican and thus is marked as Other. Second, the guardian is a man. Third, the guardian confined their dog outdoors, an animal practice that pit bull rescuers reject as inhumane and that serves as a marker of lower class. Fourth, the guardian used the pit bull primarily for income generation through breeding, again violating the animal practices of white rescuers. Fifth, the emphasis on breeding ties to broader cultural narratives about lower-income Latinx and Black men as irresponsible fathers, or men who reproduce for their own short-term benefit (whether sexual gratification or the status of having many children or puppies or the income from selling a puppy) but who then fail to or are unable to care adequately for the offspring produced by these encounters.

The narratives that pit bull rescuers craft about the dogs in their care omit any discussion of how neglectful dog guardians, including men involved in dogfighting, are themselves often trapped in poverty, may have few options for legitimate income generation, and possibly rely on their dogs for some combination of status or companionship. Instead, the narrative of the villainous original guardian is one in which rescuers construct the humans involved as uncaring, inhumane, and immoral; when dogfighting or allegations of abuse (including medical neglect) are at issue, rescuers contribute vocally to the perspective that the perpetrators are people who deserve to be punished with prison time and ostracism.[65] Even as rescuers "save" dogs from the carceral institution of a high-kill shelter, they encourage the incarceration of those individuals and entire social categories who they believe hurt animals, namely dark-skinned, urban men.

Pit bull rescuers' preoccupation with the undesirable animal practices of lower-income men of color demonstrates how whiteness relies on the construction of nonwhites as culturally deficient.[66] Their narratives maintain social distance between whites and Black people and poor Latinxs and enable the rescuer, others involved in the rescue (such as volunteers, foster homes, and donors), and the ultimate adopter to see themselves as helpers on a path of upward mobility, a narrative of white benevolence.

Taking the dog out of the ghetto means finding the "right" kind of adopters, namely those who will treat their dog as a family member and have the financial means to care for their dog at a high level for the duration of the dog's life, for example by providing specialty-brand food, toys and beds, and extensive veterinary care should any illness or injury occur. Rescuers impose strict adoption requirements, including completion of lengthy adoption applications (often two to three single-spaced pages of questions about the adopter's home, experience with dogs, and expectations) and contracts (typically three to four single-spaced pages of provisions about how a dog will be cared for). These applications require time, patience, and internet capability to complete.

On one occasion when a rescue received an application from a low-income Latinx family to adopt a pit bull, the rescue director responded, "Why would we send [that dog] right back to the kind of situation we took him out of?"

Some rescuers redline entire communities, refusing to adopt a dog into those areas at all, irrespective of the content of the application; at least one rescuer doesn't even "bother" to read applications that come in from certain low-income, predominantly nonwhite communities. Yet another rescuer conceded to me that she scans applications she receives for dogs for the name and zip code of the applicant to try to establish their ethnicity and neighborhood; she then excludes people with racialized (Spanish or "Black") names *if* these are in particular zip codes. Many rely on Google maps and real estate websites to identify neighborhoods and see images of the actual home and the neighborhood, and to make judgments about whether to adopt a dog to the home based on what they see. Thus, even as they utilize a color-blind rhetoric that implores people to judge dogs as individuals, not as members of a group, rescuers judge prospective adopters as members of groups first.

Rescuers' reluctance to place dogs in lower-income communities of color reflects their view that these households pose too great a risk of dogs ending up back in a shelter. Contra the shelter's ideas about risk, rescuers see the guardian and their community as the site of risk, not the dog. Adopting the dogs out to people in low-income communities would be returning the dogs to the site of contamination and the location of the dogs' problems (neglect, homelessness, being allowed to roam, health issues, etc.). After rescuers have invested the labor of extending the animal practices of whiteness to the dogs they rescued, they do not want to repatriate the dogs to a space—the "ghetto"—that made pit bulls Black to begin with.

MAKING PIT BULLS WHITER

Since rescuers reject placing the dogs in low-income communities of color, they must instead find homes for them in white middle- and upper-class households. This necessitates that they take dogs associated with Black and Latinx lower-class men and refashion them to be appealing to white middle-class people. The first piece of this work begins in rescuers' selection of pit bulls on the basis of appearance and behavior. Given the large number of pit bulls available for rescuing in the Los Angeles area—PAW, which is but one of many shelters in the region, typically has at least fifty pit bulls in its care on any given day—rescuers can choose carefully whom to rescue as they are likely to be able to take only between one and four pit bulls at a time. Rescuers rely on reports from shelter staff and volunteers in selecting dogs; in some cases, they may also go themselves or send representatives to the shelter to meet the dogs and evaluate them in person. Rescuers most often help pit bulls who are gray, fawn, and/or white and under sixty pounds, have "smooshy" faces (snouts that are stubby and give the dogs a childlike expression), and are particularly submissive, such as dogs who constantly roll over for belly rubs. Rescuers also seek out pit bulls who appear to be friendly toward people and toward other animals and who are under two years of age; a small subset of rescues that is focused on senior dogs and dogs with medical needs will also consider older dogs and dogs who require veterinary attention, but opportunities for dogs with these special needs are extremely limited and most will die at the shelter.

The dogs most likely to be selected to be rescued thus are those dogs who are the most compliant and most clearly conform to white middle-class expectations of behavior and appearance for canine companions.[67] These dogs meet the needs of rescuers, who fear accidentally rescuing a dog with aggression. Rescuers believe that aggressive dogs give the category of pit bull a bad name. They are also extraordinarily difficult, and sometimes even impossible, for rescuers to place into permanent homes because they do not meet the expectations of white, middle-class homes—homes that seek gentle, cooperative dogs.

Even advocates for the breed acknowledge that pit bulls cannot always be successfully refashioned to meet the expectations of contemporary consumers of companion animals, who think about their animals as family members, but also as needing to "match" their lifestyle and interests in a way that is never expected from human kin in an anthroparchy (i.e., children are not brought to shelters because they are sickly, exhibit behavior their parents find annoying, or otherwise fail to "match" their parents' needs). As with any type of dog, sometimes rescued pit bulls are domineering; physically hard to control; hyper; reactive to other dogs, people or subgroups of them (such as men or kids), cats, and/or other animals or objects; stubborn, destructive, or obsessive; and some of them have long-term physical health or behavioral problems like hip dysplasia or separation anxiety—all characteristics that, when coupled with being part of a stigmatized breed, make them very difficult to place in permanent homes. One rescuer lamented, "I can place a Shih Tzu who will rip your face off in a week or two, but a sweet-as-pie pit bull could take six months."

In my experience as a shelter and rescue volunteer, a surprisingly high number of people seeking to adopt dogs and who are open to considering pit bulls decide against pit bulls because they don't want to negotiate the stigma of having one. Time and again, when I met prospective adopters at meet-and-greets with pit bulls, they decided not to adopt one because they worried about how their family/friends/parents of their kids' friends/neighbors would react. Pit bulls activate taboos around cannibalism because of their reputation as animals who will fight other dogs to the death. Perhaps most problematically of all, because of their association with Blackness and dangerousness, many people believe pit bulls are more likely to bite humans than are other types of dogs, and are more likely to bite them badly (this latter point is demonstrated most clearly in the pervasiveness of myths about pit bulls having locking jaws). The possibility of animals biting not only arouses fear of physical pain or even death but also troublingly reverses the consumptive relationship of humans to animals. Ultimately, in spite of the rapid growth of pit bull advocacy, there appear to continue to be more pit bulls than there are *desirable* homes seeking pit bulls, and pit bull rescuers face a tall order in trying to make them more appealing to the kinds of homes they consider "right."

Because of the stigma associated with the breed—including not just people's individual reluctance to adopt pit bulls but also the restrictions imposed by landlords, insurers, and homeowners' associations—pit bulls are harder to place than other dogs.[68] Rescuers spend more money caring for adult pit bulls than for other types of dogs because they usually stay in rescue longer. Foster homes are also most scarce for adult pit bulls, so rescues have to pay for boarding, and adopters often want the dogs' behavior to be what they see as perfect, so rescuers must invest in training.[69] The difficulty of placing pit bulls contributes to rescuers' frustration with the dogs, whom some rescuers come to see as resource vacuums on their organization's funds. A discounted boarding and training program, for instance, will cost at least $50 per day, and most pit bulls from a shelter will require several weeks of work to meet the standards set by adopters for behavior—so easily over $1,000 and often much more, depending on the behavior issue.

Still, pit bull rescuers persist in their work to increase the adoption chances of these dogs and to work toward their destigmatization. Once a rescue has committed to taking in a dog, the first step in remaking pit bulls into appropriate companions for white middle-class homes is renaming them. Pit bulls who have been surrendered by their owners often enter PAW with names like Phantom, Venom, Felon, Monster, Oso (bear in Spanish), Negra (black in Spanish), Rocky, Chica (girl in Spanish), or Lobo (wolf in Spanish). Rescuers promptly abandon these names in favor of names like Bentley, Emma, Floyd, Henderson, Hope, Kermit, Madeline, Peaches, and Riley. Overwhelmingly of Anglo origin, these new names are signifiers of white, middle-class belonging. Rather than evoking violence or threat— as the names Phantom or Monster do—or using Spanish, these new names are deliberately intelligible as part of white culture.

Rescuers erase physical markers of neglect or disease as quickly as possible: they treat mange, they add extra pounds to those who are underweight and start weight loss programs for those who are overweight, they dress bitches who have been bred in T-shirts to cover up their dangling nipples, and they groom dogs and give them supplements to support glossy, glowing coats. Some of these changes are medically necessary and essential to providing humane care for the dogs. Others are mostly or entirely cosmetic. These changes help shift the dog's class position from one that embodies the neglect of low-income homes of color to one that shows the physical signs of health, well-being, and self-care associated with the middle and upper classes. Although basically all of these cosmetic corrections could be made easily and inexpensively in an adoptive home (for instance, treating mange is inexpensive and losing weight is free), rescuers make the dogs available for adoption only *after* they have achieved an ideal physical presentation as established by the rescue. In this way, the rescue controls the dogs' images and ensures that only animals who look the part of the breed ambassador are available to adopters.

Associating a companion animal with middle-class respectability also involves linking that dog to a lifestyle recognizable as comfortable and white. Rescuers endow rescued pit bulls with symbols of middle-class white pethood. They strenuously object to the dogs wearing studded or leather collars, which they describe as "trashy," "mean-looking," and "ghetto," and quickly replace these with fabric collars that are colorful and often feminine and/or comical, such as those printed with flowers or cartoons; identification tags shaped like hearts or bones complete the presentation.[70] In removing and throwing away the collar put on the dog by the former guardian and replacing it with a collar of the rescuer's choosing, rescuers assert their guardianship of the animal and the dog's linkage to white middle-class animal practices.

A key part of moving the dogs closer to whiteness is feminizing them. Rescuers must unmake the masculinized and racialized image of pit bulls as tough, powerful, dominant, and aggressive dogs and show them as sweet, submissive, and sociable, irrespective of their sex. Pit bull rescuers could instead challenge gender norms if they celebrated the physicality of the dogs and encouraged women to feel empowered to handle them (an approach that could also prove problematic for the dogs but that would subvert gender stereotypes). Instead, they largely use their contact with the dogs to maintain white norms of femininity and to extend these norms to the dogs. They envelop the dogs in idealized feminized practices, stressing that the dogs are "furkids" who require a particular kind of doting care. Of course, this care can be provided only by those with the time and resources it requires.

Several rescuers with whom I interacted have cultivated relationships with dog accessory companies so that they receive highly decorative free or discounted collars and leashes. One of my foster pit bulls received a complimentary collar from a collar manufacturer with a massive cluster of pink faux roses on the collar. The collar was not terribly practical: the huge flowers interfered with taking the collar on or off, leash walking, and playing with other dogs, and the flowers fell apart quite quickly. However, for visual purposes (including photographs the rescue and I used to promote her for adoption), the collar succeeded in transforming a black pit bull recovering from mange into an eye-catching, civilized, and highly feminized dog with giant pink blooms around her face.

Visual cues like collars reflect that the dogs are companions who have achieved middle-class status, as they possess all of the trappings of the white mainstream and its practices of animal companionhood. Using social media like Facebook and Instagram, rescue organizations post images of foster dogs that include cues of whiteness and respectability such as collars, toys, and dog beds. Cardinal rules of pit bull rescue photography include that dogs are always to be photographed in neat, clean environments that look like middle-class homes or naturescapes, not kennels or low-income homes. Sometimes the animals are photographed against solid-colored backdrops in a style reminiscent of pop art, or in well-maintained yards. When a foster parent submitted pictures of her foster dog taken in her yard, replete with rusty lawn furniture and other detritus, the rescue's director deemed the photos unsuitable and would not use them to try to market the dog. She griped that the backgrounds made the dog look like a "yard dog" who "lives in a dump." Only images with cues of a higher-class status are acceptable for trying to attract white, middle-class adopters.

In attempts to market the dogs through visual images, the depictions of the dogs' bodies are important for conveying their femininity and docility. The dogs are always shown in states of relaxation, never barking or baring their teeth. Certain camera angles minimize the muscularity of the dogs, helping them appear less tough or strong. Pit bulls with cropped ears—often seen as a marker of dog fighting, although many people crop ears for aesthetic reasons—are especially likely to be shown with children and/or in costume such as sunglasses or seasonally appropriate headbands, like reindeer antlers in the winter, and/or in highly domestic situations, such as asleep in bed or wearing dresses or flowered headpieces.

I attended an adoption event in a busy commercial district with one of my foster dogs, an exceptionally pretty and petite fawn-and-white pit bull with soulful eyes. My notes about the presentation of the pit bulls capture some of the practices involved in remaking pit bulls:

> Two volunteers [at the event] seemed to have taken on responsibility for dressing up the [pit bulls]. . . . The volunteers had a large Tupperware storage bin filled with costume elements for the dogs, including bandanas with floral patterns, paw prints, and/or pro-adoption messages; sets of butterfly, bee, and angel wings; scarves; sunglasses modified to be able to sit on a dog's head more easily; and t-shirts intended for dogs. While the other volunteers set up the pop-up tents, tables, chairs, water areas, and signage and decorations, these two volunteers moved from dog to dog, choosing a "look" for each one and then dressing them up. I was partial to a pair of purple (dragonfly?) wings, but they put them on another dog before getting to [me and my foster dog]. When they approached us, one of the women started gushing immediately: "Oooooo! She is so pretty! What a beautiful, beautiful girl!" "It looks like she's wearing eyeliner!" the other woman proclaimed. They quickly decided her "look" should be Hollywood glamor, and within a few moments, my foster dog had a vintage leopard print scarf tied artfully around her neck. "She looks darling!" one of the women declared, "Like a perfect little starlet."

Wearing scarves, butterfly wings, and other accessories undermines dominant cultural scripts of pit bulls as scary urban weapons. All dressed up, the dogs seem childlike, feminine, and appropriate companion animals for white middle-class homes.

As the new racial and class status of the dogs is developed, foster homes and rescuers craft narratives of each dog's rescue built around the themes of redemption and upward mobility and in which physical markers of the dog's past often play a role: the dogs are saved from irresponsible and neglectful homes that are coded as lower income and nonwhite, and then are transformed into respectable companions suitable for cohabitation in white, middle- and upper-class homes. Echoing centuries of white colonial and neocolonial narratives of "saving" non-Europeans, these origin stories center on the rescuer as savior.[71] They are often crafted from loose interpretations of an animal's record at the shelter or their behavior once out of the shelter. Sad or challenging origin stories allow for the greatest possible glory in redemption for the animal and the humans around her, and many stories seem to be inflated. Overwhelmingly, when a dog has any scars, wounds, or marks, rescuers attribute these to human violence rather than to animal aggression, other animal behavior, or accidents. As an observer at the shelter, I regularly saw rescuers assert that injuries on dogs they were rescuing originated from human abuse when the injuries were entirely consistent with digging under fences or being hit by a car. These abuse narratives situate the dogs as victims of their former guardians and thus place the dogs in a submissive position vis-à-vis them, rather than as agentic actors who *choose* to fight with other dogs, escape from their yards, or growl at people.

MAINTAINING WHITENESS
THROUGH PIT BULL RESCUE

Pit bulls in the United States are deeply enmeshed in human structures of race, class, and gender. Pit bull rescuers in Los Angeles participate in these structures as they actively work to extract the dogs from their position as a feared type of dog. They attempt to transform the dogs from frightening, urban dogs into docile, feminized companions. Ultimately, rescuers of pit bulls work to make pit bulls whiter by inscribing them with animal practices associated with whiteness, thereby rendering them appropriate and desirable for white homes.

Like shelter animal advocacy more broadly, much of this rescue work for pit bulls in the Los Angeles area is undertaken by middle- and upper-class white women who engage in a range of practices to make the dogs adoptable by connecting them to signifiers of middle-class, feminized, white, mainstream animal companionship or "pethood." Rescuers offer a predictable solution to the peculiar problem of pit bulls. As they go about the work of repositioning the dogs as appropriate companions in middle- and upper-class feminized white homes, rescuers are not simply helping dogs: they are also shifting the boundaries of whiteness to include the dogs, even as they maintain the boundaries to exclude the dogs' imagined former guardians.

Rescuers of pit bulls further enact whiteness by generally failing to challenge raced, classed, and gendered beliefs about Black and Latinx masculinity as problematic and dangerous and about white middle-class domesticity as ideal. Rather than confronting the structural causes for why the dogs disproportionately end up in shelters or the entrenched cultural belief that lower-class Black and Latino masculinity is dangerous, pit bull rescuers focus on saving individual animals, blaming their former guardians for their plight, and disassociating them from low-income communities of color. Pit bull rescuers reify existing ideas about difference, hold onto and propagate their beliefs that pit bulls in shelters mostly belong to young, urban, Black and Latinx men who are irresponsible owners, and work to secure a better future for the dogs they rescue, all while ignoring the circumstances and needs of the people who once cared for them. In this way, pit bull rescue involves what Charles Mills calls the epistemology of ignorance by failing to see or engage with the racial inequalities that help explain the low status that pit bulls have.[72] While much of rescuers' critique of low-income guardians of color focuses on these guardians' instrumental use of companion animals, rescuers ultimately also use the animals as instruments for reproducing whiteness.

Humans can manipulate animals and the racial meanings attached to them. Pit bull rescuers' project of moving pit bulls closer to whiteness is necessarily incomplete. While breed advocacy does seem to have shifted public views about pit bulls to make them more appealing to white middle- and upper-class people across the United States, the dogs continue to fall outside the boundaries of whiteness.[73] Antiblackness is powerful, and pit bulls will not easily leap up the racial hierarchy to whiteness.

7   Animals' Resistance to Shelter Rule

KENNEL ATTENDANT SHAUNA APPROACHED Olivia's kennel slowly. One of the primary staff members tasked with evaluating the temperaments of dogs, Shauna had seen Olivia in her kennel many times over recent days and had observed how Olivia reacted to the presence of staff near her kennel. If a staff member approached, Olivia would launch her short, stocky body repeatedly against the kennel door, her eyes staring, wide and angry, directly at the offending staff person. Invariably, that person would step back, at which time Olivia would assume a defensive position, her face and ears alert as she stood her ground, bow-legged and snarling, spit spraying from her flapping gums. The notes in her record indicated that staff should exercise "extreme caution" in attempting to interact with her, and someone had written "CAUTION" on her kennel card in large, crooked red lettering. Shauna deemed Olivia unsafe to remove from her kennel, an immediate grade of F on PAW's temperament test and a virtual guarantee that her life would end at PAW.

Volunteers had a different experience of Olivia. Although she reacted to them initially with some signs of unease—pacing in her kennel and moving away from them—when volunteers knelt next to her cage with their backs to her, she would begin to shift closer and closer to them, eventually coming over to them, exhaling a big huff, and sitting down. If volunteers proceeded slowly, they would soon be able to reach their hands through the bars and scratch the top of her head. She would take treats gently through the kennel bars and push her body against the cage door to receive more human contact.

Olivia is the kind of dog who volunteers believe can differentiate between staff and other people, presumably identifying staff from their stiff police-like uniforms versus the more casual clothing of others (volunteers are required to wear a purple crewneck T-shirt with the SCAS logo when volunteering at the shelter and most of us pair this with old blue jeans). Volunteers explain dogs' sensitivity to staff members in a number of ways. Some point to the fact that, at intake, staff administer vaccinations, which hurt, and that they subsequently clean kennels daily, which involves spraying water into the dogs' habitat; the cumulative traumas the staff enact on dogs lead some animals to dislike them and aggress upon them. Other volunteers identify a canine dislike of all people in uniforms ("My dog hates the mailman!"), as if dogs can recognize this as a universal symbol of human authority (and maybe they can). Still other volunteers suggest that dogs can "smell death" in the presence of shelter staff because these workers kill animals.

In each of these narratives, dogs resist human intrusions. Olivia, and dogs like her, reject the presence of kennel staff and refuse to let kennel staff near them because of some kind of negative feeling toward them. They deny the authority of the kennel staff, even as these dogs—presumably unwittingly—seal their own fates as "aggressive" dogs who are unsuitable for adoptive placement.

PAW's practice of caging, through which humans largely control where animals are and engage in surveillance of them, gives the impression that humans are the only subjects with agency at PAW. However, a close examination of what animals do in the shelter reveals that while caging may serve to create an illusion of control and of separation between human and nonhuman animals, nonhuman animals in fact can and do act with agency and engage in resistance. As Shelly Scott argues, "Both oppressed animals and people deal with limitations imposed on their capacity for agency by rebelliously or subversively asserting their own wills."[1] Olivia, for instance, thwarted PAW's efforts to control her body by refusing to allow staff members to touch her or remove her from her kennel. She used a strategy of intimidation to prevent staff contact with her, making the work of staff more difficult (for example, when they went to feed her or clean her kennel), stressful (because what she did was noisy and frightening), and ineffective (since she would not let them control her beyond the act of caging).

Olivia's actions—and those of so many animals I observed at PAW—demonstrate that animals can and will act with resistance in pursuit of their own interests. In this chapter, I unsettle human ideas about animal resistance, ideas that we tend to use to comfort ourselves in our justification of human exploitation of animals and perhaps to manage our own fears of animals and the revenge they might exact on us. Animals impounded at PAW resist the conditions of their confinement. Observing and analyzing animal resistance help us understand animals' own wishes and guide human contributions to a more just future for them. Resistance is one way for animals to communicate their desires to us; only by listening will we hear them.

Animals who fail to comply with the expectations of docility set by the shelter and by the public face consequences for their resistance. The shelter primarily responds to animal resistance by pathologizing it: animals who resist shelter control are wild, dangerous, and unsuitable as companion animals, and, depending on the particular manifestation of their resistance and what type of an animal they are, they must be spared from their suffering or punished for it. PAW marks resistant animals as either unsafe for placement with humans or unappealing for such placement. Either assessment makes their chances of exiting the shelter alive much lower than for animals who oblige human expectations of docile animal bodies; many dogs and virtually all cats who are withheld from public adoption are killed.

Using lenses from critical disability studies, a field of theorizing and research that holds that social organization pathologizes, confines, and marginalizes people living with disabilities, helps illuminate the complex intersections of speciesism and ableism that shape human responses to animal resistance at PAW. Through pathologizing, resistant animals come to be seen as sick and suffering; even those who are understood as simply aggressive are disabled in the sense that they have no prospect for adoption and thus suffer by being stuck in their kennels in perpetuity unless they are killed. The discourse of suffering that threads through PAW's practices of pathologizing animals reflects mainstream thinking about animals and suffering that uses suffering as a justification for shelter killing: that is, killing (or, in PAW's language, euthanasia) is humane to put animals out of their misery. As animal liberationist and disability activist Sunaura Taylor writes,

> While disability advocates have pushed away from narratives of suffering, it is everywhere within animal rights scholarship. Animal activists have done a huge amount of work simply to prove that animals can suffer. . . . Suffering has become an inevitable part of conversations about animal industries, as well as around disabilities within these industries, and for good reason. But animals are too often presented simply as voiceless beings who suffer. Exploring their lives through a critical disability analysis can help us ask who these animals are *beyond their suffering*. It prompts us to consider how the very vulnerability and differences that these animals inhabit may in fact model new ways of knowing and being.[2]

In that spirit, I turn to exploring animal resistance to lead us to new ways of thinking about animals and our relationships with them.

CONCEPTUALIZING ANIMAL RESISTANCE

Thinking about animal agency is hardly new: Charles Darwin was one of the earliest proponents of recognizing that animals act deliberately.[3] Yet humans have largely rejected the idea of various forms of agentic behavior among animals, including animal resistance, in favor of behavioral explanations for understanding what animals do, or explanations that focus on conditioned responses to stimuli.[4] Human disavowal of animal resistance persists for at least two reasons, rendering animal resistance largely invisible because of our refusal to recognize it as such. Resistance among humans is often seen as important—even when it does not result in obvious change—because it undermines existing systems of oppression and creates new systems of signification. Inherent in this kind of definition of resistance are political and cultural elements, but humans generally hold that animals have neither political consciousness nor culture.

Thus one reason for human disavowal of animal resistance is a widespread belief that resistance reflects consciousness on the part of those engaging in resistance, and animals are assumed not to possess consciousness. Most simply, consciousness refers to being self-aware. Paolo Freire more specifically focuses on critical consciousness, or the awareness of one's own oppression, which is also sometimes used as a litmus test for resistance.[5] Marxist thinking further distinguishes between false consciousness—the belief in one's own subordination—and political consciousness, or the recognition of one's true political role rooted in material relations.[6] From a Marxist or neo-Marxist perspective, companion animals who accept their subordination to humans may be experiencing false consciousness (though it is also possible they are enjoying their status as a higher class among animals given their higher status than most animals), while those aware of their subordination have developed a critical consciousness. Once critical or political consciousness is achieved, antihegemonic work can begin.[7]

Yet many human acts of resistance are not grounded in critical or political consciousness.[8] Further, it is quite possible that animals *do* have critical consciousness but do not articulate it in a way that humans are willing or able to understand. When a dog like Olivia consistently responds to the presence of shelter staff with snarling aggression, it certainly could be inferred that she is acting from a place of refusal to submit to human state authority over her body and self—a political consciousness.[9] Still, humans generally fail to see animals as having the building blocks we believe are necessary to develop a critical consciousness. The most basic of these is a sense of self. Many, if not most, humans believe animals don't have a sense of self or of identity, both central aspects of extant analyses of human resistance.[10] If some animals are unable to recognize themselves or demonstrate self-awareness in ways that humans acknowledge, so the argument goes, then they don't have an identity or a sense of self. Without an identity or sense of self, they lose their basis for resistance. Yet human experiments have identified self-awareness in many species, including dogs, and our understanding of how animals demonstrate self-awareness and identity is expanding rapidly.[11] While we may not be able to know if and how animals mobilize ideas about and practices of self and identity through resistance, this does not mean it is not happening.

Another building block for resistance is a theory of mind, or awareness that others have thoughts and feelings different from one's own. While it would be possible to resist someone or something without knowing their intention, consciousness requires an ability to understand that an actor(s) or institution is attempting to act upon you. Here, too, there is ample evidence of animals possessing theories of mind, in their interactions with other animals and often with humans.[12] Companion animals in particular are well positioned to be aware of human goals and intentions.

Animals' purported lack of reason and intelligence has been one of many justifications used to support human exploitation of animals. This is a problematic way of relating to humans with intellectual disabilities and to animals, both of whom are denied full personhood on the basis of the argument that they lack the necessary reason of neurotypical humans.[13] In arguing that animals are mindful and can act deliberately, I do not want to fall into the trap of arguing that they reason in the same ways as humans. My point is rather that animals can act deliberately and engage in resistance, *even if* they possess a different way of reasoning than we observe in neurotypical humans. Diverse ways of thinking, feeling, and experiencing are part of the complexity and beauty of our multispecies worlds and should not be used as the basis for denying members of any species autonomy and dignity.[14]

The second source of human reluctance to think about animals as engaging in resistance is that theorization and research on resistance focus heavily on signification and meaning—proxies for culture—which humans have tried to lay exclusive claim to in our quest to differentiate animals from us.[15] Here, again, there is overwhelming support that our human-centric belief that we are the only species with culture is wrong. Evidence of culture—shared customs, beliefs, and/or tools that are transmitted across generations through social learning—among animals first emerged from research on those animals most similar to us, namely primates;[16] however, subsequent research has documented cultural practices and learning in whales and dolphins, fish, and birds, among other animals.[17] Culture has been specifically identified in the context of animal shelters: in their analysis of a private cat shelter, Alger and Alger identify a culture built between and among cats and humans.[18] These studies show that animals can and do communicate with each other, often using languages (like whale song, dolphin clicks, or elephant rumbles) and passing knowledge across generations.

Further, animals use their bodies as sites of performance. Thinking back to Olivia, when she refuses to greet passersby or even growls at them, she is engaging in a performance that undermines dominant images of companion animals. She cannot control the possible interpretations of that performance—staff may see her as aggressive, passersby as scary or mean, volunteers as vulnerable and scared. Yet each of these interpretations of her performance challenges PAW's depiction of itself as an institution helping animals, undermines seeing companion animals as docile and submitting to human will, and separates her from any value as a commodified object of pet-love.[19] These *are* all cultural challenges involving signification—and all are challenges made by an animal.

I conceptualize animal resistance as acts that stand in opposition to anthroparchal power and thus demand that power respond.[20] Such acts may be individual or collective, isolated or sustained. Resistance may result in repression, resolution, or some combination: "No particular outcome or effect should be mandatory; only the *potential* of undermining power."[21] Animal resistance may be recognized as any instance of animals refusing to comply with human expectations of their behavior. It need not be violent or grandiose, but it must threaten to interfere with or undermine existing relationships of domination between humans and animals.

Animal resistance is corporeal and visible to humans. In contrast to the many forms of covert resistance documented among humans, animal resistance is easy for any human who is looking to see. However, reflecting anthrocentric beliefs, humans are most likely to interpret the act of resistance as something other than resistance: behavior, instinct, poor health, personality. Animals are rarely, if ever, understood to be acting with agency and deliberately in pursuit of challenging human dominance over them as individuals or as a group.[22] As Eva Meijer writes, nonhuman animals "cannot answer the harms done to them because the framework in which they speak is constructed in such a way that their responses are not considered relevant to the conversation, or even heard."[23]

Although animals are shut out of conversations within the sheltering industry about what is best for them, they are engaging in resistance. The specific contours of power determine who and what to resist.[24] In an animal shelter, where animals are subjected to loss of control over their bodies through caging and other forms of restraint, their primary expressions of resistance are also against caging and other forms of restraint. Inside the kennel, dogs may rush forward or run away. They may show their teeth or lunge, or they may "pancake" on the ground and refuse to walk. They may try to push past the person opening the kennel door and run away. They may spin in circles in their kennel, making it difficult to lasso them with a leash.

Cats, whose space is much more limited than dogs, also have possibilities: they can hiss, scratch, or bite, push forward in the cage and try to jump out, or hide in the small box placed in their cage for privacy.

A growing body of research shows various ways in which animals act as agents engaged in resistance, particularly when held in captivity. In her analysis of captive dolphins at a marine park, for example, Traci Warketin finds that the dolphins learn to negotiate their physical confinement in ways that are not what the park's staff desire.[25] The dolphins employ strategies to avoid being touched by humans while still managing to snatch forbidden containers of fish from them. These are not behaviors dolphins ever would have learned in the wild, nor are they trained to do this. Instead, the dolphins "transgress the routine of what was supposed to happen according to human desires and expectations, and assert their own desires and agency."[26] Irus Braverman speaks of zoo animals as engaging in reproductive strikes, refusing to mate or act out parenting behaviors encouraged by zookeepers who are seeking to secure species futures and/or additional captive animals for display or trade.[27] The documentary film *Blackfish*, which examined the conditions of confinement of orcas in marine parks and the killing of three trainers by orca Tillikum, drew national attention to animal welfare in "animaltainment" settings—or venues like Sea World in which animals are used for purposes of human entertainment—and also raised important questions about animals' capacities for meaningful resistance.[28] The documentary *Tyke Elephant Outlaw* explores similar themes in the tragic story of Tyke, a circus elephant who killed her trainer and made a run for it in Honolulu.[29] Jason Hribal identifies numerous cases of resistance by animals who have been exploited for entertainment, consumption, or research.[30] Meijer likewise recounts various cases of animals, including birds, dogs, and primates, resisting infringement upon their habitats and their direct exploitation, while Dawn Coppin analyzes the resistance of factory-farmed pigs.[31]

Taken together, these works create a long inventory of animals engaging in resistance that defies the expectations of their human guards/guardians. Anyone who listens to animals will find that almost all of them are asking to be heard and to have their lives continue; many even have ways of communicating with us that we can more readily understand.[32] Animals across species can and do engage in acts of resistance to human intervention in their lives, and impounded animals regularly resist their captors and the state of their captivity. Animals do not accept intensive confinement and ongoing violence as an acceptable way of living.[33]

Companion animals occupy a particularly interesting space in the species hierarchy for purposes of resistance. While some may argue that companion animals are the Uncle Toms of animals because of their apparent willing acquiescence to human demands, they also are afforded an opportunity to see, observe, and understand human activity that most other animals do not enjoy. They also can communicate with us: dogs in particular have been shown to recognize and be able to follow typical human gestures, such as pointing, and to recognize objects by name or symbol.[34] They are further able to acquire the trust, love, and admiration of people. Companion animals thus have unique revolutionary potential. Especially if they could convince enough humans to act on their behalf, they may be the best positioned to challenge anthroparchy as long as they are willing to cede their position of high status within the species hierarchy.

As is the case for farmed animals, guardians of companion animals—whether individuals or institutions—typically try to prevent resistance before it manifests. In the context of an animal shelter, this prevention includes specific protocols for managing animal bodies so that they are either tethered (leashed) or caged and for handling animal bodies to minimize the risk of injuries to humans, such as by wrapping leashes around animals' mouths as muzzles during veterinary checks. Administrative control involves tracking animal behavior and labeling some animals as behaviorally problematic; this alerts staff to interact with these animals in particular ways, which may then reinforce those behaviors. For example, if a dog is resistant to leashing and staff are told to walk them on a catchpole, which dogs seem universally to find scary and uncomfortable, that dog is likely to have increased anxiety about humans—and things that go around a dog's neck—in the future. The intervention multiplies harms rather than being therapeutic.

Although he engaged in a sustained analysis of power, Foucault dedicated much less attention to resistance, suggesting that there were few options for people to find their way out of the total domination of contemporary modes of (bio)power and surveillance. From a Foucaultian perspective, resistance merely engenders new forms of management. Because of animals' substantial subordination in capitalist systems with advanced technologies for enacting violence against animals, the probability of animal resistance effecting significant change seems limited. However, especially when noticed by human advocates, animal resistance can be a catalyst for major change. The marked decline in the exploitation of live animals in American circuses and the shifting use of orcas in the marine parks owned by SeaWorld are two high-profile examples of how animal resistance invited and supported interspecies justice projects.

Relationships between power and resistance change not only because of the interaction of the specific responses of a power structure to a specific act or set of acts of resistance; there may be other outside pressures, ranging from additional resistors who represent a different group or set of interests or other structural changes. PAW and SCAS have periodically shifted how they respond to animal resistance because of changes in the practices of the animal-sheltering industry. These include a growing industry-wide commitment to move away from thinking of animal shelters as sites for managing and reducing animal populations to conceptualizing animal shelters as rehoming centers focused on adoption and rescue, not killing. Shifting practices include giving impounded animals more time to find homes or rescues and making efforts to increase enrichment, including the construction of several units of multicat housing in which several cats can cohabit at once. More recently, the invitation to partner with Humane America has moved some of SCAS's and PAW's practices to align with those of the nonprofit organization, which concentrates on reducing shelter killing through the principles of the no-kill movement and through the extensive relocation of animals from high-intake shelters like PAW to shelters in areas where few animals are coming into shelters.

Of course, as evidence mounts of animals' political consciousness, culture, and resistance, humans are likely to change the requirements for what constitutes the human. Agamben conceptualizes the anthropological machine as operating so that humans alone decide what separates humans from animals, citing ever-shifting criteria, such as cognition, use of tools, culture, and family formation.[35] Whenever humans or animals challenge an alleged innate difference between them, humans employ a new difference to secure human exceptionalism. Ultimately, per Agamben, human identity rests on the exclusion of the animal, no matter what the basis of that exclusion. Still, reimagining resistance stands to shift our thinking about animals in ways that should benefit them.

Human struggles for animal rights, for their part, continue to mount challenges to the exclusion of animals from the human. My assertion of animals as conscious agents of resistance supports these efforts. If we recognize that animals are asking—or even demanding—that we cease harming them, if we acknowledge their ability to think and act as individuals and collectives, if we see them struggling against us, we will start to rethink our relationships with them and their alleged difference from us.

ANIMAL RESISTANCE AT PAW

Animals engage in a wide range of acts of everyday resistance against humans and other animals. Their resistance can be physical (including violence), relational, and/or symbolic. Companion animals provide an especially instructive case for considering animal resistance, for these are the animals most tied to humans in relationships and the ones whose behaviors we routinely have opportunity to observe. We consider them domesticated, or purpose-bred to be tame, dependent on humans for survival, and able to meet needs humans dictate. They often live very closely with us, especially the animals who constitute the overwhelming majority of animals at PAW, namely dogs and cats. Anyone who lives with a companion animal is likely to have a narrative of companion animal resistance already, even if they do not define it as such: the dog who breaks out of their crate, the indoor cat who claws through screens to get outside, the cat who flees even at the sound of their carrier being removed from the closet, the dog or cat who defecates in the new baby's room, the dog who chews up the sofa cushions.[36] These can all be acts of resistance, communication of dissatisfaction with the conditions of confinement, and efforts at being heard.

While attempts to cause physical harm to humans may be the most obvious forms of resistance animals employ, animal resistance includes a wide range of behaviors. At PAW, passive forms of resistance involve efforts at noncooperation with the shelter's regime of activity and surveillance and include strategies such as hunger striking; refusing to get up, move, and/ or walk as requested; hiding under the raised platform beds for dogs or in the privacy box for cats; going limp and requiring being carried or dragged rather than walking on all fours; and refusing to take medication when offered or administered. Active forms of resistance involve both warnings and attempts at causing physical harm to humans—growling, hissing, lunging, scratching, kicking, twisting, bucking, snapping, and/or biting among them—as well as running away, opening the guillotine door, escaping from kennels, repetitively jumping up, and uninterruptedly barking or vocalizing in other ways. While it's easier to see active strategies, passive and active strategies are both common at PAW and occur with approximately equal frequency. Consider these notes I made about interactions with dogs in adjacent kennels one afternoon:

> The first kennel I approached housed four little dogs: two Chihuahua mixes and two scruffy little dogs. When I bent down outside of their kennel, two of them came rushing over to the door, bouncing gleefully against the kennel bars. A third stayed back, right before the guillotine partition, and barked at me, leaning back on their haunches and craning their neck. The fourth remained on the inside of the kennel under the bed and would not come out even as I cooed and gave the friendly kennelmates at the front some treats.
>
> The next kennel housed a single German Shepherd. The dog's kennel was caked in feces: they had pooped and then walked in it, tracking the fecal matter all over. The dog was pacing, primarily in the outside portion of the kennel, swooping in two strides along the long side of the kennel, then curving their body into a tight turn to swoop along the other side. I clucked but they did not stop for even a moment to glance at me.
>
> Next door was a pit bull I have met before. She was asleep on the inside of the kennel when I approached, and I didn't want to wake her, but she noticed me because of the barking of other dogs nearby and came running over, her tail thumping wildly. She pressed herself against the kennel bars so I could rub her a little. I dug around in my bag and gave her a treat.
>
> In the next kennel, the guillotine door was shut, so the dog was trapped on the outside half of the kennel only. The dog, a cow-pattern pit bull, sat hunched in the back corner, head down and tail tucked. I was still down in a crouching position, and I tapped my hand [on my thigh, an action some behaviorists think mimics a wagging tail and signals friendliness]. The dog looked away from me. I sat a little longer [with the dog],

looking away down the line of kennels and avoiding eye contact, to wait to see what the dog would do. After what must have been a minute or ninety seconds, I looked back at the dog, who had now looked up at me so that our eyes briefly met. They lifted their lip to show me a glimmer of teeth and quickly looked away. I went to the other side of the kennel to open the guillotine so the dog could try to hide in the relative darkness of the indoor side.

My field notes reflect how routine animal resistance is at PAW. In this small sample of seven dogs, four responded to the imposition of my presence with some form of resistance, whether hiding, barking, pacing, avoiding, or growling. For some of these dogs, these behaviors may not be shelter specific and thus may not be resistance to the shelter. They may be engaged in resistance against human intervention in their lives more generally. I didn't meet these particular dogs before their impound, but what staff and volunteers regularly observe is that animals are friendly and happy outside the shelter but once inside the shelter become either immediately or gradually less friendly and happy.

Given all the different forms of resistance animals employ at the shelter, it appears that they, like humans, have the capacity to experiment with different forms of resistance, trying out and possibly rejecting one approach in favor of another. Humans utilize a myriad of different tools of resistance and often change them in response to the reactions that certain approaches receive or to changing structures of power. At PAW, it's not uncommon to see an animal initially ignore humans and later begin aggressing against them. Following a different pathway, some animals resist contact with humans at first and then begin to acquiesce to human control over their bodies.[37]

Because they must try to move animals regularly in the course of their regular work, one of the sites of resistance that volunteers and staff talk about the most is ambulation. To get animals to different areas within the shelter such as the RVT's office, the clinic, or the social area, or just from one side of the kennel to the other for cleaning, staff and volunteers need them to move. For dogs, this most commonly happens on a leash, but movement can alternately involve carrying a dog, walking them on a catchpole, or placing them in a rolling kennel. How an animal responds to leashing is seen as an indicator of their level of training and socialization. The overwhelming majority of dogs pull on their leash when taken out of the kennel. Exiting the kennel is a moment of significant excitement, and also an opportunity for them to ignore human demands in favor of their own. As dogs rush out of their kennels, dragging a staff member or volunteer behind them, they assert their desire to be in control and their rejection of human domination. Under the auspices of safety, humans at PAW rarely handle cats directly for long: when they are removed from their cage, the staff member or volunteer usually places them directly into a plastic box with a window, air holes, and a carrying handle and moves them to their destination more constrained and separated than most other types of shelter animals.

Oppositional actions are forms of resistance through which impounded animals refuse to participate in their own confinement and reject human expectations for docility and cooperation. Animals deliberately disrupt desired operations at PAW. When animals are either passively or actively resistant, staff must dedicate more time to completing basic tasks with them than with animals who comply with PAW's expectations of animal behavior. Handling a cat or dog who is trying to bite can be particularly treacherous and time-consuming and also causes many staff members stress as they feel fearful both about getting hurt and about hurting the animal through restraint. Staff interpret these behaviors as a lack of self-control and as indicators of violent and not fully de-wilded tendencies—in short, as *animality*.

For companion animals, whose value depends on their acquiescence to human expectations of them, or their complete domestication, engaging in resistance to the rule of law at PAW is, by extension, resistance to the commodification of their lives and bodies. In the United States, the dominant form of animal practices has sought to establish companion animals as "family members." Simultaneously, companion animals' primary value as purported family members lies in their abilities to please human senses and provide desired forms of companionship. A dog or cat who refuses to demonstrate the characteristics expected of companion animals—friendliness, docility, cooperativeness—loses that value. At PAW, I consistently observed adopters seeking out dogs and cats whom they perceived as "friendly"—animals who greet visitors at the front of their cages and who do not bark, hiss, or growl at them.[38] Dogs and cats who ignore prospective adopters, threaten them in some way, or display behaviors that prospective adopters find problematic, like repeated barking (even if not hostile), fail to meet adopters' expectations and are slower to be adopted, if they are adopted at all. A dog like Monster, who seemed indifferent to human contact and whom I never saw get up to greet any human, even the staff feeding him, does not comply with market expectations and thus rejects commodification of his life and body. Impounded animals resist the multiple ways humans attempt to control them, rejecting human authority over their routine actions *and* the assertion of a human system of valuing their lives. These animals are resisting anthroparchy and the conditions it sets forth for them.

Sometimes animals engaging in acts of resistance change once they are outside the shelter. On numerous occasions, dogs who were quite hostile to people inside the shelter turned out to be loving and friendly companions outside the shelter. Often, the change is practically instantaneous. I pulled a purportedly human aggressive pit bull mix named Ace from the shelter. The shelter staff had tried to assess him and determined that he was "trying to bite" and therefore unsafe to leave his kennel or to be adopted by a member of the public. As a volunteer with a rescue organization, I was able to remove him from the shelter and into the care of the rescue. Upon leaving the building, I walked him around the parking lot so he could go to the bathroom and then loaded him into my car. Since I had never been able to interact with him outside his kennel and might have needed help with him, another volunteer stayed with me while I walked Ace and got him in the car. When I opened the trunk to my hatchback, Ace eagerly catapulted himself into the back of the car, sniffed around the front seat area, and lay down, panting happily. When I got in the car, he stood up and licked deep into my ear and then lay back down, his body loose and relaxed. I was not afraid of him, and I did not see any aggression in him. But I had also offered him a change in setting and activity that perhaps he knew from his life before the shelter: a walk and a ride in a car. Perhaps these were sufficient to ease his resistance to anthroparchy. Perhaps these were manifestations of anthroparchy he was willing to accept.

SHELTER REPRESSION OF ANIMAL RESISTANCE

Dogs and cats are rarely understood as having motives of resistance at PAW. When they pop up the guillotine doors on their kennels to escape, snap at volunteers or staff, hiss and attempt to scratch, or flat-out refuse to walk or move into a designated area when asked, staff see their actions as reflections of their bad character, and volunteers see their actions as irrational responses to fear. Neither interpretive framework integrates the possibility that animals purposefully engage in resistance to human efforts at asserting control.

Humans tend to interpret canine behaviors such as these through biological, rather than social, lenses, chalking them up to "instinct," including instincts that are activated by particular stimuli. In fact, with companion animals, we remain deeply preoccupied by their "wild" origins and how those origins shape their behavior today. Celebrity dog trainer Cesar Millan, also known as the Dog Whisperer, helped popularize the lupomorph model of dog training, or the idea that dogs retain the pack instincts of wolves and need their human to be a "pack leader."[39] Dozens of books just in the last decade examine the history of companion animals, particularly their domestication and how their wild ancestry influences their behavior today.[40] The take-home message from most of this popular science and animal behavior literature is that in order to understand dogs and cats we must consider their evolution from wild ancestors. This presumed wildness in domesticated animals translates into the widespread acceptance of the idea that dogs and cats behave on the basis of instinct—and that this naturalness and their purported predetermined tendency toward wild animality should we humans fail to contain them stands in opposition to being human and, by extension, to the planning and strategy required of resistance.

Indeed, if the desire for freedom and autonomy is an instinct among all animals—including humans, of course—there is an instinctual basis for these behaviors. Yet how animals deploy their resistance is far more than instinct alone. Many have capacity to think about possibilities, make decisions, take the interests and needs of others into account, and act accordingly. They manipulate their environment and their relationships with animals of other species, including humans. They choose when to strike, and how.

Still, among staff at PAW, explanations focused on nature—discourses involving instinct, personality, character, and other inherent traits—dominate. A dog or cat who bites is a "bad" animal rather than an individual enacting a choice or strategy. Their behavior is understood as a reflection of their intrinsic self, not their situation. Further, it is the behaviors associated with wildness— behaviors that reject humans as companions—that PAW understands as problematic. Animals who refuse to be petted, use their bodies to protect themselves, and/or display a lack of respect for human expectations are identified as problem animals. They are seen as animals who have been unsuccessfully or not fully domesticated and who lack the docility necessary to be a human companion. The more "tame" an animal, the more adoptable, and the more likely to exit the shelter alive.

How PAW establishes a cat as feral is telling with regard to the shelter's awareness of resistance and its pathologizing of it. Feral/community cats are not a separate species from domestic cats (both are *Felis catus*), but rather simply cats who have had limited or no contact with humans and are therefore less social with humans. They are still considered domesticated because they rely primarily on human resources for food and protection (under cars, porches, or dumpsters, in junkyards and other industrial areas, etc.). Per PAW's policy manual, staff are to identify any "cat without owner identification of any kind whose usual and consistent temperament is extreme fear and resistance to contact with people" as feral. Feral status thus is defined in part precisely by resistance, although such resistance could be situational—that is, in response to how humans dominate animals in shelters. Feral cats are not made available for adoption at PAW: they are housed in a separate building from housecats and are generally killed on the first day on which PAW can legally kill them.[41]

PAW's ideas about tameness are colored by breedism, itself an outgrowth of racism and classism. Pit bulls in particular are held to a different standard of behavior than other types of dogs. Staff see a resistant pit bull, for instance, as much more problematic than a resistant Boxer, even though the dogs are physically similar in terms of size and strength and even though, during my research, both types of dogs were involved in physical attacks against humans in the shelter and in the community. But a Boxer is a purebred animal associated with middle- and upper-class suburban households, whereas a pit bull is a mongrel from the dark-skinned lower classes.

Staff, volunteers, and rescuers routinely note that a pit bull has to be "perfect" to be worthy of adoption or rescue. While other dogs can get away with a certain amount of resistance and have that resistance chalked up positively to their character—"What a hilariously surly boy!" "He know what he wants!" "She's a real queen!"—pit bulls must be compliant and agreeable. Even a generally friendly pit bull who is seen as "too dominant"—maybe because they repeatedly jump on people or tense up during a veterinary exam or prefer to rest their head on the back of other dogs when playing—will be perceived as more likely to engage in future aggression and therefore will be flagged as a threat. Such a dog is likely to still be made available to the public for adoption, but only to specialized homes. Any sign that they won't acquiesce to human demands can result in their demise at PAW. These expectations reflect PAW's discourse of public safety, which is grounded in the racial politics of pit bulls. Pit bulls can't seem to get away from their reputation as uniquely dangerous animals.

Staff identify a broader set of behaviors as pathological than do volunteers. In interpreting animals' actions, volunteers tend to center social understandings of animal behavior. For example, volunteers focus on animals acting in ways to protect themselves from immediate threats, such as biting someone when they are cornered, or acting aggressively after years of being kept outdoors on a tether. While volunteers' accounts of animal behavior allow for more consideration of social and environmental factors than do staff accounts, they generally do so in ways that also depict dogs as acting from instinctive, primal places, but ones they find acceptable. The undercurrent of their critiques of shelter interpretations of animal behavior is that PAW doesn't account for "normal" canine behaviors and the ways that the shelter disrupts the possibility of expressing those "normal" behaviors. Volunteers employ a much more expansive view of the normal—and therefore the acceptable—than staff. While staff may limit adoption opportunities for animals who try to bite the RVT, are jumpy or mouthy, or growl, volunteers see these as contextually appropriate responses and as within the normal range of companion animal behavior. Staff designated a young Husky with luscious white fur and bright blue eyes as available to rescues only because he liked to put human hands and arms in his mouth. Staff viewed the behavior as "trying to bite" and as a problem behavior that could be hazardous, while volunteers understood it as "mouthing," which they argued was common in the breed and could be exacerbated by stress and its attendant anxiety. The staff interpretation was one focused on danger and aggression, while the volunteers' interpretation emphasized the typicality of the behavior and its connection to caging.

A dog who outright bites a kennel attendant at PAW may indeed be scared, but that animal is also telling the staff to respect her and to recognize her as someone with bodily integrity and the right to maintain her boundaries. A dog who bites a kennel attendant, however, will be placed in quarantine (where the dog may not be touched or taken out by staff or volunteers for the duration of the quarantine) and then will be made available to rescue organizations only and, frequently, will be killed. Not only will the behavior elicit a highly punitive response from staff caregivers, but the behavior will be understood as one that reflects inherent flaws in the animal herself: she becomes a "biter," which is a "bad dog" (or, in the words of one staff member, "not nice").

Staff see the bite as a reflection of the animal's temperament, something that is fixed. Volunteers, in contrast, see the bite as something contextual that happens because of where the dog is and what is happening to her—it is a situational expression of resistance. They see the bite as justified because the dog was stressed and/or scared. The volunteer interpretation tends to frame bites and what staff call "attempts to bite" (which happen far more often than bites with actual injuries, but which can also trigger an animal's being made available only to partnered rescue organizations and not to the general public) as a reaction that is largely driven by fear and thus is reflexive or instinctual rather than reasoned.[42]

Animal resistance unfortunately can undermine the efforts of volunteers to help animals exit alive. Volunteers want to present every shelter animal as deserving of life; when those animals in turn behave in ways PAW finds problematic, the animals reinforce PAW's belief that some animals are unfit for placement with humans and are not truly companion animals. Volunteers attempt to challenge PAW's assessments of dogs as dangerous; in the cases of Olivia (at the beginning of this chapter) and Junebug (in chapter 6), volunteers found the dogs to behave quite differently than staff did and pushed to have the dogs reevaluated. When they were unsuccessful (as they almost always were), they organized together to try to secure rescues for the dogs.

RESISTANCE AS PATHOLOGY

PAW's primary response to animal resistance is to view it as pathological, a framing that then opens pathways toward shelter death. Companion animals share an elevated status with zoo animals: unlike low-order animals like farmed animals, fish, and insects, their suffering and deaths generally require justification through human biopolitical frames of sickness and health, safety and crime.[43] Framing animal behavior as pathological provides PAW with an explanation for why a particular animal is killed. When volunteers, rescuers, or other humans express distress that an impounded animal has been killed, effective ways for staff to frame the killing are to assert that the animal was aggressive or suffering. These frames resonate with broader discourses of public safety and compassion circulating within PAW, SCAS, and the larger sheltering industry.

Aggression and zoochosis are the two labels staff use to label animals as killable. The first is understood at PAW as an inherent trait, as something that cannot be undone, and as something that poses a threat to the safety and well-being of humans. Animals who are aggressive violate the hierarchy of human-animal relationships by threatening humans with their animal bodies. They cannot be helped in or out of the shelter environment, and PAW and SCAS consider them unsuitable for placement with the public because of the threat they pose to public safety as dogs who have been assessed as bite risks. They normally (but not always) are still made available to rescue organizations partnered with SCAS, and some of the dogs exit the shelter alive to join a rescue. Feral cats are not generally even available to rescue groups; they are seen as a public nuisance that must be exterminated.

Zoochosis, in contrast, is a contextually specific condition that could potentially be resolved by leaving the shelter. Unlike medical issues, which volunteers and some staff often see as treatable in the shelter, zoochosis—or what staff and volunteers also widely refer to as kennel stress—can best be cured by leaving the shelter. Symptoms of zoochosis include the onset of problematic behaviors after a period of impoundment, including jumping repetitively at the kennel door, or what shelter staff and volunteers call pogo-sticking; growling or snarling at shelter staff, volunteers, and/or visitors; hiding in the back of the kennel or, in the case of small dogs, under the raised platform bed; repetitive tail chasing or what staff and volunteers call spinning; self-injurious behavior such as self-biting (usually of the tail or nails/toes) that has no known underlying medical cause; snapping at the air or licking the kennel bars obsessively; and/or barking unrelentingly or in a seemingly aggressive manner.

The term *zoochosis* comes not simply from the Greek root for "animal" but from the initial recognition of this issue in zoos, where it refers specifically to wild animals in captivity who engage in abnormal and/or repetitive

behaviors as an apparent indicator of stress. The language that originated
with zoo animals makes sense to members of the shelter industry, who,
like zoo workers, see themselves as engaged in the protection and care of
animals.[44] While domesticated dogs and indoor cats arguably are always
in captivity and never wild, the shelter environment usually presents them
with a much stricter level of confinement than they would experience in a
home environment. At an underfunded and understaffed shelter like PAW,
some dogs may not leave their kennel enclosures for weeks at a time; they
are restricted to a space of about forty-five square feet (half of that when the
guillotine door is closed for cleaning, at night, or when the shelter is crowded
and kennels are split) with only food and water bowls and a raised platform
bed; they have no toys, and their only forms of distraction are their observations of what happens around them. Small dogs may have the company of
kennel mates; dogs over thirty pounds typically do not. Depending on their
location in the facility, there are other dogs on three or four sides of them,
and the kennel design means that humans can look in on two sides at any
time without warning. The dogs have limited privacy and nowhere they can
hide from prying eyes or the cacophony of the shelter's sonoric architecture.

The diagnoses of aggression and zoochosis are often codetermined. Any
behavior a shelter staff member feels is atypical can be designated as kennel
stress, and with some forms of kennel stress the staff simply refer to a dog
as "now aggressive." That is, there is an idea within the institution that even
dogs who once were good can "turn" and become "bad" or aggressive if kept
in a shelter environment for too long—so aggression can be a symptom of
zoochosis or an independent diagnosis, depending on the timing of the
onset of symptoms. If an animal is aggressive from the moment of entry,
they are aggressive; if their aggression develops after days or weeks at the
shelter, they have zoochosis, and aggression is the presenting symptom.

From the perspective of most volunteers, impounded animals are living
under temporary conditions of extreme stress that do not mimic those of
their future homes. Most staff assert that, given the volume of incoming
animals, flagging those animals who respond poorly to the shelter environment is a reasonable strategy for population management and likely culls
the animals most likely to pose a risk to the human community. While staff
readily acknowledge that zoochosis is an outcome of the stressful conditions
at PAW, they never frame kennel stress as an issue for which the shelter

should be held accountable. It is *the individual dog or cat* (and many cats who are, at intake, found to be tame cats are later reclassified as aggressive) whose response to the shelter environment is problematic; the shelter environment itself is not seen as problematic.

Dogs who are in any way unruly and whose bodies and attitudes do not align with the level of docility expected by staff are viewed as problem animals. Just like farmed animals who refuse to follow human instruction, shelter animals who seem to defy the authority of staff members are quickly identified as problem animals.[45] Escaping from the kennel, for example, is grounds for being designated as a behaviorally problematic dog. Some dogs figure out how to use the safety latch on the inside of the kennel to release themselves, making it very difficult for the shelter staff to contain them (although the kennels in one building in the shelter do not have this interior release, so the dog could simply be moved into this building rather than be punished for the behavior). For the first few years of my fieldwork, dogs who could lift the guillotine door between the indoor and outdoor parts of their kennels were also considered to have a behavior problem that made them likely candidates to be killed. This particular behavior is very annoying to staff who clean the kennels because it facilitates the dog escaping when one half of the kennel is being cleaned. Making the staff's jobs more difficult is an unacceptable behavior, and one that places dogs on the list for death even if that behavior is unlikely to be one that emerges in a domestic context (private homes generally don't use guillotine doors to contain animals).

Being designated as behaviorally problematic triggers multiple processes that increase the eventuality of shelter death for any given animal. Most especially, once a dog or cat has been identified as having aggression or zoochosis, the amount of time that the dog is given at the shelter is substantially reduced, sometimes to just a day after the diagnosis is made. Staff enter information about animal behavior into the computer system, and that information is then available to the kennel supervisor when they review the computer-generated list of animals legally eligible to be killed. In some instances, particularly when volunteers have already been involved with a particular dog, staff notify volunteers about the shortened time line for live release. When volunteers have not already been involved with a dog, the dog is just killed. Exhibiting pathology is a fast track to shelter death.

Jake is but one of several hundred dogs I came to know at PAW who lost their lives because they were deemed to be suffering from aggression and/or kennel stress. A handsome young German Shepherd with the classic black-and-tan coloring, Jake resisted the shelter's authority over him from the outset, rejecting being controlled on a leash by shelter staff, slipping up the guillotine door and attempting to escape during feeding and cleaning, and, eventually, refusing any human contact by intimidating humans from behind his kennel bars by lunging and growling. Once a staff member had flagged him as having problem behaviors in the computer system, each subsequent observation of such behaviors in his record became part of a spiral of documentation of his purported aggressiveness leading toward death. At no point did any staff member actually *try* to get him out of his kennel and into a play area: on the basis of his in-kennel behavior alone, he was determined to be unsafe for placement into an adoptive home. After a week at PAW (including the period of his mandatory hold), Jake was taken to the Euth Room and killed.

Alice was a pudgy fawn Chihuahua mix who didn't want human contact at the shelter. She hid under her bed, and if staff forced her out she snarled and snapped at them. Two volunteers who specialize in working with resistant small dogs were able to build trust with her, and she would allow them to hold and stroke her. Everyone else kept their distance. Alice's behavior was flagged as aggressive, and, in spite of appeals from the volunteers who held her, she was killed.

Lobo was a young pit bull and German Shepherd mix who turned his back on humans by turning instead toward his tail. He chased his tail constantly, never stopping to interact with the people or other dogs around him. The shelter staff classified him as suffering from zoochosis. Some volunteers conjectured that he had a neurological problem (but he was never sent to a private veterinarian for evaluation); others suspected he had a type of canine obsessive-compulsive disorder. Another way of looking at Lobo's behavior is through the lens of resistance: by showing that intensive confinement can make you crazy, Lobo's tail-chasing provided an ideal way to draw attention to the problematic conditions of his captivity; to challenge the views of staff, visitors, and volunteers who might find those conditions of caging acceptable; and to avoid contact with humans without actually attempting to hurt anyone else, human or animal. Alas, the shelter killed him.

That the shelter responds to acts of resistance by meting out diagnoses of aggression and/or zoochosis reflects anthroparchal rejection of the right of companion animals to behave in ways that humans find undesirable and an ableist assumption that dogs who have zoochosis are sick and not deserving of (or possibly not even safe for) a home. Even those animals whom PAW designates as aggressive are killed in part to save them from suffering. In this logic, keeping them alive in the shelter is inhumane given that they have little or no hope of exiting alive as they are not available for adoption to the public.

Reflecting the intersections of helping, policing, and killing, those animals PAW identifies as pathological—whether suffering from kennel stress or making themselves a threat to humans or other animals through aggressive behavior—are killed, in the name of either ending suffering (helping) or protecting public safety (policing). The hierarchies of anthroparchy mean that while humans who are identified as mentally ill are today routinely managed through medication, therapy, and possibly confinement, animals who are diagnosed as mentally ill are killed. Animals humans consider mentally diseased in the shelter have no opportunity for treatment, no chance to correct their deviance, no prospect for another chance. This is where the responses to human and animal resistance diverge most markedly: humans often have prospects for accepting discipline, for being rehabilitated, or for retreating into subcultures where they can live without treatment or can continue to resist. Under anthroparchy, animals typically don't have those choices. Their resistance—which PAW sees as mental illness, as too much animality, as aggressive, as unsafe—is their downfall.

8   Waiting, Wondering, and Wavering

ON A TYPICAL WEEKDAY AFTERNOON at PAW, the line for service wends out through the lobby and down the front path toward the parking lot. Those in line fiddle with their cell phones, shift their weight from one foot to the other, and sometimes make small talk with one another. Three lucky people secure the only chairs available in the waiting area; everyone else is left to stand. Many of them watch the activities around them as people with dogs, cats, and other animals come and go. Even those using their phones look up when people come in or out with different kinds of animals, or when someone who has made it to the front of the line becomes visibly upset in their interactions with front desk staff.

People stand in the front line at PAW for various reasons. Some have come to complete basic administrative tasks, like paying a licensing fee for their dog. Others want to adopt an animal at the shelter. Some are hoping to find their lost pet and think the front desk staff will help them with that. Others know their companion animal is impounded at PAW and are trying to get them back. Those in line generally have the markers of everyday people: mass market clothing and shoes, tired faces, children clawing at their arms and legs. Occasionally, a wealthy person—almost always a woman—comes from the western part of Los Angeles to adopt an animal, and the markers of her class status blind everyone else in the lobby, who stand gawking at the woman's expensive shoes, designer clothing, long, thin legs, and surgically modified body and/or face.

When I began volunteering at PAW, what I noticed about the experience of being at the shelter was how quickly things happened, and with a general sense of urgency—at least among volunteers—but also how slowly many events unfolded, such as getting through the line in the front office or getting a temperament test completed for a pit bull I wanted to help. PAW was simultaneously an intensely fast-paced environment and a place where I practiced my skills at patience as I never had before, anywhere. For impounded animals, I noticed that time often moves too quickly because PAW gives them only a limited amount of time to find homes or rescues; when the shelter determines they have run out of time, they literally die. Yet at other moments, time at PAW moves too slowly for those (including animals) who are seeking any kind of service from the shelter. PAW is a place of waiting, where people and animals are forced to defer to the institution's schedule, sometimes for hours or even days or weeks for a response to their needs.

PAW operates on two seemingly competing time lines: one that seeks to move impounded animals along as quickly as possible, and another that offers services to people and animals too slowly. Table 1 details some of the key functions at PAW that occur either too quickly or too slowly. Whether acting too quickly or too slowly, PAW sets the time line for action within its own boundaries. It maintains sovereignty over time. Like other types of total institutions—prisons, hospitals, schools—PAW dominates through its control over time.

At PAW, volunteers, members of the public, and animals find themselves both being rushed and being forced to wait. Time organizes activity at PAW absolutely. It is a near-constant referent at PAW; in fact, time comes up in virtually every conversation between volunteers and between volunteers and staff, and often also between staff members and between staff and members of the public. Here are some examples of topics or conversations having to do with time, taken during a single afternoon of fieldwork in 2015:

> Leila was really worried about [a dog named] Max and asked me how much time he has left. She wondered if we could get him extended, so she could keep working on him. Even two more days could be a big help as she has one rescue she thinks might assist.

Jane asked me how my interaction with some adopters last weekend went. She asked how long they had to wait [for service from staff]; when I told her the adoption took almost five hours, she was horrified and wondered aloud what's wrong with PAW that they can't process adoptions more quickly.

Kathy and I discussed which of the six dogs we are networking right now are most urgent, and which we think the shelter might give more time to. We selected three to make requests for with the staff, and hope the other three will be okay for another few days, when maybe we can ask about them. We agreed that asking for more time for all six at once was not likely to go over well with [a staff member].

Chris was around for a while visiting the dogs, and told me that Ginger's owners have been visiting her almost daily since she was impounded about six weeks ago. She told me they are trying to get Ginger back. I asked her why it was taking so long. She shook her head and said she had offered to help the guardians by talking to the staff.

I stopped in to see [staff member] Jesus just to say hi and see what's new. He warned me that we [volunteers] are going to be getting a lot of emails [from staff] about dogs who need to exit because they've been here too long.

[Kennel attendant] Alejandro asked me if I knew about anyone interested in the senior Miniature Pinscher. He said he was worried the dog would get sick and pointed out she's already been at the shelter for almost two weeks. I told him I don't work with small dogs very much, but promised to reach out to people who do. While we were talking, I sent myself a text message reminder so Alejandro would know I planned to do this soon.

When I left, the line in the front lobby was out the door. I felt lucky I wasn't pulling a dog because I guessed the waiting time would have been close to an hour.

Each of these interactions I documented invokes time: needing more time, feeling concerned about how much time has been taken, being worried about not having enough time, trying to be strategic about how to ask for time. At PAW, time talk is routine, reflecting the importance of time in this social setting.

TABLE 1. The Pace at PAW

PAW Moves Too Quickly When...	Moving toward killing an animal, especially cats and pit bulls
	Giving notice that a particular animal is sick or stressed and must exit
	Taking disciplinary action against volunteers
	Developing and instituting new policies or practices in response to events/incidents
PAW Moves Too Slowly When...	Providing service to people in line, waiting for property checks, or trying to adopt/rescue
	Completing temperament tests for "dominant breed" dogs
	Working toward institutional change that would lower intakes, improve conditions of confinement, and reduce killing
	Trying to improve staff numbers and competence
	Training new volunteers
	Asking for help from volunteers or the public

In their analyses of how residents of a heavily polluted shantytown in Buenos Aires called Flammable think and feel about environmental degradation and its health effects, Javier Auyero and Débora Swistun artfully illuminate how control over time is a form of domination. Corporate polluters and the political leaders who support them muddle time by creating narratives of the past, maintaining their own accounts of what occurred when, and promising future changes. Auyero and Swistun's analysis points to the need for a temporography of domination, or "a thick description of the ways the dominated perceive temporality, of the ways they act on these perceptions, and of the ways these perceptions and actions (and inactions) serve to challenge or perpetuate their domination."[1] Auyero and Swistun find that frustrated waiting time and hopeful waiting time characterize life in Flammable. At PAW, people and animals experience frustrated and hopeful waiting time—time waiting either in frustration about slowness or in the hopes of something positive happening—and they also experience desperate hurrying time, or accelerated time that threatens to be insufficient for what needs to be done during it.

Each of these types of time serves as a distractor. As Kathryn Gillespie demonstrates in her work focused on the violence perpetrated against bovines in the dairy industry, "Boredom and monotony have a way of glossing over the reality of what is before you."[2] At PAW, both the boredom of waiting *and* the anxiety of hurrying keep volunteers and many clients distracted from the conditions of confinement and the practice of killing. There is little time for volunteers simply to look around, process how things are, and make strategic plans for action. They cannot set their own time lines. Instead, the constant barking, the smell of urine, feces, and fur, and the obvious distress of so many animals trapped in cages too small to give room for them to exercise fade into the background as volunteers hurry—or wait in frustration—to get done what they feel needs doing.

PAW imposes each of these experiences, which volunteers, members of the public, animals, and even staff *feel*, for time is an experience caught up with emotion. The experience of time can leave people relaxed, anxious, angry, and/or despairing. Volunteers routinely talk about their emotional experiences of time, the feeling of being rushed, anxious, nervous, harried, and hurried on the one hand and ignored, pushed off, slowed down, and demeaned on the other. In controlling the time of others, PAW triggers these emotions, some of which subsequently foment resistance or submission.

So far in this book, I have documented numerous ways PAW tries to help people and animals while also inflicting distress on them. In this chapter, I conduct a temporography of PAW to illuminate the way time operates as a form of domination and how the public, volunteers, and animal rescuers try to resist that domination at PAW. I map out the different dimensions of time at PAW and analyze how the locus of time and power shapes the shelter environment and the people and animals in it, often with the effect of stalling longer-term prospects for change. PAW retains exclusive control over how time moves, including over who is served at what time. This reduces the agency of clients, volunteers, and impounded animals. The control of time becomes a key mechanism through which the shelter dominates its clients, volunteers, and impounded animals, and control over time was one form of domination that neither human nor animal resistance could wrest from PAW during my fieldwork. The analysis reveals the centrality of time for organizing all activity at PAW, as well as the ways in which powerful actors can manipulate understandings of time to promote acquiescence among those subjected to a particular time line. In an analysis that dovetails with my analysis of volunteer resistance to shelter death in chapter 4, I also discover that negotiations around time between staff, volunteers, and rescuers involve tensions around class and power within the shelter.

RACING AGAINST THE CLOCK

One of the first lessons I learned as a new volunteer at PAW was the urgency of getting impounded animals *out* of the shelter. This is the experience of desperate hurrying time: the feeling of dread that there is not enough time to do what is needed because PAW won't provide the time. Desperate hurrying time is time that feels chaotic, busy, and often out of control. Volunteers describe the experience of their time at the shelter as "pumping," "bursting," "racing," "pounding," "nonstop action," and "exhausting." Many notice that they forgo their own bodily needs, like eating or going to the bathroom, while at the shelter and operating in desperate hurrying time. Ultimately, this type of time is also highly distracting and distressing: it leaves volunteers fatigued and overwhelmed (or, as one volunteer refers to her state after a day of volunteering, "shelter zonked") and with the feeling that they are too tired to take on anything else, like organizing for longer-term change. Because desperate hurrying time is, in its essence, about immediacy, it keeps volunteers focused on the short term—whether the current moment or possibly a few hours into the future.

Volunteers feel a near-constant pressure to help animals find adopters or rescues as quickly as possible so they won't be killed. Even cats whom PAW made available for adoption—so who were not labeled as feral—rarely received more than a week at the shelter before being killed. Because of the pervasiveness of kennel cough and other infectious diseases, volunteers see any animal as being at risk for shelter killing at any time, since all it takes for an animal to be killed is to show a symptom. If a staff member, volunteer, or rescuer expresses interest in a particular dog and that dog remains healthy and unstressed in the shelter (per PAW's assessment), the dog can potentially remain for several weeks or, starting with greater regularity since 2016, even months, but an animal's safety is never guaranteed. Volunteers therefore see any animal in the shelter as in urgent need of assistance.

The race to get animals out of the shelter alive is fraught with anxiety as volunteers and rescuers genuinely fear a dog or cat will be put down while they are in the process of trying to save them. Many volunteers and rescuers told me about lying awake at night worrying about an impounded animal. Others reported other symptoms of stress they attributed to the rushed time line to save animals, including loss of appetite, headache, issues with concentration at work, and, in one case, panic attacks. Volunteers rush to their computers at PAW's opening hours to check the status online of animals they care about; if an animal "goes offline" first thing in the morning, it almost always means they have been killed because PAW normally kills animals in the mornings before the shelter opens to the public. Texts, emails, phone calls, and group messages with other volunteers and rescuers on social media platforms both serve as a network of support and heighten the anxiety and worry about shelter killing.

Staff, for their part, maintain the sense of urgency in a number of ways. They may reach out to an individual volunteer or a group of volunteers to ask for help placing an animal. They may refuse a volunteer's appeal to extend the time for a particular animal, increasing the urgency for that specific animal and contributing to a general sense that all animals are in a hurry to leave because the staff may decline any request at any time. Usually, staff decline requests for more time when an animal has a health or behavioral issue, like kennel cough or aggression, but the reasons vary enough to seem to volunteers quite random. This arbitrariness increases the sense of uncertainty among volunteers and rescuers about time and the shelter's intentions.

Emergency appeals are particularly distressing for volunteers and rescuers because they are the hardest to address, and volunteers feel they set unreasonable expectations for the time line of an animal's exit. An emergency is, by definition, a situation in which time is of the essence. When staff identify one or more dogs whose situation has reached emergency status—usually because they are sick and, per PAW's veterinary team, either are not getting better or could threaten the health of the larger shelter population—they send out a mass email appeal to volunteers and sometimes also to rescuers informing them of the emergency. Reflecting the species hierarchy, appeals for cats are extremely rare and usually are issued only for unweaned kittens. The appeals typically give the animal in question only a few hours or sometimes a day to get out of the shelter. Many of the managerial staff start their shifts at 6 a.m., so these emails often go out early in the morning, indicating that rescue is needed by noon of the same day; sometimes the deadline is the end of the business day. Occasionally, especially when the animals experiencing the purported emergency are puppies or kittens, the shelter staff will call select volunteers (rather than send a mass email) to notify them of them the emergency; with unweaned animals, the time line is usually just a few hours since these animals must be fed at frequent intervals and deteriorate quickly. Whether the animals have a few hours or a whole day, volunteers face very tight time frames in which to enlist a rescue organization, locate a foster home, secure funds for any necessary veterinary care, and make logistical arrangements.

Staff almost always reject volunteer pleas for more time for an animal for whom the shelter has issued some kind of emergency communiqué. From the staff perspective, an emergency is the end of the road for an animal. Sometimes, volunteers will beg lower-level staff to talk with the veterinarian or the manager to appeal for more time for a particular animal. Most often, the lower-level staff refuse these requests; even if they do talk with a higher-up, the request for additional time is routinely denied.

Volunteers resent the pressure the shelter places on them to save animals. Emergency appeals noticeably reduce volunteer morale, as expressions of anger toward the shelter rapidly increase following these appeals. The sending of emergency appeals also solidifies volunteers' view that PAW and SCAS don't actually want to help animals and that they don't appreciate volunteers. Volunteers see appeals not as helpful efforts at assisting animals in need but as threatening and unfair gestures toward animals and volunteers that wrongly shift responsibility for saving animals from the shelter to its volunteers. Once I had been volunteering for about a year and had reached the point where I was included on emergency appeal emails, one of the most senior volunteers at the shelter advised me that "what they're doing is trying to make *us* responsible for getting the animals out. If they asked us to help and we couldn't, it's *our* fault the dog died." After we had received an email from the staff informing us that a small dog with kennel cough had to be rescued by shelter closing that day, one volunteer vented to me, "They can't just manipulate us like this! Making up these random deadlines—it's just a way for them to make excuses for euthing [*sic*] a dog."

In another conversation with a volunteer about last-minute appeals from the shelter to save dogs, she said, "I feel sick whenever I get those emails. And I get so mad! It's not *my* job to help animals—it's *theirs!*" Still another volunteer reflected on the experience of receiving email appeals from staff: "They're just trying to make *us* feel responsible when the dog ends up dead." One volunteer encouraged me to ignore the email appeals, stating that "the shelter is just trying to fuck with us," a view many volunteers share: the "emergencies" often are animals with illnesses that can be easily and inexpensively treated. Volunteers believe that PAW issues these appeals as a way to stress volunteers and to deflect responsibility for shelter killing away from the staff and the shelter and onto volunteers and rescuers who fail to save the animal in time.

But adoption and rescue require time. PAW receives many visitors who come to the kennels with the intention of adopting and have not selected a particular dog of interest beforehand. The rate of foot traffic at the shelter varies significantly: weekdays before 4 p.m. tend to be quite quiet, while Saturdays are usually the busiest day, often bringing several hundred visitors to the shelter. Events outside the shelter's control—school vacation periods, major holidays, the weather (including both rain and temperatures above ninety degrees, the latter of which are common in the Los Angeles area from April to October), large sporting events (like the Super Bowl)—can depress adoptions, while some of these events—most especially July Fourth—increase intakes. Rarely, special events increase adoptions: during the research period, PAW participated in three major off-site adoption events annually and several smaller ones at which cats and dogs had good chances of adoption. Volunteers especially prize weekends, as the chances of adoption are the highest, so they routinely ask staff to extend a particular animal through another weekend; they also push to have animals they like included in adoption events when they are scheduled. While having more time or going to an event is no guarantee of adoption, an animal obviously cannot be adopted if dead.

Volunteers typically focus their efforts on finding rescues for animals for whom an emergency appeal has gone out because the time line is generally too short to expect to find a qualified adopter and because the emergency is usually medical and most adopters don't want to adopt animals with known health issues. Finding a rescue group to take an animal also takes time. Volunteers craft written email or text appeals and send them to rescuers whom they know or call them directly. They also post about the animals on their social media. A rescue organization has to commit to helping a particular animal by agreeing to "back" the animal, or to pay for veterinary care, training or behavior modification, food and other living expenses, and any other costs until the animal is adopted into a permanent home, a process that the rescue also oversees. Many rescues will not agree to rescue an animal unless they have secured a committed and qualified foster home *and* a certain amount of money to defray costs. They often expect shelter volunteers to do the work of securing fosters and donations, which is both time-consuming and an additional stress. I am aware of many cases in which shelter volunteers themselves contributed funds, often hundreds of dollars or even a thousand dollars, toward the rescue of a particular animal. Raising money is usually the easier part. People on social media can pledge to contribute a certain amount if an animal is rescued, and the group or organization that rescues the dog collects the funds once the dog is out of the shelter. This method at PAW was more widely used for dogs than for cats. Finding a foster home can be much more difficult, especially for cats and for dogs over forty pounds. Many people who volunteer to foster turn out not to be suitable placements. Several volunteers foster for rescue organizations (myself included) but can accommodate only one or two animals or litters at a time, a number that never meets the demand for fosters.

When an episode of desperate hurrying time ends, it may culminate in a moment of celebration (if an animal has been saved), or grief (if an animal has died), or of just stopping (if there has been no resolution). The volunteer experiences a sense of relief (coupled with other emotions) irrespective of outcome because the episode is over. They then may move into a period of disengagement from the shelter, or may enter a new cycle of desperate hurrying time, or may be pulled into frustrated waiting.

"SPEED THINGS UP ALREADY!"

Time can drag on at PAW. It's not uncommon for clients to wait forty-five minutes or even an hour to make it to the head of line at the front desk. There they watch as staff move with excruciating slowness to process requests. The computer system freezes routinely, interrupting transactions and forcing everyone human to wait. Even when it is working properly, office staff make no obvious efforts to complete tasks quickly.

Bureaucratic processes draw out even the most mundane transactions at PAW, so that people and animals are subjected to frustrated waiting time at the shelter. The waiting creates visible signs of distress and anger among people stuck in line at the front desk to be helped. This interaction between a man who waited in the lobby for about twenty-five minutes before being called up is typical:

> The man in the cowboy boots finally is at the head of the line. He approaches the counter warily; Lupe [the staff member behind the desk] is shuffling some papers and does not look up as she asks, "What can I do for you?" He replies that his dog got loose and is at the shelter; he is waiting for a property check so he can get his dog back, but no one [from PAW] has called him to schedule it. "What's the ID number?" Lupe responds. He looks at his phone and tells her the number, which she types into the computer with loud clacks on the keyboard. It looks as if she is scrolling through the record on her screen, reading the notes in the file. "Yeah," she says, twisting her mouth to the side. "I can see you need a property check. But you have to wait for them to call you." "I have been waiting a week already," the man replies. Lupe looks unmoved as she continues staring at the screen. "My dog is just stuck here," the man tries again, not hiding his desperation. "Is there no way to speed things up already?" Lupe shrugs. "It can be a few weeks, sir. You just have to wait."

In this interaction, the man hoping to free his dog from the shelter is forced to wait both for assistance at the front desk and for a visit from a field officer. While he waits, he is separated from his companion animal and is accruing fees, both conditions that could explain his seeming desperation in wanting PAW to hurry up. He is being punished for allowing his dog to get loose, which PAW sees as a threat to the health and safety of the dog and of the public. As with a criminal waiting for trial, the state will decide when he will have his chance to clear his name; however, unlike a criminal, he has no legal basis for demanding a quick and speedy trial.

Forcing someone to wait is a simple strategy of domination,[3] and it is a tool PAW has mastered. At PAW, members of the public seeking services, volunteers, and animals are all made to wait. The individuals enforcing that waiting are the shelter staff who are state agents. Although they occupy a low social status outside the shelter as lower-income workers with little education who are almost all nonwhite, the state grants them the authority to make others wait. The staff at the front desk are notorious among even other staff—especially managers—for their inefficiencies in assisting clients. Although they are the most public face of the shelter, there are no incentives in terms of job promotion or compensation to do a good job, as they are at the top end of a career ladder. For some, their lower social status outside the shelter may also contribute to a willingness to try to assert control over others when given the opportunity to do so. The experience of working with many hostile or inappropriate clients (I have more than once intervened when a front desk staffer was being sexually harassed) may further undermine their motivation. The computer system upon which they depend is temperamental and not terribly user-friendly, contributing to aggravation that they may then redirect on clients, volunteers, and even other staff members.

For volunteers, the waiting times prospective adopters must negotiate in adopting are a near-constant source of aggravation (I actually started volunteering at this shelter precisely because I myself found it so difficult to adopt). Prospective adopters may have to wait in line multiple times in a single visit, extending what could be a visit of an hour or so into a four- or five-hour-long (or longer) affair. When staff were working with a family one weekend afternoon to help them adopt a dog, the mother became so frustrated that she mock-banged her head against the wall, mouthing the yelling of "Oh my fucking God! Hurry up!" while her young kids weren't looking. In order to meet an adoptable animal, visitors are required to start at the front desk, the most congested area of the shelter. Once a staff member at the front desk has confirmed an animal's availability, they summon a kennel attendant or volunteer to assist in introducing the animal to the prospective adopters in a ritual referred to as "a social." Sometimes adopters are told they cannot meet an animal because staff are too busy to help them, or because the animal has kennel cough, or because it's too dark or rainy or hot or cold. They are then told to come back at another time, which can drag the process out longer or cause the adopter to go elsewhere in search of a companion.

For animals, having adopters and former guardians wait poses an immediate danger: if people find it difficult to adopt animals or have animals returned to their homes because of how long they have to wait, animals are more likely to be killed. Volunteers generally come into the shelter with an orientation toward helping people and animals, and they see keeping human or nonhuman animals waiting as unnecessary and even inhumane. Volunteers believe that keeping prospective adopters waiting reduces how many animals are adopted: not only do the adopters who come to the shelter in person not adopt because of the wait, but some of them then go on to post negative reviews online or tell others in person about the shelter's long wait times, thereby deterring other future adopters.

For dogs identified as dominant breeds, waiting for the SCAS-mandated temperament tests is particularly grueling. Only after the test is complete—which sometimes takes months—may they come out of their kennels with volunteers. These large dogs tend to be energetic, playful, and people centered, and during the long wait for the test, many of them start to engage in resistance to their confinement, barking incessantly or lying down and refusing to get up.

Frustrated waiting time means volunteers and clients often feel that they are suspended in time, waiting for something to happen and not knowing if and when it might happen. Animals must feel the same way, not knowing exactly where they are or why, and so experiencing a suspension of sorts of both time and space. Waiting is a "relational process, characterized by uncertainty, confusion, and arbitrariness."[4] For animals who may be longing to leave their cages or to eat or to play, the regular foot traffic past their cages gives them hope of getting out even as they, too, are made to wait. For some of them, the only time they will leave their cage will be to go to the Euth Room.

Volunteers also believe that keeping an animal waiting can increase the stress of their stay; for instance, taking too long to feed the animals or clean their kennels makes the day less pleasant for them. Volunteers consistently report that they feel the "least we can do" is meet the animals' basic needs as efficiently as possible, given the otherwise "depressing" conditions of their impound, such as the small kennels and the lack of climate control for dogs in hot weather. Therefore, volunteers typically hurry in completing tasks. When they see people who might be prospective adopters in the kennels, they stop to ask if assistance is needed. They move briskly and purposefully.

Volunteers often feel that their own work is thwarted by frustrated waiting. A particular point of aggravation is the time it takes to pick up and to return the keys that open the kennels. On arrival at PAW, volunteers who want to access animals must see the staff member in charge at that time to sign out a kennel key. Often, none of the staff know who the person in charge is or where they are. Although staff have radios, they refuse to use them to get keys for volunteers. Once the volunteer has found the staff person in charge, they routinely have to wait to be able to talk with them. The staff person might be in the middle of another task, away from their desk to attend to issues in another office space or in the kennel buildings, or taking a break at their desk, in the break room, or outside. Getting kennel keys within fifteen minutes of arrival at PAW is considered excellent time, and it routinely takes thirty or more minutes. Returning the keys can be as or more complicated. Later in the day, many staff members have often left (most sign off at 4 p.m. although the shelter is open past 4 p.m. every day of the week), and the question of who can accept a key back becomes seemingly unanswerable. Because volunteers must leave their driver's license or their own keys as collateral for the kennel key they checked out, they can't simply walk away (some long-term volunteers trade in dummy keys as collateral for the kennel keys so they can leave the dummy key behind if they can't find anyone to check the kennel key back in).

While waiting to receive or return the kennel keys may seem like a minor detail, it is fraught with meaning. First, this kind of waiting is a universal experience PAW volunteers have. All volunteers need kennel keys to start and end their shifts, and all of them are forced to wait. Second, by imposing this waiting, PAW conveys that it devalues the time—and therefore the overall contribution—of shelter volunteers. Third, because the keys provide access to the animals, delaying access to the keys can be read as an assertion of PAW's control over the animals in its care. Because PAW holds the keys and volunteers are not, for example, simply each issued their own key or given access to a lockbox with keys so they can bypass the ritual of waiting to get keys from a managerial staff member, PAW reminds volunteers that their presence is by courtesy, their admittance conditional, and their access to animals only with PAW's permission.[5] By denying volunteers keys, PAW is denying them the ability to do the work they see as most important and preventing them from engaging with the population of impounded animals. The wait to receive keys involves PAW's control over time, space, and human and animal bodies. Volunteers recognize this as a form of domination; volunteer Alanna declared a common sentiment one day after waiting for keys: "They are just trying to keep us in our place with these keys."

Volunteers, unlike staff, are also at the shelter during their leisure time. Wasting leisure time is particularly irritating to them. I heard common complaints that the staff should do more to cooperate with volunteers given that volunteers are "here on my own time," "donating my time," and "just trying to help even though I am not getting paid."

PAW's imposition of frustrated waiting time contributes to stress and aggravation with the daily functioning of PAW and to a sense that PAW is unchanging and unchangeable when volunteers think about PAW over longer periods of time. A common refrain I heard from fellow volunteers refers to the lack of change at PAW; volunteers state, "This place will never change," "Nothing ever changes here!" and "It's like time stands still at PAW."

UNCERTAINTY

Uncertainty is a driving force at PAW, and one that the institution encourages by undertaking actions in ways that don't make sense in terms of time. PAW mobilizes time effectively as a tool of domination by acting arbitrarily: when, how, and why things happen is never predictable, which leaves the public, volunteers, and others who interact with the shelter on uncertain ground. For instance, when the shelter abruptly puts down an animal who volunteers believed was safe from shelter death, that action contributes to heightened anxiety about time and what the "normal" amount of time for animals to stay alive at the shelter is.

When I started volunteering, other volunteers warned me never to trust the time lines that I assumed were correct, or even that staff promised to me. They reminded me, over and over, that an animal could be put down at any time, even if the animal had just arrived or if someone was waiting to adopt or rescue them. For this reason, animal rescues never announce that they have rescued an animal—even if they have told the shelter when they are coming for that animal and the animal has been sent to the shelter clinic to be spayed or neutered—until that animal is "out of the building," or OTB. Any volunteer or rescuer who is active at PAW will repeat the mantra: an animal is *never* safe until they are OTB, even if that animal seems adoptable and healthy. Only when an animal is no longer in PAW's custody can they be seen as safe from the threat of shelter killing.

My first encounter with this reality came in November of 2012 when I had been volunteering for less than a year and still felt I was learning the norms and practices of the shelter. I spent a Sunday afternoon at PAW, where I met a delightful dog named Lovey. She found herself at the shelter because her guardian had passed away and none of her guardian's friends or family would care for her. At a little over a year old, she was athletic and a bit bouncy with deeply intelligent eyes, and I admired her immediately. Clearly confused about her change in circumstances, Lovey was vigilant when I took her out the play area, looking intently through the chain-link fence and down the road. She was generally uninterested in me during our first encounter, but when a prospective adopter was eager to meet her and I took her out a second time, she leaned into my legs and rested her head on my lap, as if asking to be pet. She had soft, cream-colored fur, half-upright ears, and a long, lean, almost delicate body. Lovey was a Labrador mix, light-colored, young, friendly, and pretty—the perfect candidate for adoption. But four days later, she was taken from her kennel by a staff member and led to the Euth Room to be killed.

I was a combination of dumbstruck, angry, sad, and betrayed when I learned Lovey was dead. I also felt like a fool because I had not asked a member of the staff the day I met her to make a note that I was trying to help Lovey. Had I taken the time to stand in line and talk with a staff member, Lovey quite possibly would have lived and been adopted. Yet I took for granted that such a young, attractive dog would *not* be likely to be targeted for shelter killing after fewer than four days at the shelter (one day of which was the Thanksgiving holiday, so that the shelter was closed for adoptions). This occurred before I began fieldwork, but I share the experience here because it is the trial by fire that every volunteer experiences. Those who do ask questions about what happened to an animal or why rarely receive an answer; I contacted the shelter manager four times to find out why Lovey had been killed and never received an explanation.

My experience is typical: every volunteer with whom I have spoken about salient experiences as a volunteer remembers the first animal they really cared about who was lost to shelter killing, and almost all of those narratives include the shock that *PAW did not keep the animal for as long as they expected*. Lien, who for several years was among the most omnipresent dog volunteers, broke into tears on the morning I had to tell her that I had just found out a dog she expected to pick up later that day for a rescue had been put down that morning. She had notified the shelter, but a staff member had forgotten to make a note in the computer. Louise's first experience with the surprise of shelter killing was before she even started volunteering: she came to meet a dog at the shelter hoping to adopt, and the dog was killed shortly after they met. In all of these instances, volunteers protested to each other that *the dog did not have enough time* and that the shelter made a mistake in killing them.

Uncertainty is also an issue when PAW issues emergency appeals for animals it considers in urgent need. Here the uncertainty is whether PAW is serious that an animal will be killed if not adopted or rescued by the specified time. At least half of the time, PAW allows animals to continue to stay at the shelter after the deadline stated in an emergency appeal has passed. That is, while staff issue a deadline of 2 p.m. or the end of the business day, when no one shows up they may let the animal stay longer. Sometimes the additional time is just a day or two; in some cases it has been a month. This leads volunteers and rescuers to doubt the veracity of emergency appeals. In fact, sometimes after such appeals arrive on email, volunteers begin communicating with one another, starting with the most pressing questions: Does PAW really mean it? How can we know? PAW's assertion of urgency, their capacity to kill animals at will, and their refusal to share their thinking with volunteers and rescuers mean that those trying to get animals out of the shelter must always assume the worst.

PAW also sometimes kills animals who volunteers believe are safe because PAW itself has promoted them for adoption. Homer, a handsome young German Shepherd, was selected to appear on a local morning news show as the Pet of the Week. His segment aired on Monday; he was dead by the end of the week. Volunteers were flabbergasted that a dog whom PAW sent to be on a television show would be killed so soon after. None of us had thought to request an extension for him because we all assumed he would be safe given that he had been on television. This kind of seemingly arbitrary killing on a time line that violates the usual norms of time at PAW unsettles volunteers' beliefs about how much time PAW gives animals, increasing their sense of urgency to help all animals exit the shelter.

Excluded from the process of decision-making about shelter killing and perpetually unclear about how PAW selects animals to be killed and when leaves volunteers confused and unsure about PAW's motives and reasoning. PAW claims transparency as it provides new volunteers with a policy manual that includes the Euthanasia Policy. The policy provides careful detail of the chain of command for making euthanasia decisions and instructions for staff on how to update the computer record as an animal moves through the process of being identified as a candidate for killing (what the shelter refers to as "reviewing") and is then killed. It does not, however, include any information on how or why animals are selected, what conditions would lead to killing, or whether and how time factors into shelter killing. Volunteers thus have a poor understanding of why the shelter kills *when* it does: Is it because of capacity issues? Staff-animal ratios? Some arbitrary cutoff that designates an animal has been at the shelter for "too long"? Something else? After every killing, volunteers conjecture about why it happened, but they never have a definitive answer, only speculation. PAW not only controls the time line for killing but also hides how the time line is determined. Obscuring this process further enhances the institution's control over those it dominates.

BREAKS IN WAITING

Impounded animals (particularly dogs) and volunteers experience occasional breaks in their experience of time at PAW as moving either too quickly or too slowly. These events interrupt ongoing grievances. Animals experience breaks in waiting through nonroutine interactions with staff and volunteers. Dogs are almost always at their happiest when out in one of the shelter's small play areas, where they have at least five or six more times more space than in their kennels, the ability to see out across the parking lot and up the road, different scents to smell, and at least one human there with them who can be a source of affection and attention. Their body language communicates their happiness: bounding across the Astroturf, wagging their tails, dropping into play bows, jumping up on or nuzzling the human(s) to request physical contact. Because of the low levels of staffing and the variable schedules of volunteers, dogs never know if and when they might be taken to the play area; it is always a surprise, which makes it all the more of an interruption in normal time. Many dogs resist going back to their kennels after time in the play area, suggesting that they have a preference for the play areas. For them, time in the play areas is fun and interesting compared to their time in their kennels. Many dogs show similar happiness when taken out of their kennels to visit the shelter clinic. Research suggests that dogs possess a sense of time and behave differently in response to being left by their guardians for different amounts of time.[6] For them, as for volunteers, breaks in their routine help reduce the stress of being at the shelter.

For humans, breaks in waiting most commonly occur when volunteers and/or members of the public are involved in a "feel good" moment, such as watching (and often helping) a dog or cat be adopted or rescued. Seeing a pet leave PAW alive (or "through the front door," as volunteers generally refer to live releases), especially when with adopters of whom the volunteers approve, offers a moment of satisfaction; if the pet is one a volunteer has been championing, the feeling can approach euphoria. Although these moments typically occur *in spite of* the shelter management, rather than *because of* it, they nonetheless generate positive feelings about the shelter as being a place from which animals can be saved, as well as positive feelings about being involved at PAW. Shelter animal advocates frequently repeat their mantra, "It's all about the dogs," and when a dog is adopted they will state, "This is why I do this."

When involved in such moments, volunteers tell other volunteers about the experience through e-mails, group messages on Facebook, phone calls, or text messages; I routinely receive joyful news from other volunteers announcing that a particular animal was adopted or rescued. These events provide important interruptions in the experiences of desperate hurrying and frustrated waiting. Following such events, volunteers are less likely to report negative feelings about the shelter or to promote ideas for change within the shelter system.

My notes capture a conversation with two volunteers during a period when management was putting down particularly high numbers of dogs:

> "I can't believe they put him down," Lien commented, shaking her head. "He was such a good dog, so sweet and friendly. And there is plenty of space [in the kennels]! Why not give him more time [to be adopted]?" "[The manager] is bloodthirsty!" Chris replied. "She hates the dogs!" Lien wrings the leash in her hands and looks down. "But Joe was adopted!" Chris exclaims. "How awesome is that?" Lien lifts her head and smiles at me and Chris, and we grin back. "That's what it's all about!" Lien reminds us.

This exchange illustrates how when a volunteer experiences both a positive and a negative event in the same day at PAW—such as one favorite dog being put down and another being adopted—they focus on the positive case. During an aggravating period when many dogs are put down and the volume of positive outcomes seems low, volunteers return to previous positive moments, reviewing photographs they took on their cell phones, spreading the good news about a pet who was saved, or celebrating communication from an adopter who has sent pictures.

Another group of grievance interruptions occur through the actions of the shelter, though these actions are not taken in response to volunteer demands. Staff at PAW quite regularly are shuffled to or from other shelters that are part of SCAS; these moves can be demotions, promotions, or just parallel moves. When unpopular staff members—who can include managers, kennel attendants, and veterinary staff—are moved, volunteers express happiness, hope, and anxiety, as they do when unfamiliar staff members arrive. While not offering the same kind of short-term high as seeing a pet leave the shelter, the high rate of turnover at the shelter keeps volunteers on ever-shifting terrain that holds out the promise of change (both positive and negative), particularly when there are significant staffing changes among managers. When a manager whom volunteers found particularly difficult to work with was reassigned to another SCAS department, volunteers celebrated via text message and later in person, exchanging joking high fives and singing "Ding-Dong, the Witch Is Dead." "Whoever is next *has* to be better," one volunteer exclaimed, to agreement from a small group standing together. "So let's give them a chance and hope for the best!" This type of response to grievance interruption results in a logic of waiting that ultimately inhibits collective action on the part of volunteers as it bleeds into hopeful waiting.[7]

HOPEFUL WAITING

Volunteers, members of the public, and impounded animals are subjected to hopeful waiting that involves the anticipation of something good happening. Volunteers in particular and, to a lesser degree, members of the public who interact with the shelter, are subject to an institutional narrative of positive change, and they integrate aspects of this narrative into their own understandings of PAW and SCAS. Through the narrative of positive change, PAW and SCAS assert that they are committed to reducing shelter death, improving the quality of the shelter experience for animals and people, and working on implementing new programs, policies, and practices that will help accomplish these goals.

The building block of this narrative is what I call future talk, or discourse that centers on or invokes the future. Future talk is frequent and powerful at PAW: staff—especially managers—often acknowledge that problems exist and promise that they will be addressed. These promised changes can be seemingly very minor, such as a promise by one shelter manager that large dogs would be offered more in-kennel enrichment in the form of Kong toys in their kennels (a promise that was never realized). Others can be much more significant, such as plans to overhaul the way dogs' temperaments are assessed (a promise that was realized at the end of 2018, at least three years after staff first started promising it).

Future talk is routine at PAW. For example, when volunteers make specific requests to the management for reform of shelter practices—like asking that temperament tests be done more quickly so dogs can be adopted, or holding more off-site adoption events at which animals are more likely to be adopted than in the shelter itself—the shelter management and staff respond by stating that the shelter shares the goal and is "working on it." Rarely do staff reply with "No, that's not going to happen." Instead, PAW's practice is to acknowledge the request for change and then promise it will be happening. Even though volunteers can see from their volunteer work that change does not happen and that in fact none of the staff are "working on it," volunteers find it difficult to challenge promises of imminent change and are sometimes appeased by a sense that the power holders within SCAS share their goal of reducing shelter killing of adoptable pets. Others are more cynical about change: Genie, one of the shelter's longest-term volunteers, often laughingly comments that she must be "Mrs. Gullible" for thinking the shelter will ever change. Shelter volunteers also routinely joke about how they are "gluttons for punishment" because they continue to volunteer when nothing ever improves at PAW. I continued as a volunteer for years after fieldwork and often wondered the same thing about myself.

Promising change and keeping volunteers in a state of hopeful waiting is powerful in undermining volunteers' thoughts of organized collective action. In my over three years of fieldwork at PAW, there were no discernable improvements in the treatment of impounded animals, nor was there any substantial difference in the rates of pets who left the shelter alive (according to shelter statistics, the euthanasia rate actually *increased* slightly from the 2013–14 fiscal year to the 2014–15 fiscal year, in spite of a 12 percent decrease in the number of impounded animals, and then started to decrease). However, PAW management maintained a narrative of innovation and hope that offered constant placation of volunteers' demands and a sense that staff and volunteers were unified in their vision for the future of the shelter. This often included making claims that conditions *had* gotten better. One SCAS manager (so not someone who worked at PAW, but someone I would encounter there periodically when she visited from SCAS headquarters) especially aggravated me and other volunteers with her perky insistence each time she came to PAW that "things around here just keep getting better!"—a claim with which volunteers did not agree.

However misleading, keeping volunteers suspended in hopeful waiting is effective in securing their submission. By way of one example of how the narrative of change can drag out hopes, beginning in June 2014, the shelter management started responding to most volunteer concerns with the promise that the shelter management had created a new position for a volunteer coordinator and that once the position was filled, that person would address volunteer concerns and help improve the volunteer experience at the shelter and, in turn, the experience of impounded animals. The volunteer coordinator was to serve as a liaison between volunteers and staff, coordinate volunteer efforts, and expand the volunteer, adoption, and fostering programs, all of which would presumably improve the volunteer experience and reduce shelter killing. The search for someone to fill that position was under way for ten months, with the time line to complete the search pushed back at least four times. In spite of a large applicant pool that included some qualified volunteers, a candidate who had no experience working in an animal shelter or coordinating a volunteer program, but who already worked within the same larger government bureaucracy of which SCAS is but one part, was ultimately hired. Volunteers were immediately skeptical of the new hire, whom they (and I) saw as lacking relevant experience. Discontent grew when the new volunteer coordinator, a man, treated women volunteers in ways they found sexist and demeaning. The new staff member further alienated volunteers by starting out with strong opinions about what the volunteers and the shelter needed when he had no experience with either; volunteers, who had retained some hope that a volunteer coordinator would listen to them, felt silenced. Within three months of starting at PAW, he vanished; more than a month later, volunteers were informed that his unexpected medical leave was now a resignation and that he would not be returning to PAW. In September 2015, shelter management assured volunteers that a new coordinator would be brought on promptly; the job ad was posted about seven months later, in March 2016, with an expected start date for a new hire no sooner than June 1, 2016; a new hire finally started in March 2017.

Although the volunteer coordinator hiring effort dragged on for years, the promise that a new employee would fix problems about which volunteers were concerned fed into a wait-and-see mentality among shelter volunteers, who held on to hope that change would occur once someone was hired. Frequent changes in management—the general manager position changed hands five times in less than three years—similarly contribute to hopeful waiting: with each announced departure, volunteers hope that the next manager will be an improvement over the former one. Sometimes, in fact, they are, making the narrative of positive change even more believable. The narrative of positive change, coupled with frequent changes in staffing at the shelter, encourages volunteers to keep up their hopeful waiting for something meaningful to happen, even as they recognize that their waiting, in the words of one volunteer, "makes fools of us—for years!"

FIGHTING TIME AT PAW

How time passes is established through systems of power. At PAW, volunteers, clients, and animals often find themselves being rushed and/or forced to wait, two key ways in which PAW exercises power over members of these groups. Like other dominated groups, volunteers, clients, and animals at PAW "are condemned to live in a time oriented to others."[8] In the social milieu of PAW, time for clients, volunteers, and impounded animals moves simultaneously too quickly and too slowly. PAW and SCAS, and by extension, the state, impose these contradictory time lines on several key groups that include both human animals and nonhuman animals. In turn, members of these groups often resist PAW's and SCAS's time lines and try to establish alternate time lines, with varying degrees of success. Members of the public resist the waiting by complaining and expressing frustration and anger toward staff and the institution. I observed this dozens of times but also noticed that members of the public typically left their complaints with the front desk staff rather than asking to speak to a manager or other higher-up. Volunteers attempt to accelerate how quickly adopters are helped and dogs are temperament tested, while also resisting the limited time that animals are given to live at the shelter by trying to extend that time—that is, to extend the period of time during which any individual dog and all dogs collectively are considered "safe" at the shelter. Volunteers and the public generally seek to speed up that which is slow and slow down that which is quick.

Members of dominated groups may accept the time lines they are offered, buying into how dominators tell them events unfolded and accepting promises for change. Yet time also can become contested terrain when those subject to domination assert their own understandings of time. In a bureaucratic environment like PAW, the most common expression of this type of resistance comes from members of the public waiting for assistance at the front desk: whether glaring angrily at the staff behind the counter, complaining quietly or, more often, loudly to neighbors in line about the long wait, storming angrily out of the lobby without completing the task that brought them to the shelter, or, occasionally, complaining directly to the staff about the waiting time, members of the public routinely demonstrate their dissatisfaction with how time is ordered at PAW.[9] Coupled with volunteers' and rescuers' frequent transgressions of PAW's time lines, their violations of how PAW orders activity, and their near-constant demands that PAW do things more quickly and more slowly, I could argue that there is a full-scale time insurrection at PAW. Yet simultaneously the public, volunteers, rescuers, and even staff acquiesce to PAW's time line, excusing it as an outcome of underfunding, understaffing, or just being a government bureaucracy.

Volunteers struggle against the time windows provided by PAW to put together an exit plan for specific animals. Yet volunteers and concerned members of the public also articulate a clear desire for changes to speed up at PAW, especially with regard to promises of improvements. As one volunteer summed up during one of my very first days volunteering at PAW, "If only they would do everything as quickly as they kill animals here."

It's curious how volunteers—who so readily assert their social capital in resisting the shelter's practice of killing—seem so acquiescent in the face of the shelter's domination over them through time. While they do sometimes try to circumvent waiting, especially by taking advantage of relationships with individual staff members, they don't seem to have any real expectation of different or better conditions in terms of time. Their submission may be explained by the repeated experience of being subjected to desperate hurrying, forced waiting, and hopeful waiting; socialization from other volunteers, who regularly discuss problems with time; preexisting stereotypes about state-run offices as inefficient or problematic in terms of time; a lack of a morally urgent transgression comparable to killing; and the absence of a concrete target for grievances about time.

Volunteers see themselves largely as at the mercy of PAW's and SCAS's time lines. In no other realm of shelter life did I consistently observe volunteers to be so accepting of their domination. While some found ways to circumvent particular forms of waiting—for example, by visiting a friendly staff member with a cubicle to ask a question for an adopter rather than taking a number and waiting in the long front lobby line, which was the shelter policy—they did not see these practices as actually undermining the operation of time. That is, their getting this information in five minutes instead of thirty minutes helped them on that one occasion but didn't change time for anyone else in any meaningful way. Compared to their resistance to shelter killing especially, how volunteers respond to PAW's domination through control of time is far more acquiescent. Killing and time are deeply intertwined: it wouldn't, for example, matter if the shelter put down animals if it did so on a radically different time line, for example when their guardians and their guardians' veterinarians determined it was necessary to end suffering at the end of their lives. Yet killing eclipses time as an issue at PAW.

Shelter volunteers appear to be in the best position to engage in organized action for shelter reform at PAW. They understand how the shelter works, are generally familiar with its power structure, recognize the challenges the shelter faces, and have the resources and know-how to engage in advocacy and protest. Instead, shelter volunteers have not yet organized collective action to promote shelter reform, although they do discuss this possibility periodically. One key reason for the absence of mobilization is PAW's domination of time. PAW neutralizes impulses for change through forced waiting, desperate hurrying, and the regular use of future talk as part of hopeful waiting, promising again and again and again that conditions for animals and people are on the cusp of improving.

9 A New Revolution

I PUSHED MY FEET OUT ABOVE MY HEAD and stretched, relishing the feeling of each muscle lengthening and of the cool air tickling through my nostrils. I blinked my eyelids slowly closed, kept them that way for a few long seconds, and then opened them again, noticing the brightness of the light as it poured into my eyes. I lifted my head and shook it. Looking out across the field, I could see a cluster of lumps I knew to be sleeping dogs. The sudden bodily memory of their fur and skin in my mouth as we played made the breath surge out of me in a kind of slow snort. I contemplated getting up to greet them, but the sun felt so pleasantly hot on my side. I knew I had time before anyone expected anything of me, and so I just lay there, warm and elongated.

Later, when the sun started to shift down in the sky, the humans came back. When I heard their voices, I clambered to my feet and moved across the field to the buildings. Crossing the walking path, I sniffed the air to see who—human and animal—had arrived. I found the musky scent of the woman I liked drifting in the air, and turned toward her door, which, happily, was slightly ajar. I pushed the door fully open with an indiscreet bang; almost immediately, I heard her calling, "Oooh! Is that you, my big buddy?" I hurried toward her voice in the kitchen, my tail wagging with anticipation. I skidded around the corner and found the woman resting on a chair, a tall glass on the table beside her. "Ah, my Monster man!" she said happily, opening her hands to me so I could push my head onto her lap. She pulsed her hands along the back of my neck and down my spine. "Who likes a little massage?" she said in a bright voice that made my ears itch with pleasure. She continued rubbing me as I gazed up at her with a wide smile.

When she stood up to start making dinner, I went and lay on a cushion in the corner. I wondered if any of the other dogs who regularly spent time with this woman would be coming today. As I watched her working, following the movements of her hips and arms as she shifted around her tasks at the counter, her device started to sing. She pressed a button, and a man's voice greeted her in Spanish. "I am just calling with a routine check-in on the *compañeros* around there." "Ah, yes!" she replied and began telling the man on the device about Monster, Chin-Chin, Homer, Ginger, and Marva. When she was done, the man reminded her that the Outreach Team would be coming to see us in three weeks. She smiled and tapped the device to end their talk.

"See how it is, Monster?" she said, looking at me. "The doctors are going to come and make sure you are well, and then you can keep coming here, or going wherever." She knelt down and placed her lips gently on my forehead. "I like it that you come here," she murmured into my fur, the sound humming with a tickle through my skull. I wagged my tail appreciatively, feeling a wave of gratitude for the warmth of her skin against mine. When our bodies moved apart, I bounded happily back over to a large cushion on the floor and sat down to wait for the evening meal, which I knew would be announced throughout the community with a long whistle. The other dogs would probably arrive by then, too, and we would greet each other and gather around the eating area. I knew the woman's door remained open so I could leave to eat and come back whenever I was ready to, after romping with the other dogs or spending time with other humans. Maybe tomorrow or the next day, I would move on to the family with the tiny child who liked to have me sleep beside them at night. For now, I was content, safe, watching and listening as the woman went about her routines, knowing that some of my friends and my dinner would be here soon.

MONSTER'S UTOPIA

This world of Monster's is a utopia—one where he lives with the choice of which animals or humans to be a companion to, and with the guarantee of always having food, shelter, veterinary care, and attention. Monster's new world is a world in which animals have been decommodified, their value based on their unique and distinctly nonhuman contributions to the world, whether as community companions like Monster or as noncompanion animals (i.e., "wild" animals). No longer subject to systemic violence and no longer private property, they live peacefully with each other and with humans. This is a pseudoreturn to the world of village dogs, but one where dogs and cats (and other domesticated animals who may live more separate from humans) are guaranteed food and care, may select guardians if they so choose (and may leave them should they so choose), and live in communities that have been spatially reorganized to account for their needs—for example, by eliminating surface roads in favor of walking and biking paths and elevated or underground trains.

In imagining this world, I draw on multiple sources of knowledge and thought. First are my own observations of companion animal dogs and cats, both at PAW and outside it. Companion animals endure stresses as a result of their relationships with humans—stresses associated with limits humans impose on their freedoms, such as being confined indoors and being left alone for extended periods. I sought to engage with what companion animals would want if they could choose a new way of living. Second are perspectives on different models of social justice. I believe other worlds are possible and require imaginative thinking.[1] To that end, I conceptualize Monster's utopia as a space created with the input of multiple species that allows nonhuman animals to enjoy a good life. Monster's utopia is a world in which he seeks out people as *his* companions, where he is part of a community and not a piece of property, and where spatial and social relations have been reorganized to accommodate him and all other human and nonhuman animals.

Some abolitionists—or people who support ending all human uses of animals—have argued that the only way for humans to have nonexploitative relationships with companion animals is to end their reproduction altogether, creating a world without companion animals.[2] The argument in favor of allowing all domesticated species to die often refers to domesticated animals' vulnerability as one reason for their problematic position and as a justification for why we should allow them to die out. Vulnerability should not be a reason to push any group to extinction. Instead, we need to find better ways to restrict the power of those less vulnerable and to encourage—and create structures for—the care of those who are more vulnerable. We need to develop new models for recognizing interdependence and engaging in care.

When arguments in favor of letting domesticated species die out focus on domesticated animals as human moral failures who are vulnerable and unable to care for themselves, they fail to consider the possibilities of alternatives in which animals are empowered to participate in democratic politics and to act as decommodified subjects. Many species of animals have language and mechanisms for communicating, and there are numerous extant proposals for recognizing and extending their democratic citizenship.[3] In some places, this is already happening.[4] While democratic participation for nonhuman animals would require human mediation, it would also push humans toward new ways of thinking about democracy, communication, language, power, negotiation, and human domination over animals—all of which could substantially transform both political institutions and the broader society.

Imagining Monster's utopia is useful in that it can help move us toward envisioning alternate ways of organizing human-animal relationships and thinking about what is possible. In this book, I have shown how PAW, a high-intake public animal shelter, operates as part of the regimes of the welfare, carceral, and anthroparchal state. Animals and people who come into contact with PAW enter a nexus of multiple forms of power centers. The conditions of confinement, the ways the shelter interrupts human-animal relationships, and PAW's practices of ending animals' lives rely on biopolitical justifications centered on regulating human and animal bodies and selves. PAW's welfare, carceral, and anthroparchal regimes result in contradictory actions, trying to help animals and people while also causing them obvious harm. PAW attempts to displace blame for the killing of shelter animals onto so-called irresponsible owners, the guardians whom most staff and volunteers see as creating the need for animal shelters. The narrative of irresponsible owners also maintains dominant ideas about low-income and often nonwhite people that obscure the very real and very important connections many poor people of color have with companion animals in their care.

Volunteers—almost all women—believe that, while irresponsible owners are part of why animals end up in shelters, a major issue is that the shelter kills animals. They resist the shelter's practice of killing animals, while simultaneously giving care to animals and constructing kinship-like bonds with them. Their resistance to shelter killing includes diverse challenges to the various logics PAW uses to justify killing, including the practice of mourning killed animals to make their lives socially intelligible. Impounded animals, too, engage in resistance, rejecting PAW's efforts to render them docile companions in line with contemporary market demands for ideal love objects. Impounded animals are agentic actors who resist the circumstances of their confinement and the violence and control of anthroparchy, even though their efforts at resistance result in their being pathologized and often killed.

PAW maintains domination in part through its control over time. Looking closely at PAW's temporal power reveals a complex and contradictory set of time lines that force animals and people both to hurry and to wait. By placing impounded animals, volunteers, rescuers, and clients seeking services within its own temporal order, PAW keeps members of these groups in various types of time—desperate hurrying, frustrated waiting, and hopeful waiting—that suspend their investment in and capacities for organized, sustained resistance.

Although there are moments of joy, laughter, and solidarity at PAW, I have focused in this book on the themes most consistent at PAW: domination, defiance, and conflict. I hope this will not always be how PAW—or any shelter—operates. I believe there are many possibilities for meaningful change, some of which started to unfold even as I finished my fieldwork but continued to volunteer. Monster's utopia presents a vision of what a different world for animals and humans might look like, one in which humans and animals work together collaboratively in queer networks of kinship centered on choice, care, and dog love and its attendant sensory pleasures, or what Weaver terms "intimacy without relatedness."[5]

Animal shelters like PAW raise at least five different issues that this kind of utopian thinking can help us address. The first issue, which has been the center point for animal welfarists to date, is shelter killing. The no-kill movement especially has pushed for an end to the killing of adoptable companion animals by focusing on shelter practices of killing. Central to what advocates call the no-kill equation are shelter managers with a commitment to reducing shelter killing, broader community commitment to lowering the shelter death rate, proactive spaying and neutering programs, and aggressive adoption programs that include off-site events, adoption incentives like free or reduced adoption fees, and transports to other shelters with low volumes of incoming animals. In many communities, these practices have reduced shelter killing, and they have at PAW too. One of the nation's largest companion animal welfare groups announced that 2018 marked the first year in which under one million companion animals were killed in shelters, which represents a massive reduction in shelter killing over the last few decades.[6]

Second, shelters reveal the challenges many companion animals experience in securing stable homes. The crisis is especially acute for cats: fifty to seventy million cats in the United States are considered feral,[7] some subsection of which are house cats who have lost their homes. Dogs are much less likely to live as strays for more than a few weeks or months at a time; roughly three million dogs find their way to shelters each year. Many of these are animals who have experienced a significant disruption in their lives, by losing their home or ending up in a shelter, and who have human guardians who may also have experienced disruption.

Third, shelters normalize human domination over animals. They exemplify that even the animals we claim are most precious to us lose their value when detached from a specific human guardian. Animals at many shelters live in conditions similar to those at PAW: in small cages with limited, if any, meaningful contact with humans or other animals. Even as shelters increasingly strive to enhance shelter life with what they call enrichment opportunities for impounded animals, the animals remain confined and subject to constant surveillance, and their fates are subject to the whims of human caretakers. These practices reflect broader ideologies about humans' right to control and exploit animals, whether for companionship, food, or territory. Ending human violence against them, and against the communities they come from, will necessarily involve pushing against powerful capitalist ideologies of human entitlement to all that is part of the "natural" world, and against powerful notions of sovereignty that empower states to determine which animals live and die.

Fourth, shelters normalize violence against humans *and* animals. Incarceration, caging, disciplinary power, disruption of kinship bonds, normalizing judgments, violence, and killing are all enacted on animals in much the same ways as they are on humans. Each of these practices of domination seeks to control the movements, location, and behavior of animals. But even more significant than the ways in which individuals are affected is the way the entire population is: we come to accept practices of power—such as caging—as the only or best way to do things. Inflicting suffering on animals makes violence part of our everyday lives. The structure of contemporary violence against animals—which is predominantly hidden from humans, whether in abattoirs or the Euth Room—allows us largely to ignore this violence even as we know it is happening and see the products of that violence in our grocery stores, restaurants, and own refrigerators and plates. We can't continue to treat animals as an Other that may be subjected to systematic, socially accepted violence and simultaneously expect that other forms of violence will fade away.[8] As long as we police, cage, and kill animals, we will continue to do so to humans as well.

Fifth, shelters like PAW reinforce inequalities among and between humans and animals. Dean Spade reminds us that contemporary modes of power are dispersed across multiple regimes of control that ultimately affect everyone and render certain populations—including women, LGBITQ people, and marginalized people of color—particularly vulnerable.[9] Extending Spade's analysis beyond the realm of the human, it is easy to see how human regimes of domination over animals rely on the same logics and practices as regimes of domination involving people. Further, it is precisely animals who are associated with or attached to marginalized humans whose lives are most precarious and who are most likely to find themselves policed, caged, and/or killed.

THE HUMANE COMMUNITIES REVOLUTION

In light of these complex issues, I propose a new revolution in companion animal sheltering that I call the Humane Communities Revolution. The Humane Communities Revolution centers on a "a generous, life-affirming biopolitics" guided by feminist approaches to care, which reject dualisms (human/nonhuman, man/woman) and are "*for* caring and empathy while never letting power off the hook."[10] This road map addresses the particulars of animal sheltering and uses those particulars to extend to a vision of human-animal relations that brings animal abolition into partnership with movements for the liberation of women, Black and other people of color, gender/queers, and others who live at the margins under neoliberal capitalism. The vision is an abolitionist one, though I believe persons who adopt a welfarist approach will find this approach provocative, engaging, and useful.[11]

Ending the practice of shelter killing must be a critical goal for everyone working in the sheltering industry. The no-kill movement has had a remarkable effect on the industry in a relatively short period of time, forcing even resistant sheltering systems (like SCAS) to respond and shifting the shelter industry's emphasis toward increasing adoptions.[12] Many shelters, including PAW, need to continue working on reducing shelter killing but lack necessary resources and especially facilities to improve the conditions and outcomes of impounded animals. If members of the public want shelter killing to stop, public resources must be made available to improve and build appropriate facilities for homeless animals.

Further, more effort needs to be expended on keeping animals out of the shelter in the first place. Yet rather than focusing on what does bring animals into shelters, the no-kill approach focuses almost entirely on what happens *in* shelters (with the exception of continuing to endorse spay/neuter access).[13] Advocates for shelter animals must now turn to reducing the number of shelter intakes by expanding efforts at reducing intersectional precarity so that humans and animals can maintain relationships of care. The city and county of Los Angeles have well over eighty thousand unhoused people.[14] Hundreds of thousands more people experience the various types of precarity I have discussed in this book, including poverty, high levels of policing, incredibly high housing costs, and undocumented immigration status. The City of Los Angeles aspires to construct hundreds of low-income housing units by 2030, a goal that is to be realized through the conversion of existing apartment buildings and motels, the construction of completely new housing, and a program to incentivize homeowners to rent guest houses (casitas) to unhoused people. These programs should also make central the relationship between humans and animals by ensuring that all city-funded properties for unhoused people accept companion animals and that additional incentives are in place for small-property owners to permit companion animals in their rentals.

Because they are so grossly overrepresented among dogs in shelters, a central goal must be ending housing discrimination against pit bulls. Nationally, only 24 percent of rental apartments allow dogs on the premises, and many of these have restrictions by size and breed.[15] When I called the managers of a dozen apartment buildings in one of the communities PAW serves in 2017, all of them told me pit bulls were not allowed there.[16] Even states like California, which has passed legislation prohibiting local government agencies from implementing BSL, have made no effort to expand protections for these dogs. Requiring landlords of certain types of properties to allow all dogs and cats (up to local limits) in rentals and prohibiting insurance discrimination against dogs on the basis of breed rather than behavior would make more housing available to people with any companion animal, including pit bulls. Local governments could offer incentives to landlords—such as small reductions or rebates on their property taxes—to consider applicants with companion animals.

The insurance industry contributes to the problems facing pit bulls especially because these dogs are often excluded from insurance policies for rental properties and sometimes also from homeowners' insurance policies. Consumers can attempt to put direct pressure on companies by insuring their own properties (automobiles, homes, etc.) only with companies that do not have breed-specific discriminatory practices. However, policy intervention is more likely to be effective in pushing for change in the norms of this industry. It's time for policy makers in the state of California and elsewhere to prohibit insurers from discriminating against animals on the basis of their breed. Shelters and animal rescues can support animal-inclusive housing in a number of ways, including offering low- or no-cost training programs, educational and outreach programs for landlords, and bite prevention education.

Another goal for shelter animal advocates should be economic justice through wage increases and lower housing costs. Both the City of Los Angeles and the State of California have moved to increase the minimum wage so that by 2023 virtually all California employees will be entitled to a minimum wage of fifteen dollars per hour. The 2019 passage of statewide rent control may also help to stabilize housing costs, but it's unlikely to be enough to make costs affordable or to help those toward the bottom of the economic structure. The minimum wage needs to continue to rise beyond 2023, and the (re)development of affordable housing must be a priority. Recent research has shown that increases in the minimum wage result in significant decreases in reports of child abuse.[17] While additional research is needed to extend these findings to companion animals, it is reasonable to expect that increases in wages for workers would also result in more companion animals having higher qualities of life.

Community cats also need attention. TNR has come under extensive fire from wildlife advocates, who have shown the detrimental effects of free-roaming cat populations on bird life and biodiversity.[18] TNR currently isn't working for cats or for birds because it is not nearly expansive enough. We need a comprehensive effort to manage and reduce populations of community cats. Animal control agencies need to implement (for instance, within SCAS) and expand TNR and find ways to create spaces for community cats that minimize risk to local birds. Massive outdoor catteries, the placement of noisemaking devices or BirdBeSafe collars on community (and all outdoor) cats to warn prey, and/or the relocation of community cats to areas with fewer birds or less sensitive bird species would be among the options.

Community involvement and transparency must be central goals in the sheltering industry. Every animal shelter should have a structure that includes a board of community advisers, people who can serve as bridges between the shelter and the people it serves, and as one type of supervisory body of shelter activities and programs. Just as local elected leaders hold meetings and/or open houses with constituents, so too should shelter managers or directors. Shelter volunteers should also have a seat at the table for making policy decisions within SCAS and other shelter systems. For too long, animal shelters—including many nonprofits contracted to offer public services—have been black boxes, hostile arms of the state that intervene in human-animal relationships in often problematic ways. Communities will offer their local shelters greater support if they are included and represented in shelter activities.

Animals should be represented on these boards, via human agents or through trials of new programs to which they have an opportunity to respond. In her case for interspecies democracy, Meijer lays out numerous ways in which animals can be included in democratic decision-making, including through microboards.[19] Given that animals are the primary inhabitants and clients of shelters, the animal-sheltering community should be at the forefront of efforts to bring animals into discussions of how shelters operate.

Humane sheltering also requires more than policy solutions: it requires a change in hearts and minds. To move toward a world that is equitable and secure for human- and nonhuman animals, we must shift current power relations among humans and between human and nonhuman animals. The project of justice for animals requires justice for people, and vice versa; we must examine the "largely unexplored potential for a shared politics between human and nonhuman interests."[20] As long as we rely on the human-animal divide to establish who is Other and use claims of animality as a basis for exclusion and exploitation, we will maintain the logics that justify the exclusion and exploitation of women, people of color, queers, the disabled, nonhuman animals, prisoners, and others whose bodies and lives have all too often been pushed from the human side of the human-animal divide to the animal side. The only way to avoid this is to challenge structures that maintain the divide, always attentive to the possibility that we are reinforcing some forms of domination in order to alleviate or end others.[21]

During the time frame in which I wrote this book, white supremacy experienced a surge of public support from elected politicians, Black Americans continued their struggle against state violence, women spearheaded activism around sexual violence, young people challenged the inertia of government and business leaders to tackle global climate change and gun violence, and immigrants to the United States found themselves subject to detention, family separation, and expulsion.[22] I see little evidence that white supremacy, heteropatriarchy, nationalism, or the violence they rely on has diminished in the United States. We face multiple global crises, including the rise in ethnonationalism and the devastation of global climate change. All of these are immediate and pressing problems. The only way to tackle them is through radical reimaginings of intersectionality, democracy, and inclusion. The small steps will be through new activist praxis that brings humans and animals together to push for shared goals of policy and redistribution and the rejection of animal bodies as products. The big steps—and the hard ones to take—will be those that bring us closer to ensuring that all living creatures on earth can live and thrive.

Notes

CHAPTER 1: MONSTER'S WORLD

1. This figure is an estimate because there is no centralized system for tracking shelter intakes or outcomes nationally. The Humane Society of the United States has a research branch that I believe provides the most accurate estimate; for 2013, the Humane Society estimated that 3.4 million companion animals died in US shelters. Humane Society of the United States, "Our Policies" and "Pets by the Numbers."

2. Calvo (now Cudworth), "'Most Farmers Prefer Blondes,'" discusses anthroparchy as a system. See also Probyn-Rapsey, "Anthropocentrism," 51–52, for a discussion of the politics of the terminology used to describe human relationships with animals.

3. Jones, Haley, and Melton, "Per Capita Red Meat."

4. For more on the lives of chickens in factory farms, see Garcés, *Grilled*; Striffler, *Chicken*.

5. Irvine, *If You Tame Me*, includes an ethnography of a nonprofit humane society serving a predominantly white, middle-class community that serves as an excellent contrast to PAW.

6. Wolch, Brownlow, and Lassiter, "Constructing the Animal Worlds"; Jerolmack, "Primary Groups"; Jerolmack, "Animal Practices, Ethnicity."

7. Foucault, *History of Sexuality.*

8. Guenther, "Volunteers' Power and Resistance."

9. Scott, *Weapons of the Weak*; Vinthagen and Johansson, "'Everyday Resistance.'"

10. Foucault, *History of Sexuality.*

11. Srinivasan, "Biopolitics of Animal Being."

12. Irvine, "Animal Sheltering," provides a solid review of the history and practice of animal sheltering in the United States.

13. The use of gas chambers has been largely rendered obsolete in the US, with twenty-two states banning their use and nineteen states having no ban but also no known use of gas chambers as of the end of 2016. Gas chambers are still in use, particularly in the US South. See Jaskot, "Closing the Door."

14. Bergh, "Henry Bergh's Views," 2.

15. Zawistowski et al., "Population Dynamics."

16. Bergh, "Henry Bergh's Views."

17. Zawistowski et al., "Population Dynamics," 202.

18. Davis, *Gospel of Kindness*. Reflecting the widespread emphasis of early animal welfarists on reducing animal suffering rather than on changing humans' exploitation of animals altogether, Henry Bergh patented the knocking bolt, a device slaughterhouses use to this day to kill or render unconscious four-legged animals for slaughter so that they hopefully experience less pain when subsequently having their throats slit and their blood drained. For a detailed review of the device in use, see Pachirat, *Every Twelve Seconds,* especially chap. 6.

19. Rowan and Kartal, "Dog Population." I discuss the politics of sterilization in greater depth in chapter 2.

20. Rowan and Kartal, "Dog Population"; Parlapiano, "Spaying, Neutering," provides a journalistic overview of trends.

21. This is not an open-admission shelter but rather takes select animals from the City of San Francisco's open-admission shelter. Maddie's does not itself pick up or take in stray animals.

22. Best Friends Animal Society, "No Kill."

23. No Kill Advocacy Center, "No Kill Equation"; foster programs place animals in private homes. At many shelters, such programs utilize foster homes only for unweaned animals and those with medical needs and typically return the animal to the shelter once of age or recovered. Private rescue organizations with foster programs typically keep animals in foster homes until adoption.

24. With a revenue of about $45 million, the North Shore Animal League has a substantially smaller budget than Best Friends Animal Society's $85 million or the ASPCA's whopping $217 million budget. The No Kill Advocacy Center has a budget of barely $100,000.

25. In many ways, the move toward no-kill has had the same effects on American shelters that the shift toward conservation has had on American zoos, whose efforts, as Irus Braverman notes, have become increasingly "cooperative, collective, and global." Braverman, *Zooland*, 5.

26. Robinson, *Evolution*.

27. Marra and Sentella, *Cat Wars*, provides an excellent explanation of the hazards community cats pose to biodiversity.

28. Irvine, "Animal Sheltering."

29. Rowan and Kartal, "Dog Population." Best Friends Animal Society, in a post on their website entitled "Together, We Can End the Killing by 2025," claims that seventeen million companion animals were killed in US shelters in 1984, when they

began advocating for reducing shelter deaths; I have been unable to substantiate this claim elsewhere, but it points to the immense disagreement in data on animal sheltering in the United States. Even today, I think national kill data are educated estimates.

30. Rowan and Kartal, "Dog Population"; Humane Society of the United States, "Our Policies."

31. Winograd, *Irreconcilable Differences*; Winograd, *Redemption*.

32. Pit bulls are a type of dog rather than a breed. Pit bulls include American Pit Bull Terriers, American Staffordshire Terriers, Bull Terriers, Staffordshire Bull Terriers, and mixes thereof, including dogs who share physical attributes of one or more of these breeds but who may not have any genetic ties to them.

33. Nocella et al., "Introduction."

34. Singer, *Animal Liberation*.

35. Best, "Rise"; McCance, *Critical Animal Studies*; Nocella et al., "Introduction."

36. McCance, *Critical Animal Studies*.

37. This book also contributes to a nascent field Heidi Nast proposed in 2006, critical pet studies, and engages with several of the key questions about guardian–companion animal relationships that Nast poses. Nast, "Critical Pet Studies?"

38. See, e.g., Lee and Geyer, *One at a Time*; Zheutlin, *Rescue Road*.

39. Humane Society of the United States, "Pets by the Numbers." American Society for the Prevention of Cruelty to Animals, "Pet Statistics" suggests the percentage of companion animals in homes who came from shelters or rescues could be as low as one-quarter to one-third. There is general agreement in the sheltering industry that adoption has risen markedly in popularity in the last decade.

40. Alger and Alger, *Cat Culture*; Harboldt, *Bridging the Bond*; Irvine, *If You Tame Me*; Markovits and Crosby, *From Property to Family*.

41. Measuring the size of shelter populations in the United States remains challenging. One of the more comprehensive data sources is Shelter Animals Count, a database maintained by the Humane Society of the United States. For their 2016 data set, 2,225 shelters and rescues reported data on their own operations; there may be more than 10,000 shelters and rescues in the US. Although government shelters like PAW constituted only 9 percent of responding organizations, they reported a far greater share of animal intakes than all other shelter types combined in the three states with the highest number of intakes (California, Texas, and Florida). Shelter Animals Count, "2016 Animal Sheltering Statistics."

42. Foucault, *Discipline and Punish*; Foucault, *History of Sexuality*.

43. Foucault, *History of Sexuality*, 138.

44. Wadiwel, "Biopolitics," 92; Coppin, "Foucauldian Hog Futures."

45. Kim, *Dangerous Crossings*; Boisseron, *Afro-Dog*; Ko and Ko, *Aphro-Ism*.

46. Kim, *Dangerous Crossings* and "Murder and Mattering."

47. Agamben, *Homo Sacer*; Kim, "Murder and Mattering," 11, emphasis in original.

48. Ortner, "Is Female to Male"; Hartsock, "Feminist Standpoint."

49. Birke, "Intimate Familiarities?"; Adams, *Sexual Politics of Meat*.

50. Adams, *Sexual Politics of Meat*, graphically links the masculine practices of hunting and butchering to the late twentieth-century practices of pornographic violence. Butchered animals and butchered women are linked by an overlap of cultural images of sexual violence against women and the fragmentation of nature and the body in Western culture.

51. Adams and Donovan, "Sexism and Speciesism."

52. Gaarder, "Where the Boys Aren't."

53. See also Weaver, "Pit Bull Promises."

54. Weaver, "Pit Bull Promises."

55. Chen, *Animacies*.

56. Kim, *Dangerous Crossings*, 24.

57. Joy, *Why We Love Dogs*.

58. Foer, *Eating Animals*; Joy, *Why We Love Dogs*.

59. Kirksey and Helmreich, "Emergence of Multispecies Ethnography," 545.

60. Haraway, *When Species Meet*; Weaver, "Pit Bull Promises."

61. In working with an intersectional lens, I am aware of critiques of intersectionality that note its tendency to "privilege general categories over particularities" and attend carefully to the specific intersections at work at PAW. Boisseron, *Afro-Dog*, 25.

62. Dave, "Witness"; Gillespie, "Witnessing Animal Others"; Gillespie, *Cow with Ear Tag #1389*.

63. This represents a break from dominant approaches in the field of ethology, which tends to focus on behavioral responses to stimuli and values emotional disengagement from animals, who are seen as research subjects.

64. Dave, "Witness."

65. Tyler, *CIFERAE*; Wadiwel, *War against Animals*; Meijer, *When Animals Speak*.

66. Arluke and Sanders, *Regarding Animals*, 87.

67. Doubleday, "Scale-Blocking Grief."

68. Gruen, *Entangled Empathy*, 3.

69. García, "Grieving Guinea Pigs," also discusses mourning and grieving as political acts that constitute witnessing; I take up this theme in depth in chapter 5.

70. Haraway, *When Species Meet*, 80.

71. I say "when appropriate" because sometimes I would be working with another volunteer when it was very noisy or chaotic or we were engaged in physical labor, and talking about the research simply didn't make sense. I did not actively seek to keep my work a secret from volunteers. Since this research took place in a public setting and posed no foreseeable risks to participants beyond the risks associated with the activities they were already engaged in, not talking about the research was also well within federal and disciplinary norms for fieldwork.

72. The Human Subjects Review Board at my university approved my research protocol through an expedited review process standard for protocols that pose limited risks to participants/subjects. Interestingly, the board did not express any concerns or

ask any questions about the animals in my research, which stands in marked contrast to Gillespie's experiences reported in *Cow with Ear Tag #1389.*

73. Guenther, "Politics of Names"; Jerolmack and Murphy, "Ethical Dilemmas and Trade-Offs."

74. Haraway, *When Species Meet.*

75. Moore and Kosut, "Among the Colony," 520.

76. Kirksey and Helmreich, "Emergence of Multispecies Ethnography."

77. Animal Studies Group, *Killing Animals.*

78. In California, the debate about municipal codes changing wording from *owner* to *guardian* has sometimes been heated. In 2003, San Francisco pioneered this effort. Opponents argued that legally a guardian has a substantially different and less controlling relationship over their charge and that this change in language would create unanticipated legal complications for guardians of companion animals. See, for example, the California Veterinary Medical Association's position against the language of companion animal guardians, "CVMA's Owner vs. Guardian FAQ."

CHAPTER 2: HELPING/POLICING/KILLING

1. SCAS designates the following breeds as dominant: Akita, American Bulldog, American Pit Bull Terrier, American Staffordshire Terrier, Bull Terrier, Cane Corso, Caucasian Mountain Dog, Chow Chow, Dogo Argentino, Jindo, Pit Bull, Neopolitan Mastiff, Presa Canario, Rottweiler, Shar Pei, Staffordshire Bull Terrier, Tibetan Mastiff, and Tosa Inu.

2. SCAS assumes animals enter the shelter without vaccines, and all incoming animals are vaccinated.

3. State of California, SB 1785.

4. Reeve, Spitzmüller, and DiGiacomo, "Caring-Killing Paradox."

5. Hannah, "Biopower, Life"; Ojakangas, "Impossible Dialogues on Biopower"; Rabinow and Rose, "Biopower Today."

6. Erika Cudworth first developed the concept of anthroparchy in 2005, in *Developing Ecofeminist Theory.*

7. Morin, "Wildspace"; Morin, "Carceral Space."

8. Morin, "Carceral Space," 1328.

9. Coppin, "Foucaultian Hog Futures"; Thierman, "Apparatuses of Animality."

10. I take up SCAS's and PAW's practices around dominant breeds in chapter 6.

11. I base these rough estimates on data from the page "US Pet Ownership Statistics" on the American Veterinary Medical Association's website, https://www.avma.org/KB/resources/statistics/pages/market-research-statistics-US-pet-ownership.aspx, in conjunction with reviewing population estimates from several other sources.

12. A renovation of the kennel buildings began in 2016 and was still under way as of September 2019; this project mainly involved new paint and doors, resurfacing

or replacement of roadways and paths, and the reorganization of some work spaces, not improved features or more space for animals.

13. Braverman, *Zooland*, provides an in-depth analysis of the care animals in zoos receive.

14. As I discovered, obtaining raw data from SCAS is extremely difficult and for me proved impossible. SCAS staff explain this as a function of the software system the shelter uses. SCAS does post statistics for each of its shelters by fiscal year on its website. Animal advocates question the reliability of these data because many believe that SCAS removes animals who are deemed unadoptable from their data, an allegation SCAS officials denied in public presentations I heard during my fieldwork.

15. NKLA is an initiative of Best Friends Animal Society and aimed to have made Los Angeles a no-kill city by the end of 2017. For purposes of this initiative, and as widely accepted in the shelter industry, Best Friends defines "no kill" as a 90 percent live release rate. As part of this effort, Best Friends took over management of one of the city's shelters and opened a new adoption center, partnered with local rescues to offer them financial incentives to rescue animals, developed fostering programs for unweaned animals, and initiated the NKLA Super Adoption events.

16. Foucault, *Security, Territory, Population.*

17. See also Braverman's *Zooland* for detailed discussion of pastoral power in the context of zoos.

18. SCAS has a head veterinarian for the full shelter system who oversees the creation and implementation of veterinary policies for PAW and the other SCAS shelters. Their work is heavily informed by research and reports stemming from the Koret Shelter Medicine Program at the University of California, Davis (https://www.sheltermedicine.com/).

19. The most common zoonotic diseases at the shelter are sarcoptic mange, ringworm, and giardia. These conditions are not usually a basis for killing an animal, but they necessitate handling only with gloves on. Animals who have these conditions may not go into the social areas. They generally have a lower chance of adoption. Thus, while PAW doesn't kill them specifically because of the illness, the illness places them at elevated risk of being killed, since they may not be adopted in a timeframe PAW finds acceptable.

20. Shelter volunteers routinely contest PAW's justification of killing in the interest of the health of the shelter population. This is because PAW fails to engage in many routine disease-prevention strategies recommended by shelter medicine specialists. Volunteers believe the shelter should employ these strategies, which include quarantining, specialized cleaning protocols, and improvements in ventilation, before turning to killing animals.

21. Residents in unincorporated areas of the SCAS service area can have up to five cats, but most of the cities that contract animal control services through SCAS—and that are the primary producers of animals that come into PAW—have a limit of

three cats. In 2017, SCAS raised the limit on the number of dogs from three to four, again affecting only unincorporated areas.

22. Fly strike is a dermatitis caused by stable flies biting the ears. At PAW, we most often saw this in dogs with large, pointy ears like German Shepherds. The condition was apparent through the complete loss of fur on the ear tips.

23. Davis, *Gospel of Kindness*; Irvine, "Animal Sheltering."

24. Local ordinances categorize animals who stray on public or private property as animal nuisances.

25. PAW does periodically receive or pick up animals that could be designated as wild, such as pigeons, raccoons, opossums, and skunks.

26. For me and other volunteers, the act of returning dogs to their kennels is often emotionally distressing because it makes us act directly as the cager. I have seen volunteers cry after returning a dog to their kennel. The experience of putting a dog back in their kennel after time in the social area can be especially distressing when the dog does not want to go back in the kennel. I distinctly remember returning to her kennel one obese pit bull after I had sat with her for nearly an hour in the social area, playing fetch and cuddling. I was certain she would die at the shelter because of her age, breed, and appearance. The shelter was quiet that evening, and no one was around to help me get her back into her kennel. I tugged on her slip lead while pushing at her butt with my feet, desperately hoping to avoid having to pick her up, which I feared would aggravate my chronic pain. I attempted a leashing maneuver that involves looping the leash under a dog's hips to facilitate lifting them, also to no avail. Breathlessly begging her to move, I finally bent over and heaved the enormity of her up over the kennel lip, blocking the kennel opening with my body to prevent her from turning around and barging back out. When I had finally squeezed her fully in and slid my legs out of her kennel to secure the door, my lower body bowed to the ground and I found myself on my knees, my head resting against the kennel bars and tears streaming down my face. I was overwhelmed with sadness that she would die, and angry with her for making it so difficult to put her back—an anger that I knew, even as I knelt there crying, was actually a rage toward the shelter and toward the world for allowing her to die.

27. CalWorks is a welfare program in California that provides temporary assistance to needy families and requires a work component. Community service workers are individuals who have been sentenced by the courts to complete community service. Both groups of workers tend to be highly transient, sometimes working at the shelter for only a few weeks or months. Unlike volunteers, their activities are tightly regulated by shelter staff. They primarily complete cleaning tasks and have limited one-on-one interactions with animals.

28. One manager during the period of fieldwork insisted that animals receive only one meal each day in order to reduce the frequency of their bowel movements and therefore make the kennels cleaner. The one-meal-a-day policy was highly contentious among staff and volunteers: many of them thought one meal per day was too little and was mean or even cruel to dogs already in the unfortunate

situation of being in a shelter, whereas some others thought the policy was not a big deal.

29. I volunteered for more than four years before I became aware this safety training even existed.

30. I am aware of four volunteers to whom SCAS management granted access to the system during the period of my research.

31. Pachirat, *Every Twelve Seconds*.

32. Elias, *Civilizing Process*.

33. Agamben, *Homo Sacer*; Wadiwel, "Cows and Sovereignty."

34. McKenzie, "Evaluating the Benefits"; Kustritz, "Pros, Cons."

35. Srinivasan, "Biopolitics of Animal Being," 113.

36. The shelter is not equipped to sterilize certain types of animals, such as pot-bellied pigs or reptiles, so these animals are released unfixed. Most communities for which SCAS is contracted to provide services, as well as the unincorporated areas over which SCAS has sole jurisdiction, have "mandatory" spay/neuter ordinances for residents; however, only animals being discharged from the shelter can be sterilized there. These "mandatory" ordinances allow relatively easy and affordable loopholes for working and service animals, competition animals (or animals who are licensed with breed registries and who are likely being used for breeding purebred or pedigreed animals), and animals with health issues that place them at risk during surgery. Guardians who wish to keep their animals without sterilizing them must submit a simple form with documentation from a veterinarian, breed registry, or other appropriate agency and must pay an increased license fee: depending on where they live, the fee for an unsterilized cat is $10 as compared to $5 to $7 for a sterilized cat, and the fee for a sterilized dog is $18 to $72 for an unsterilized dog as compared to $9 to $27 for a sterilized dog. Under the ordinance, female dogs may have no more than one litter per year and no more than five litters in their lifetimes; however, SCAS has no mechanism for tracking which dogs are having litters when, and I have never heard of this clause being enforced in any way.

37. Braverman, *Zooland*; Gillespie, *Cow with Ear Tag#1389*; and Parreñas, *Decolonizing Extinction*, all provide analytically rich discussions of human interventions in animal reproduction.

38. Silliman et al., *Undivided Rights*, provides a helpful overview of reproductive justice issues and activism.

39. PAW and Humane America have developed more aggressive fostering promotion for unweaned kittens especially; this has allowed more unweaned kittens to go to foster homes for bottle feeding.

40. Unaltered female cats go into estrus during the warmer months, usually beginning in March of each year. With a gestation period of about sixty days, high-intake shelters in southern California begin to fill with kittens in late April through June. Female cats may go into estrus multiple times during the warm season. Thanks to southern California's mild climate, kitten season can continue until October or even November, although the peak period of intakes is in April through June.

CHAPTER 3: THE MYTH OF THE IRRESPONSIBLE OWNER

1. State of California, SB 1785.

2. See chapter 1, note 23, for an overview of foster programs.

3. Alvado did not have Beso neutered. As I discuss later in this chapter, animal shelter and rescue staff and volunteers regard this as a marker of irresponsible owners.

4. I discuss how pit bulls themselves have become carriers of criminality in chapter 6. This loop mimics the relationship between individuals and communities Mills identifies in *The Racial Contract*: you are an irresponsible owner because you come from that neighborhood, and that neighborhood is bad because it's full of irresponsible owners like you.

5. As I discuss further in chapter 6, pit bulls are widely associated with poor men of color, making them particularly vulnerable to shelter death.

6. Hancock, *Politics of Disgust*; Gilens, *Why Americans Hate Welfare*.

7. Brown and Dilley's "Ways of Knowing" discusses examples of temporary disruptions in responsible dog guardianship. Responsible guardianship is a routine achievement that is accomplished in interaction with animals. Achieving responsible guardianship is difficult for those whose animals end up at PAW.

8. DiGiacomo, Arluke, and Patronek, "Surrendering Pets to Shelters"; Irvine, "Problem of Unwanted Pets"; Kass et al., "Understanding Animal Companion Surplus"; Patronek et al., "Risk Factors for Relinquishment"; Salman et al., "Human and Animal Factors."

9. DiGiacomo, Arluke, and Patronek, "Surrendering Pets to Shelters"; Irvine, "Problem of Unwanted Pets"; Patronek et al., "Risk Factors for Relinquishment."

10. Data from the most comprehensive national research on animal shelters find that 62.7 percent of shelter animal intakes in the United States are into government shelters (33.9 percent) and shelters with government contracts (28.1 percent). Further, government shelters have by far the highest numbers of intakes. See Shelter Animals Count, "2016 Animal Sheltering Statistics."

11. Staff and volunteers often laugh together when unusual types of animals come into the shelter as "strays." When turtles, tortoises, horses, pigs, and bearded dragons arrive as strays, staff and volunteers jokingly conjecture about how the animal may have gotten lost.

12. M. Desmond, *Evicted*, offers a detailed analysis of eviction and inequality in the US.

13. Safe Parking LA, "Safe Parking LA."

14. In "Problem of Unwanted Pets," Irvine provides an excellent discussion of how animal shelters' bureaucratic practices obscure the real reasons animals end up in the low-intake, low-kill shelter where she conducted research.

15. These reasons have only some alignment with those identified by Irvine in "Problem of Unwanted Pets," perhaps because of the marked differences in the type of community served.

16. This number was raised to four dogs shortly before the completion of the fieldwork.

17. After several years of decline, California's homelessness crisis accelerated starting in 2015. In 2017, 55,000 of California's estimated homeless population of about 155,000 people lived in Los Angeles County. Cal Matters, "Homeless in California," US Department of Housing and Urban Development, "Housing Assessment Report."

18. Clear, *Imprisoning Communities*.

19. Shelter Animals Count, "2016 Statistics." Data by species are not available for 2014; in 2016, 16.6 percent of dogs and 2.5 percent of cats represented through a national survey of public and private shelters were returned to their guardians.

20. The culture-of-poverty perspective, which holds that poor communities—particularly poor communities of color—adopt pathological beliefs and practices that in turn support the continued perpetuation of poverty, was articulated in the works of Oscar Lewis and Daniel P. Moynihan in the 1960s and has retained traction as a framework for making sense of inequality in the United States. See Lewis, *La Vida*; Moynihan, *Negro Family*.

21. Sparks et al.'s "Race and Ethnicity" presents findings of research by HSUS on racial and ethnic differences in spaying and neutering of companion animals. Among low-income guardians to companion animals, whites who engaged with HSUS Pets for Life program sites, which target low-income communities, were most likely to have companion animals who were spayed or neutered (85.4 percent), followed by Latinx (70.3 percent), and then Black (68.2 percent) animal guardians. However, the HSUS research also found that Latinx people who were offered vouchers for spay/neuter services were significantly *more* likely to accept them on the first effort than white or Black people, suggesting that low-cost or free spay/neuter outreach programs may be particularly well received among Latinx animal guardians. This counters the view among staff and volunteers at PAW of Latinx people as resistant to spaying and neutering.

22. All salary data are taken from public records.

23. N. Taylor, "In It."

24. Per Humane America's data, their program across multiple SCAS shelters assisted seven thousand animals from 2014 through June 2016. Spay/neuter assistance constituted the single biggest type of assistance requested and provided at 43 percent, followed by veterinary/medical assistance at 27 percent. The high rate of requests for spay/neuter assistance again dispels myths that people in PAW's service area don't want to spay or neuter companion animals in their care.

CHAPTER 4: THE STRUGGLE FOR SHELTER ANIMAL SURVIVAL

1. Guenther, "Volunteers' Power and Resistance."

2. Eliasoph, *Politics of Volunteering*, provides an important critique of volunteerism.

3. Vinthagen and Johansson, "Everyday Resistance" 5.

4. Hollander and Einwohner, "Conceptualizing Resistance."

5. Vinthagen and Johansson, "Everyday Resistance."

6. Gaarder, "Where the Boys Aren't."

7. Markovits and Crosby, "From Property to Family."

8. Gaarder, "Where the Boys Aren't."

9. Other volunteers and I tend to find these statements problematic and annoying. Even as they celebrate shelter volunteerism, comments that others would not be able to "handle" volunteering at PAW suggests that shelter volunteers are somehow emotionally different from other people. The perception of volunteering as being too emotionally difficult and therefore to be avoided also allows people to continue looking away from animal killing in all of its many manifestations. While of course not everyone should be expected to have an interest in volunteering at shelters, the way nonvolunteers construct shelter volunteerism undermines volunteers' hopes of demythologizing public animal shelters.

10. Men volunteers at PAW work exclusively with dogs; I am not aware of any man who was significantly involved in working with impounded cats during my research.

11. I use the term *relational resistance* to emphasize the centrality of relationships in this type of resistance. This is analytically distinct from relational aggression, or a purportedly gendered pattern of indirect behaviors intended to harm others. In *Beyond Bad Girls,* Chesney-Lind and Irwin have cogently argued that the attention among psychologists toward relational aggression among girls reinforces gender stereotypes and has a questionable empirical basis. I use the term *relational* to stress that this resistance is grounded in relationships, not to draw an analogy to relational aggression, which is a distinct concept.

12. Volunteers and staff generally believe that so-called black dog syndrome makes it less likely for adopters to be interested in black dogs in general and large black dogs especially. Research by Milliken, Humy, and Woodward, in "Give a Dog a Bad Name," exploring the effect of color, size, and breed on people's perceptions of dogs, finds that size and color are not strong predictors of human assessments of dog's friendliness and dominance but that breed is. However, this research relies on college students' assessments of photographs of dogs, not actual adoption trends from shelters or behavior of people seeking to adopt or buy dogs, which may limit the applicability of the findings to shelter adoption scenarios. Further, PAW staff and volunteers would not view a black Labrador Retriever—the large black dog used in Milliken, Humy, and Woodward's research—as an animal who would struggle to find an adopter. Rather, black pit bulls, Shepherds, and mixed-breed dogs are those whom volunteers and staff see as less likely to be adopted than light-colored dogs of the same breeds or mixes.

13. There were also a handful of Latinx women volunteers; I am aware of only one Black volunteer during my fieldwork. Several volunteers seemed to come from working-class backgrounds, but they mostly appeared to have achieved occupations and lifestyles associated with the middle class.

14. The volunteer pool at PAW is racially and religiously more diverse than the sample examined by Neumann in "Animal Welfare Volunteers," which may be explained by the shelter's location in the Los Angeles area.

15. Florida, *Rise of the Creative Class.*

16. Research on the factors that render some dogs more appealing to humans than others fails to support the widespread belief among staff and volunteers at PAW that people are not as likely to ascribe positive characteristics to black dogs. While further research on what helps make dogs adoptable is needed, in this discussion I focus on those attributes staff and volunteers see as important in explaining why some dogs are in high demand at PAW while others secure no human interest and are killed. For analyses of canine attributes that humans view positively, see Milliken, Humy, and Woodward, "Give a Dog a Bad Name," and Protopopova et al., "Effects of Social Training."

17. During my fieldwork, PAW participated in multiple transport programs coordinated by outside organizations that took dogs and cats from PAW (and sometimes other shelters) to low-intake, low- or no-kill shelters in other areas like Oregon and Utah where shelter intakes do not satisfy demand for rescued animals. One of these programs excluded pit bulls over six months of age and any dog over three years of age, generally did not take any cats, and offered only two or three spaces to large dogs. Another transport program would take only one or two adult pit bulls per month and only those with perfect scores on their temperament evaluations. Transport programs never take animals with known health issues. These transport criteria reflect ideas about adoptability, and only the most adoptable dogs are sent to out-of-state shelters.

18. Balcom and Arluke, "Animal Adoption," and Irvine, "Animal Problems/ People Skills," discuss aspects of how shelter workers and volunteers assess people seeking to adopt or interact with shelter animals.

19. Irvine, *If You Tame Me,* includes a detailed analysis of how adopters select dogs at a private shelter. See especially chap. 5.

20. Twining, Arluke, and Patronek, "Managing the Stigma."

21. Marder et al., "Food-Related Aggression"; Patronek and Bradley, "No Better"; Rayment et al., "Applied Personality Assessment."

22. Morris, *Blue Juice.* Even outside the shelter, euthanasia is sometimes contested, as when animal guardians ask veterinarians to euthanize companion animals whom veterinarians see as likely to recover.

23. Volunteers accord the veterinarians more respect than the RVTs because they have higher levels of training and are less visibly involved in the day-to-day care of the animals at the shelter. The veterinarians work mostly in the clinic at the front of the shelter, a building with locked doors that is used primarily for spaying and neutering exiting animals. Many volunteers don't even know who the veterinarians are because of their limited physical presence in the kennel buildings.

24. The veterinary subfield of shelter medicine focuses specifically on managing shelter animals with the goal of preventing disease outbreaks and reducing shelter suffering and death related to disease, especially contagious disease. PAW and SCAS veterinarians generally point to the University of California, Davis's Koret Shelter Medicine Program as a source of information and guidance (although, as far as I

know, the Koret Shelter Medicine Program has not consulted directly with any SCAS shelter). As a volunteer and as a researcher, I therefore read the materials provided on the Koret Shelter Medicine Program's website and routinely identified discrepancies between best practices promoted there and PAW's actual practices.

25. Wagner, Hurley, and Stavisky, "Shelter Housing for Cats."

26. For most of the research period, small dogs with health issues were housed in a room shared with cats, which violates shelter medicine's recommendations for housing shelter animals by species and never placing animals of different species within hearing or visual distance.

27. Volunteers object to these practices because even animals who test positive for or who have been exposed to some diseases—such parvo virus—may not develop the disease.

28. Marlor, "Bureaucracy, Democracy, and Exclusion."

29. Electronic communications fell outside the scope of my original research protocol, and I obtained consent from the author of this message to use it in my work because it provides such a useful and concise example of a legal strategy.

30. My fieldwork doesn't speak precisely to whether or how much volunteer involvement lowers shelter death, or if increases in the number or hours of volunteers at the shelter decrease shelter deaths; however, on the basis of the large number of successful interventions I have observed, I believe that volunteer advocacy at PAW significantly reduces shelter deaths. This is not to say all interventions are successful. Still, failed interventions involve volunteers challenging shelter practices and discourses in ways that could, over time, shift how the shelter operates.

31. Animal practices may be a source of solidarity or conflict. See Jerolmack, "Animal Practices, Ethnicity," as one recent example of animal practices as a basis for community solidarity.

32. My fieldwork engaged with interactions between staff and volunteers but did not involve private conversations with many staff about how they *feel* about volunteers and their interventions. However, I expect that volunteers problematize the shelter experience for staff and also serve as validators for the many staff who also would like to lower death rates. Volunteers could become allies for staff in facilitating shifts in organizational practices.

33. J. Scott, *Weapons of the Weak.*

34. See also Aptekar, "Visions of Public Space."

CHAPTER 5: THE TRANSFORMATIVE POWER OF GRIEF

1. Animal Studies Group, *Killing Animals*; DeMello, *Mourning Animals*; J. Desmond, *Displaying Death.*

2. Haraway, *When Species Meet.*

3. Redmalm, "Pet Grief," 19.

4. Butler, *Frames of War*, xix.

5. Stanescu, "Species Trouble," 569.

6. J. Desmond, *Displaying Death*, 93.

7. Gillespie, "Witnessing Animal Others."

8. S. Taylor, *Beasts of Burden*.

9. Weaver, "Pit Bull Promises," contains beautiful descriptions and analysis of how shelter volunteers and animals come to know each other. See also Dave, "Witness."

10. Weaver, "Becoming in Kind," 690–91.

11. Haraway, *When Species Meet*; Nast, "Loving . . . Whatever."

12. Nast "Loving . . . Whatever."

13. See Irvine, *If You Tame Me*, chap. 5, for a detailed discussion of adopters' decision-making processes in a nonprofit, low-kill humane society.

14. See Gillespie, *Cow with Ear Tag #1389*, and Govindrajan, *Animal Intimacies*, for examples of the emotional distress animals experience when their familial ties are broken.

15. Data on the acquisition of companion animals are disjointed at best. According to the ASPCA, "Pet Statistics," and HSUS, "Puppy Mills," 1.6 million dogs and 1.6 million cats are adopted from shelters each year in the United States, while around 2 million dogs are born in so-called puppy mills each year, most of whom are presumably sold. In Los Angeles, the pressure to rescue is significant enough that people who buy dogs from breeders or pet stores routinely justify their purchase by arguing that conditions at the breeder's or the pet store were so poor that they were, in effect, rescuing the dog they purchased.

16. Howe, "How Generational Change Boosts."

17. Collard and Dempsey, "Life for Sale?"; Haraway, *When Species Meet*.

18. Pribac, "Grieving at a Distance."

19. Pribac, "Grieving at a Distance."

20. Gillespie, "Witnessing Animal Others," 576.

21. Statistics for the 1970s, '80s, and '90s were not available to me. To date, SCAS continues to fail to provide statistics in keeping with the 2004 Asilomar Accords.

22. Pierce, *Last Walk*.

23. For a detailed account of rendering as it pertains to farm animals, see Gillespie, *Cow with Ear Tag #1389*, 113–18.

24. Peterson, "Canine Rescue."

CHAPTER 6: THE PECULIAR PROBLEM OF PIT BULLS

1. Even some rescuers see pit bulls as fundamentally different from other dogs. I encountered this in my research. See also Dickey, *Pit Bull*, esp. 242–45, for a discussion of debates among pit bull advocates that echoes much of what I heard among Los Angeles area rescuers.

2. Cohen and Richardson, "Pit Bull Panic"; Dickey, *Pit Bull*.

3. Dickey, *Pit Bull*; Nair, "Racism"; Twining, Arluke, and Patronek, "Managing the Stigma"; Weaver, "Pit Bull Promises"; Weaver, "'Becoming in Kind.'"

4. Boisseron, *Afro-Dog*; Dayan, *With Dogs*; Dickey, *Pit Bull*.

5. Kim, *Dangerous Crossings*; Kim, "Abolition"; Kim, "Murder and Mattering"; Kim, "Wonderful, Horrible Life."

6. Boisseron, *Afro-Dog*; see especially the introduction and chaps. 1 and 2.

7. Boisseron, *Afro-Dog*; Kim, *Dangerous Crossings*.

8. Andrews, "Beasts"; Nast, "Pit Bulls, Slavery."

9. For discussions of pit bulls as "America's dog," see Dickey, *Pit Bull*, and Levine and Poray-Wybranowska, "American Bully."

10. Dickey, *Pit Bull*.

11. Nast, "Pit Bulls, Slavery," 140.

12. Wacquant, "From Slavery." As Wacquant notes, the racial composition of American prisoners had inverted by 1980, changing from predominantly white inmates to predominantly Black inmates. The year 1988 marks the point at which Black men started to constitute half of the prison population in the United States.

13. Levine and Poray-Wybranowska, "American Bully," 155.

14. Kalof and Taylor, "Discourse of Dog Fighting"; Kim, *Dangerous Crossings*; Tarver, "Dangerous Individual('s) Dog."

15. Levine and Poray-Wybranowska, "American Bully"; Cohen and Richardson, "Pit Bull Panic."

16. Kalof and Taylor, "Discourse of Dog Fighting," documents how many residents of Black neighborhoods came to fear pit bulls.

17. Nast, "Pit Bulls, Slavery."

18. Davis, *Gospel of Kindness*.

19. Fiala, "Dog Breeds"; Rosenberg, "Golden Retrievers Are White."

20. Junod, "State"; Levine and Poray-Wybranowska, "American Bully."

21. Kim, *Dangerous Crossings*, 266.

22. Foucault, *Security, Territory, Population*.

23. Levine and Poray-Wybranowska, "American Bully," suggest that BSL is best understood as "Body Specific Legislation," since it targets an appearance rather than a breed.

24. Cohen and Richardson, "Pit Bull Panic"; Medlin, "Pit Bull Bans."

25. Dayan, *With Dogs,* discusses local bans on pit bulls, including the prohibition of such dogs in New York City Housing Authority properties inhabited by low-income people.

26. On the relationship between breed and bite risk, see American Temperament Test Society, "ATTS Statistics"; Cohen and Richardson, "Pit Bull Panic"; Duffy, Hsu, and Serpell, "Breed Differences." On the effects of BSL, see Chiam et al., "Retrospective Review"; Nilson et al., "Effect"; Rosado et al., "Spanish Dangerous Animals Act."

27. See Dickey, *Pit Bull*, 253, for an analysis of the small proportion of insurance claims and settlements that involve dog bites. Per Dickey, only 0.9 percent of homeowner's insurance payouts were for dog bites (from dogs of all breeds).

28. PitBullInfo.org, "Facts and Information."

29. Dickey, *Pit Bull*; Lepper, Kass, and Hart, "Prediction of Adoption."

30. Data by breed of dog in US shelters nationally is scant and often contradictory. Pit bulls are widely identified as the most common dog in US animal shelters.

They are popular among adopters as well, but apparently not in numbers proportionate to the rate at which they enter shelters.

31. Boisseron, *Afro-Dog*; Dayan, *With Dogs;* Kim, "Wonderful, Horrible Life"; Kim, *Dangerous Crossings*; Tarver, "Dangerous Individual('s) Dog"; Weaver, "'Becoming in Kind.'" Although Vick's affluence at the time of his arrest would seem to break the mold of lower-class Black men being involved in dogfighting, Vick was raised in a poor home; his kennel name, Bad Newz, referred to the public housing project in which he grew up.

32. Kim, "Wonderful, Horrible Life."

33. During my time at PAW, the shelter did not receive a pit bull as part of a dogfighting case. SCAS did receive such animals at other shelters. SCAS normally kills any dog impounded as part of a dogfighting investigation who appears to have been bred for or involved in fighting. Between 1995 and 2015, sixteen defendants were charged with illegal dogfighting in Los Angeles County.

34. Collins, *Black Feminist Thought.*

35. Dayan, *With Dogs*, has also rightly noted the involvement of lower-class rural white men in dogfighting, but especially in the context of Los Angeles this population is not visibly involved.

36. Evans, Gauthier, and Forsyth, "Dogfighting," and Kalof and Taylor, "Discourse of Dog Fighting," both evidence how dogfighting is a man's activity, and Evans, Gauthier, and Forsyth especially attend to how participation in dogfighting enhances and threatens masculinity.

37. Black people constitute less than 3.5 percent of the population of PAW's service area and less than 1 percent of the population in the community that produces the highest number of intakes into PAW. In comparison, Black people constitute about 9 percent of the population of the City of Los Angeles, 11 percent of the County of Los Angeles (including the City), 6.5 percent of the population statewide, and 12 percent of the population nationwide.

38. Telles and Ortiz, *Generations of Exclusion*, provides a starting point into this literature.

39. Bonilla-Silva, in "We Are All Americans!" and "From Bi-racial to Tri-racial," clearly articulates the organization and logic of this racial hierarchy; see also Ortiz and Telles, "Racial Identity," for a succinct discussion of the history and contemporary experience of racism against Mexican Americans.

40. Sexton, "People-of-Color-Blindness," Kim, "Murder and Mattering," and Wilderson, *Red, White and Black*, adopt an Afropessimist perspective and provide an entrée into this area of scholarship.

41. Gómez, *Manifest Destinies*, traces the construction of Mexican Americans as a racial group in the United States and illuminates important connections between the Mexican American experience and the subordination of Black Americans.

42. Tarver, "Dangerous Individual('s) Dog," 281.

43. See note 12 above.

44. Peterson, "Canine Rescue"; Rowan and Kartal, "Dog Population."

45.   On pit bull identification, see Hoffman et al., "Is That Dog," and Olson et al., "Inconsistent Identification." The ASPCA published on its website two reports by Weiss, "Filling the Pit" (2014) and "Rising from the Pit" (2017), since deleted, that discussed shelter dogs by breed type and that claimed pit bulls to be the most common type of dog in US animal shelters. In my research, I have seen a range of claims about the size of the homeless pit bull population, including claims that US shelters euthanize 3,000 pit bulls a day (Junod, "State") or, alternately, 750,000 each year (Dickey, *Pit Bull*). The shifts in data reflect both the nebulousness of the category of pit bulls and the rapid decline in shelter killing in the 2000s.

46.   Kim, "Murder and Mattering," esp. 3, eloquently discusses how this kind of perception of animals as all body leads to human violence against animals.

47.   Tullis, "Softer Side."

48.   Gorant, *Lost Dogs*; Dennett, *Champions*.

49.   See, for example, Tullis, "Softer Side," and Meltzer, "Trouble with Pibbles."

50.   Clarke, Mills, and Cooper, "'Type' as Central"; Hoffman et al., "Is That Dog"; Olson et al., "Inconsistent Identification"; Weaver, "'Becoming in Kind.'"

51.   Gunter, Barber, and Wynne, "What's in a Name?," examines the effects of breed bias on adoption attractiveness; for some examples of articles on not labeling within the animal sheltering community, see Voith, Ingram, et al., "Comparison of Adoption Agency"; Voith, Trevejo, et al., "Comparison of Visual and DNA"; Hoffman et al., "Is That Dog."

52.   SCAS designates the following breeds as dominant: Akita, American Bulldog, American Pit Bull Terrier, American Staffordshire Terrier, Bull Terrier, Cane Corso, Caucasian Mountain Dog, Chow Chow, Dogo Argentino, Jindo, Pit Bull, Neapolitan Mastiff, Presa Canario, Rottweiler, Shar Pei, Staffordshire Bull Terrier, Tibetan Mastiff, Tosa Inu.

53.   Dowling-Guyer, Marder, and D'Arpino, "Behavioral Traits Detected"; Marder et al., "Food-Related Aggression"; Mohan-Gibbons et al., "Impact"; Patronek and Bradley, "No Better"; Rayment et al., "Applied Personality Assessment."

54.   Patronek and Bradley, "No Better."

55.   It's no coincidence that dogs who are given longer periods for adoption tend to have fewer physical characteristics associated with pit bulls. Elsie, for example, had very long, floppy ears reminiscent of a hound and a long, pointy snout, and she was a bright copper color not typically seen in pit bulls. She was also smaller and less muscular than most dogs identified as pit bulls tend to be.

56.   Tarver, "Dangerous Individual('s) Dog."

57.   Boisseron, *Afro-Dog*, 43.

58.   The relationship between breed and bite risk is highly contentious, largely because pit bulls themselves have become a political lightning rod and often stand in for Black people or minorities in public debates. In spite of my extensive efforts to locate such work, I am not aware of any research in any country that shows that pit bulls are more likely to bite than any other type of dog. In temperament evaluations of dogs by breed, pit bulls perform very well—but these tests don't necessarily mimic

real-life situations. Some proponents of BSL argue that the issue isn't that pit bulls are more likely to bite but that they are more likely to cause serious injury when they do bite. Here, again, the evidence seems scant when controlling for the number of different types of dogs.

59. Volunteers regularly discussed with each other the issues facing pit bulls as a category of dog but only occasionally expressed these concerns to shelter managers.

60. *Rehabilitation* refers to veterinary attention, as many rescued dogs have health issues, as well as to behavioral work that may involve minor behavior modification in a foster home or serious behavior modification through residential training programs.

61. Boisseron, *Afro-Dog*, 42.

62. Weaver, "Pit Bull Promises."

63. Weiner, "Whitening," 360.

64. Twine and Gallagher, "Future of Whiteness," 6.

65. Several scholars have examined the Michael Vick case, documenting the vitriol with which advocates for animals called for Vick to lose his National Football League contract permanently, be sentenced to a longer sentence term—possibly even life in prison—or even be put to death. See, for example, Kim, "Wonderful, Horrible Life"; Tavers, "Dangerous Individual('s) Dog"; Dickey, *Pit Bull*, 248. I also routinely heard and read similar sentiments among PAW volunteers and within the Los Angeles pit bull rescue community.

66. Bobo, "Racial Attitudes and Relations"; Elder, Wolch, and Emel, "Race, Place."

67. Some rescuers also rescue pit bulls with cropped ears. While ear cropping serves a practical function for fighting dogs, most dogs in PAW's service area have cropped ears for aesthetic reasons. Rescuers take these dogs for a few reasons, including out of a belief that these dogs are less likely to be adopted out of the shelter and are more likely to be adopted from the shelter into the "wrong" kind of home (i.e., by people who want tough-looking dogs). Some rescuers also seem to find working with cropped-ear pit bulls as an indicator of their own power. Others also find cropped ears aesthetically pleasing.

68. A study based in the UK, Clarke, Mills, and Cooper's "'Type' as Central," finds that the type of dog that people see a dog as being significantly influences how they rate their behavior, including aggressiveness. This likely influences how adoptable people find a dog.

69. See Dickey, *Pit Bull*, 242, for a similar account of pit bull rescuers feeling that the dogs need to have perfect behavior to be adoptable.

70. Twining, Arluke, and Patronek, "Managing the Stigma."

71. Abu-Lughod, "Do Muslim Women."

72. Mills, *Racial Contract*.

73. This point has been widely made in US journalism, including through feature articles in *Time* and the *New York Times*. See, for example, Meltzer, "Trouble with Pibbles"; Tullis, "Softer Side."

CHAPTER 7: ANIMALS' RESISTANCE TO SHELTER RULE

1. S. Scott, "Racehorse as Protagonist," 46.

2. S. Taylor, *Beasts of Burden*, 42.

3. Darwin, *Descent of Man*; McFarland and Hediger, "Approaching the Agency."

4. See Horowitz, "Behavior," for an overview of animal behavior.

5. Freire, *Pedagogy of the Oppressed*.

6. Lukacs, *History and Class Consciousness*.

7. Gramsci, *Selection*. Of course, resistance and acquiescence are rarely fixed states, and instead actors move between them.

8. Hollander and Einwohner, "Conceptualizing Resistance."

9. Such consciousness would also presumably require animal subjectivity. See Govindrijan, *Animal Intimacies*, especially 20–26, where Govindrijan describes animals as "empathetic, intentional, interpretive, and intelligent beings" (22), for a discussion of animal subjectivity.

10. Mumby, "Theorizing Resistance."

11. Cazzolla, "Self-Recognition"; Irvine, *If You Tame Me*.

12. Safina, *Beyond Words*.

13. S. Taylor, *Beasts of Burden*.

14. In addressing the relationship between intent and resistance, I find myself on contested ground. In Western culture, reason and rationality stand in opposition to emotion, irrationality, and superstition, with the former considered the domain of human men and whites and holding greater social value than the latter, which has been relegated to women, people of color, and animals. Early scholarship on collective action and resistance foregrounded this dichotomy, and dominant responses to social resistance often trivialize and condemn resistance as irrational and emotion driven. See Le Bon's *The Crowd*, originally published in 1895, which conceptualizes collective action as the outcome of people taking on a collective mind and losing control over their own minds. In a similar vein, contagion theories hold that people "catch" irrational ideas from one another. Social scientific scholarship on social movements sought to restore reason to activism, revealing explanations far more complex than being overcome by emotion to elucidate why and when people engage in resistance. This approach largely sidelined the role of emotions, and scholars engaged in a significant correction in the early 2000s by bringing emotions back in to show how feelings can motivate and inform social action. For examples of scholarship addressing the role of emotions in resistance, see Aminzade and McAdam, "Emotions and Contentious Politics"; Flam and King, *Emotions and Social Movements*; Gould, *Moving Politics*; Guenther, "Impact of Emotional Opportunities."

15. This literature is vast. Two well-known examples of discussions of resistance that focus on signification are Hebdige's *Subculture* and Butler's *Gender Trouble*.

16. Laland and Hoppitt, "Do Animals Have Culture?"; McGrew, "Culture in Nonhuman Primates?"

17. Whitehead and Rendell, *Cultural Lives of Whales*; Balcombe, *What a Fish Knows*; Aplin, "Culture and Cultural Evolution."

18. Alger and Alger, "Beyond Mead"; Alger and Alger, *Cat Culture*.

19. Nast, "Loving . . . Whatever."

20. Hollander and Einwohner, "Conceptualizing Resistance"; Vinthagen and Johansson, "'Everyday Resistance.'"

21. Vinthagen and Johansson, "'Everyday Resistance,'" 18, emphasis in original.

22. Several research efforts document guardians of companion animals who interpret their "pets" as occupying subjective states and/or having minds of their own. See, for example, Fox, "Animal Behaviours"; Irvine, "Power of Play"; Sanders, "Understanding Dogs."

23. Meijer, *When Animals Speak*, 123.

24. Vinthagen and Johansson, "'Everyday Resistance.'"

25. Warkentin, "Whale Agency."

26. Warkentin, "Whale Agency," 35–36.

27. Braverman, *Zooland*.

28. Cowperthwaite, *Blackfish*.

29. Lambert and Moore, *Tyke, Elephant Outlaw*.

30. Hribal, *Fear of the Animal Planet*.

31. Meijer, "Political Animal Voices"; Meijer, *When Animals Speak*; Coppin, "Foucaultian Hog Futures."

32. Meijer, "Political Animal Voices"; Meijer, *When Animals Speak*.

33. Coppin, "Foucaultian Hog Futures"; MacKinnon, "Of Mice and Men."

34. MacLean, Krupenye, and Hare, "Dogs"; Kaminski et al., "Domestic Dogs"; Pilley, *Chaser*.

35. Agamben, *Homo Sacer*.

36. Fox, "Animal Behaviours," discusses how human guardians to companion animals interpret and negotiate such actions.

37. This latter approach is less widely seen because most animals who aggress against humans are killed before they have the opportunity to modify their actions. However, sometimes a staff member or volunteer will secure time for a highly resistant animal because they connect with them in some way or had contact with a previous guardian and believe the animal can be adopted.

38. Irvine, *If You Tame Me*, 101–6, provides an excellent discussion of how behavior factors into prospective adopters' adoption choices. Irvine identifies two types of adopters, those who are seeking a certain type of dog (the "planners") and those who come to the shelter with limited commitment to a particular breed or appearance (the "impartial"). I observed similar patterns among adopters at PAW, albeit with a much greater proportion of adopters arriving as planners than as impartial.

39. Jackson-Schebetta, "Mythologies and Commodifications."

40. The *New York Times* published at least one in-depth story each year between 2013 and 2018 focused on scientific discoveries pertaining to the evolution of dogs from wolves and/or foxes, as well as dozens more articles about human-dog relationships more generally. For some examples of publications on dogs' evolution (including popular science), see Wang, Tedford, and Antón, "Dogs"; Budiansky, *Truth about Dogs*; and Peirotti and Fogg, *First Domestication*. Searching for books on dog evolution online will turn up dozens of results published just since 2000.

41. PAW's practice of killing all feral cats has continued in spite of a visible and vocal TNR community in PAW's service area and the close public-private partnership with Humane America, which supports TNR. Many volunteers find it problematic that Humane America has not exerted greater pressure on PAW to stop killing feral cats and has not made the stopping of such killing a term of their partnership.

42. In PAW's view, the only difference between an attempt to bite and a bite is the outcome. An attempt to bite is unsuccessful, such as snapping and not reaching the target, or snapping and landing on protective clothing or gear. A bite results in injury to the target, with bites that draw blood considered more serious than those that result in scrapes or bruising.

43. At the start of my fieldwork, PAW also routinely killed animals just to manage the size of the population of impounded animals. Pressure from volunteers and changing industry standards to provide substantive justifications for the killing of impounded animals have moved the shelter toward increasingly providing justifications for killing other than space.

44. Braverman, *Zooland*.

45. Calvo, "'Most Farmers Prefer Blondes'"; Gillespie, *Cow with Ear Tag #1389*; Pachirat, *Every Twelve Seconds*.

CHAPTER 8: WAITING, WONDERING, AND WAVERING

1. Auyero and Swistun, "Tiresias in Flammable Shantytown," 18; see also Auyero and Swistun, *Flammable*.

2. Gillespie, *Cow with Ear Tag #1389*, 107; see also Pachirat, *Every Twelve Seconds*.

3. Bourdieu, *Pascalian Meditations*.

4. Auyero, "Patients of the State," 14.

5. It is not insignificant that when volunteers get in trouble, staff reprimand them when they are checking out or turning in their keys. Further, at least twice, volunteers were placed on suspension from PAW. In neither case did the SCAS volunteer coordinator call or email the volunteers; rather, when they showed up to volunteer, they were simply told they could no longer access keys. This is a particularly humiliating and mean way to alert volunteers of the change in their status as it occurs in front of other people and without warning. It also again reflects a lack of respect for volunteers' time, since many volunteers drive thirty or more minutes to reach PAW.

6. Rehn and Keeling, "Effect of Time."

7. Guenther, "How Volunteerism Inhibits Mobilization," challenges the widely held assumption that volunteerism promotes democracy by instead showing how workers' status as volunteers inhibits organized resistance and institutional change at PAW.

8. Auyero and Swistun, "Tiresias in Flammable Shantytown," 18.

9. PAW has a sign on the wall inviting customers to call their customer feedback line. I was unable to get data on what percentage of calls are complaints or compliments.

CHAPTER 9: A NEW REVOLUTION

1. See Meijer, *When Animals Speak*, for a rich discussion of animal democracy.

2. Francione, "Animal Rights."

3. Donaldson and Kymlicka, *Zoopolis*; Meijer, *When Animals Speak*.

4. Meijer, "Political Animal Voices."

5. Weaver, "Pit Bull Promises," 353.

6. Best Friends Animal Society, "No-Kill"; Castle, "Number of Animals Killed"; Parlapiano, "Spaying, Neutering and Rescuing," reports a higher number—two million—of companion animals killed in shelters.

7. Robinson, *Evolution*.

8. Brueck, *Veganism*.

9. Spade, *Normal Life*.

10. Hannah, "Biopower, Life," 1035; MacKinnon, "Of Mice and Men," emphasis mine.

11. Francione and Garner, *Animal Rights Debate*, provides a detailed overview of both of these perspectives. In contrast to abolitionism, the welfarist approach—which is what currently guides basically all of the sheltering industry in the United States—focuses on the welfare and quality of life of animals while maintaining their exploitation.

12. While SCAS has continued to reject the language of no-kill—despite the embrace of it in nearby Los Angeles city shelters—SCAS has moved toward greater cooperation with Humane America to reduce killing and has incorporated playgroups for dogs, which have enhanced the impoundment experience for dog-social and dog-tolerant larger dogs. As of late 2019, SCAS claims to be implementing a new philosophy pointedly *not* called no-kill to try "balance animal comfort and public safety."

13. The role of low-cost spay/neuter programs has not been clearly established. Some research studies (Frank and Carlisle-Frank, "Analysis of Programs"; Scarlett and Johnston, "Impact") have shown that, contrary to the dogma in the animal-sheltering industry, increasing access to low-cost spay and neuter does not reduce shelter intakes or euthanasia. This suggests the possibility that issues other than so-called pet overpopulation are responsible for animals entering shelters, and this is why, unlike many of my fellow volunteers, I don't place spaying and neutering at the top of my list of what needs to be done to slow shelter intakes.

14. Los Angeles Homeless Services Authority, "2018 Greater Los Angeles."

15. Dickey, *Pit Bull*, 252.

16. One of the managers said he would consider a pit bull if a registered therapy dog. As a coordinator for adoptions for a local rescue, I also routinely encountered rentals that would not permit pit bulls, including a luxury property (in Los Angeles and outside PAW's service area) at which the renters were paying over $10,000 a month for a two-bedroom apartment.

17. Raissian and Bullinger, "Money Matters."

18. Marra and Santella, *Cat Wars*.

19. Meijer, "Political Animal Voices"; Meijer, *When Animals Speak*, especially 207–11.

20. Wadiwel, "Biopolitics," 92.

21. Kim, *Dangerous Crossings,* 287, ends on a similar note. I am grateful to an anonymous reviewer for drawing my attention to the need to articulate clearly that we cannot allow efforts at ending violence against humans to rely on anti-Blackness.

22. Like Claire Kim in "Abolition," I reject the assertion that animals are the "new" victims of injustice and that the "old" victims have been displaced because the conditions of their domination have been erased.

Bibliography

Abu-Lughod, Lila. "Do Muslim Women Really Need Saving? Anthropological Reflections on Cultural Relativism and Its Others." *American Anthropologist* 104, no. 3 (2002): 783–90.

Adams, Carol J. *The Sexual Politics of Meat*. New York: Bloomsbury Academic, 2010.

Adams, Carol J., and Josephine Donovan. "Sexism/Speciesism: Interlocking Oppressions." In *Animals and Women*, edited by Carol J. Adams and Josephine Donovan, 11–31. Durham, NC: Duke University Press, 1995.

Agamben, Giorgio. *Homo Sacer: Sovereign Power and Bare Life*. Stanford, CA: Stanford University Press, 1998.

Alger, Janet M., and Steven F. Alger. "Beyond Mead: Symbolic Interaction between Humans and Felines." *Society and Animals* 5, no. 1 (1997): 65–81.

———. *Cat Culture: The Social World of a Cat Shelter*. Philadelphia: Temple University Press, 2002.

———. "Cat Culture, Human Culture: An Ethnographic Study of a Cat Shelter." *Society and Animals* 7, no. 3 (1999): 199–218.

American Society for the Prevention of Cruelty to Animals. "Pet Statistics." 2014. http://www.aspca.org/about-us/faq/pet-statistics.

American Temperament Test Society. "ATTS Breed Statistics." 2017. https://atts.org/breed-statistics/.

Aminzade, Ron, and Doug McAdam. "Emotions and Contentious Politics." In *Silence and Voice in the Study of Contentious Politics*, edited by Ronald R. Aminzade, Jack A. Goldstone, Doug McAdam, Elizabeth J. Perry, William H. Sewell Jr., Sidney Tarrow, and Charles Tilly, 14–50. New York: Cambridge University Press, 2001.

Andrews, Thomas G. "Beasts of the Southern Wild: Slaveholders, Slaves, and Other Animals in Charles Ball's *Slavery in the United States*." In *Rendering Nature: Animals,*

Bodies, Places, Politics, edited by Marguerite S. Shaffer and Phoebe S. K. Young, 21–47. Philadelphia: University of Pennsylvania Press, 2015.

Animal Studies Group, ed. *Killing Animals*. Urbana: University of Illinois Press, 2006.

Aplin, Lucy M. "Culture and Cultural Evolution in Birds: A Review of the Evidence." *Animal Behavior* 147 (2019): 179–87.

Aptekar, Sofya. "Visions of Public Space: Reproducing and Resisting Social Hierarchies in a Community Garden." *Sociological Forum* 30, no. 1 (2015): 209–27.

Arluke, Arnold, and Clinton R. Sanders. *Regarding Animals*. Philadelphia: Temple University Press, 1996.

Armbruster, Karla. "'Good Dog': The Stories We Tell about Our Canine Companions and What They Mean for Humans and Other Animals." *Papers on Language and Literature* 38, no. 4 (2002): 351–76.

Ashcraft, Karen Lee, and April Kedrowicz. "Self-Direction or Social Support? Nonprofit Empowerment and the Tacit Employment Contract of Organizational Communication Studies." *Communication Monographs* 69, no. 1 (2002): 88–110.

Auyero, Javier. "Patients of the State: An Ethnographic Account of Poor People's Waiting." *Latin American Research Review* 46, no. 1 (2011): 5–29.

Auyero, Javier, and Débora Swistun. *Flammable: Environmental Suffering in an Argentine Shantytown*. Oxford: Oxford University Press, 2009.

———. "Tiresias in Flammable Shantytown: Toward a Tempography of Domination." *Sociological Forum* 24, no. 1 (2017): 1–21.

Balcom, Sarah, and Arnold Arluke. "Animal Adoption as Negotiated Order: A Comparison of Open versus Traditional Shelter Approaches." *Anthrozoös* 14, no. 3 (2001): 135–50.

Balcombe, Jonathan. *What a Fish Knows: The Inner Lives of Our Underwater Cousins*. New York: Farrar, Straus and Giroux, 2017.

Bergh, Henry. "Henry Bergh on Fox-Hunting." *New York Times*, November 27, 1875.

———. "Henry Bergh's Views on Pigeon Shooting." *Chicago Tribune*, January 28, 1872.

Best, Steven. "The Rise of Critical Animal Studies: Putting Theory into Action and Animal Liberation into Higher Education." *Journal for Critical Animal Studies* 7, no. 1 (2009): 9–51.

Best Friends Animal Society. "Best Friends Animal Society 2017 Fiscal Year and How Animals Were Saved." 2018. https://bestfriends.org/about-best-friends/financial-information.

———. "No-Kill for Cats and Dogs in America's Shelters." 2019. https://bestfriends.org/2025-goal.

———. "Together, We Can End the Killing by 2025." 2018. https://support.bestfriends.org/site/SPageNavigator/2025_Proof_Points_Page.html;jsessionid=00000000.app232b?NONCE_TOKEN=4CF6BCE5B4616A0D598861BF25006F05.

Birke, Lynda. "Intimate Familiarities? Feminism and Human-Animal Studies." *Society and Animals* 10, no. 4 (2002): 429–36.

Bobo, Lawrence. "Racial Attitudes and Relations at the Close of the Twentieth Century." In *America Becoming: Racial Trends and Their Consequences*, edited by Neil J. Smelser, William Julius Wilson, and F. Mitchell, 262–99. Washington, DC: National Academy Press, 2001.

Boisseron, Bénédicte. *Afro-Dog: Blackness and the Animal Question*. New York: Columbia University Press, 2018.

Bonilla-Silva, Eduardo. "From Bi-racial to Tri-racial: Towards a New System of Racial Stratification in the USA." *Ethnic and Racial Studies* 27, no. 6 (2004): 931–50.

———. "Rethinking Racism: Towards a Structural Interpretation." *American Sociological Review* 62 (1997): 465–80.

———. "We Are All Americans! The Latin Americanization of Racial Stratification in the USA." *Race and Society* 5 (2002): 3–16.

Bourdieu, Pierre. *Pascalian Meditations*. Stanford, CA: Stanford University Press, 2000.

Braverman, Irus. *Zooland: The Institution of Captivity*. Stanford, CA: Stanford Law Books/Stanford University Press, 2013.

Brown, Katrina, and Rachel Dilley. "Ways of Knowing for 'Response-Ability' in More-Than-Human Encounters: The Role of Anticipatory Knowledges in Outdoor Access with Dogs." *Area* 44, no. 1 (2012): 37–45.

Brueck, Julia Feliz. *Veganism in an Oppressive World: A Vegans-of-Color Community Project*. [US]: Sanctuary Publishers, 2017.

Budiansky, Stephen. *The Truth about Dogs: An Inquiry into the Ancestry, Social Conventions, Mental Habits, and Moral Fiber of Canis Familiaris*. New York: Viking, 2000.

Butler, Judith. *Frames of War: When Is Life Grievable?* London: Verso, 2009.

———. *Gender Trouble: Feminism and the Subversion of Identity*. New York: Routledge, 2006.

California Veterinary Medical Association. "CVMA's Owner vs. Guardian FAQ." 2019. https://cvma.net/government/legislative-issues/legislative-archives/owner-vs-guardian/cvmas-owner-vs-guardian-faq/.

Cal Matters. "Homeless in California: What the Data Reveals." June 2018. https://calmatters.org/housing/2018/06/homeless-in-california-what-the-data-reveals/.

Calvo, Erika. "'Most Farmers Prefer Blondes': The Dynamics of Anthroparchy in Animals Becoming Meat." *Journal for Critical Animal Studies* 6, no. 1 (2008): 32–45.

Castle, Julie. "Number of Animals Killed in Shelters Drops to Record Low; Number of No-Kill Communities Nearly Doubles as the Country Gets Closer to No-Kill by 2025." 2019. https://bestfriends.org/blogs/number-animals-killed-shelters-drops-record-low-number-no-kill-communities-nearly-doubles?utm_source=facebook.com&utm_medium=social&utm_term=Number+of+animals+killed+in+shelters+drops+to+record+low;+number+of+no-kill+commun.

Cazzolla, Gatti R. "Self-Recognition: Beyond the Looking-Glass and What Dogs Found There." *Ethology, Ecology and Evolution* 28, no. 2 (2015): 232–40.

Chen, Mel Y. *Animacies: Biopolitics, Racial Mattering, and Queer Affect.* Durham, NC: Duke University Press, 2012.

Chesney-Lind, Meda, and Katherine Irwin. *Beyond Bad Girls: Gender, Violence, and Hype.* New York: Routledge, 2008.

Chiam, Su C., Nicholas S. Solanki, Michelle Lodge, Malcolm Higgins, and Anthony L. Sparnon. "Retrospective Review of Dog Bite Injuries in Children Presenting to a South Australian Tertiary Children's Hospital Emergency Department." *Journal of Paediatrics and Child Health* 50, no. 10 (2014): 791–94.

Clarke, Tracey, Daniel Mills, and Jonathan Cooper. "'Type' as Central to Perceptions of Breed Differences in Behavior of Domestic Dog." *Society and Animals* 24, no. 5 (2016): 467–85.

Clear, Todd R. *Imprisoning Communities: How Mass Incarceration Makes Disadvantaged Neighborhoods Worse.* Oxford: Oxford University Press, 2007.

Cohen, Judy, and John Richardson. "Pit Bull Panic." *Journal of Popular Culture* 36, no. 2 (2003): 285–317.

Collard, Rosemary-Claire, and Jessica Dempsey. "Life for Sale? The Politics of Lively Commodities." *Environment and Planning A* 45, no. 11 (2013): 2682–99.

Collins, Patricia Hill. *Black Feminist Thought.* New York: Routledge, 2008.

Coppin, Dawn. "Foucaultian Hog Futures: The Birth of Mega-Hog Farms." *Sociological Quarterly* 44, no. 4 (2003): 597–616.

Cowperthwaite, Gabriela, dir. *Blackfish.* United States: Magnolia Home Entertainment/CNN, 2013.

Cudworth, Erika. *Developing Ecofeminist Theory: The Complexity of Difference.* Basingstoke: Palgrave Macmillan, 2005.

———. "Killing Animals: Sociology, Species Relations and Institutionalized Violence." *Sociological Review* 63 (2015): 1–18.

Darwin, Charles. *The Descent of Man and Selection in Relation to Sex.* Chicago: Rand, McNally, 1874.

Dave, Naisargi. "Witness: Humans, Animals, and the Politics of Becoming." *Cultural Anthropology* 29, no. 3 (2014): 433–56.

Davis, Janet M. *The Gospel of Kindness: Animal Welfare and the Making of Modern America.* Oxford: Oxford University Press, 2016.

Dayan, Colin. *With Dogs at the End of Life.* New York: Columbia University Press, 2018.

Deckha, Maneesha. "Postcolonial." In *Critical Terms for Animal Studies*, edited by Lori Gruen, 280–93. Chicago: University of Chicago Press, 2018.

DeMello, Margo, ed. *Mourning Animals: Rituals and Practices Surrounding Animal Death.* East Lansing: Michigan State University Press, 2016.

Dennett, Darcy, dir. *The Champions.* [US]: Firefly Film Works, 2015.

Desmond, Jane C. *Displaying Death and Animating Life: Human-Animal Relations in Art, Science, and Everyday Life.* Chicago: University of Chicago Press, 2016.

Desmond, Matthew. *Evicted: Poverty and Profit in the American City*. New York: Crown Books, 2016.

Dickey, Bronwen. *Pit Bull: The Battle over an American Icon*. New York: Penguin, 2016.

DiGiacomo, Natalie, Arnold Arluke, and Gary Patronek. "Surrendering Pets to Shelters: The Relinquisher's Perspective." *Anthrozoös* 11, no. 1 (1998): 41–51.

Donaldson, Sue, and Will Kymlicka. *Zoopolis: A Political Theory of Animal Rights*. Oxford: Oxford University Press, 2013.

Doubleday, Kalli F. "Scale-Blocking Grief: Witnessing the Intimate between a Conflict Leopard and Confinement." In *Vulnerable Witness: The Politics of Grief in the Field*, edited by Kathryn Gillespie and Patricia J. Lopez, 91–101. Berkeley: University of California Press, 2019.

Dowling-Guyer, Seana, Amy Marder, and Sheila D'Arpino. "Behavioral Traits Detected in Shelter Dogs by a Behavior Evaluation." *Applied Animal Behaviour Science* 130, no. 3–4 (2011): 107–14.

Duffy, Deborah L., Yuying Hsu, and James A. Serpell. "Breed Differences in Canine Aggression." *Applied Animal Behaviour Science* 114, no. 3–4 (2008): 441–60.

Elder, Glen, Jennifer Wolch, and Jody Emel. "Race, Place, and the Bounds of Humanity." *Society and Animals* 6, no. 2 (1998): 183–202.

Elias, Norbert. *The Civilizing Process*. Hoboken, NJ: Blackwell, 2008.

Eliasoph, Nina. *The Politics of Volunteering*. Cambridge: Polity Press, 2013.

Evans, Rhonda, DeAnn K. Gauthier, and Craig J. Forsyth. "Dogfighting: Symbolic Expression and Validation of Masculinity." *Sex Roles* 39, no. 11/12 (1998): 825–38.

Fiala, Irene. "Dog Breeds: The Canine Version of a Socially Constructed Race." *Humanities and Social Sciences Review* 2, no. 4 (2013): 137–44.

Flam, Helena, and Debra King. *Emotions and Social Movements*. New York: Routledge, 2005.

Florida, Richard. *The Rise of the Creative Class*. New York: Perseus Book Group, 2002.

Foer, Jonathan Safran. *Eating Animals*. New York: Back Bay Books, 2010.

Foucault, Michel. *Discipline and Punish: The Birth of the Prison*. Translated by Graham Burchell. New York: Pantheon, 1977.

———. *The History of Sexuality*. Translated by Robert Hurley. New York: Vintage Books, 1990.

———. *Security, Territory, Population: Lectures at the College de France, 1977-78*. Edited by Michel Senellart, Francois Ewald, Alessandro Fontana, and Arnold I. Davidson. New York: Picador/Palgrave Macmillan, 2009.

Fox, Rebekah. "Animal Behaviours, Post-human Lives: Everyday Negotiations of the Animal-Human Divide in Pet-Keeping." *Social and Cultural Geography* 7, no. 4 (2006): 525–37.

Francione, Gary L. "Animal Rights and Domesticated Nonhumans." 2007. https://www.abolitionistapproach.com/animal-rights-and-domesticated-nonhumans/.

Francione, Gary L., and Robert Garner. *The Animal Rights Debate: Abolition or Regulation?* New York: Columbia University Press, 2010.

Frank, Joshua M., and Pamela L. Carlisle-Frank. "Analysis of Programs to Reduce Overpopulation of Companion Animals: Do Adoption and Low-Cost Spay/Neuter Programs Merely Cause Substitution of Sources??" *Ecological Economics* 2, no. 1986 (2006): 2–8.

Freire, Paolo. *Pedagogy of the Oppressed.* New York: Herder and Herder, 1970.

Gaarder, Emily. "Where the Boys Aren't: The Predominance of Women in Animal Rights Activism." *Feminist Formations* 23, no. 2 (2011): 54–76.

Gallagher, Charles A. "Racial Redistricting: Expanding the Boundaries of Whiteness." In *Challenging Racial Thinking*, edited by Heather M. Dalmage, 59–76. Albany: State University of New York Press, 2004.

Garcés, Leah. *Grilled: Turning Adversaries into Allies to Change the Chicken Industry.* New York: Bloomsbury Sigma, 2019.

García, María Elena. "Grieving Guinea Pigs: Reflections on Research and Shame in Peru." In *Vulnerable Witness: The Politics of Grief in the Field*, edited by Kathryn Gillespie and Patricia J. Lopez, 40–53. Berkeley: University of California Press, 2019.

Gilens, Martin. *Why Americans Hate Welfare: Race, Media, and the Politics of Antipoverty Policy.* Chicago: University of Chicago Press, 1999.

Gillespie, Kathryn. *The Cow with Ear Tag #1389.* Chicago: University of Chicago Press, 2018.

———. "Witnessing Animal Others: Bearing Witness, Grief, and the Political Function of Emotion." *Hypatia* 31, no. 3 (2016): 572–88.

Gómez, Laura. *Manifest Destinies: The Making of the Mexican American Race.* 2nd ed. New York: New York University Press, 2018.

Gorant, Jim. *The Lost Dogs: Michael Vick's Dogs and Their Tale of Rescue and Redemption.* New York: Penguin Random House, 2011.

Gould, Deborah. *Moving Politics: Emotion and ACT UP's Fight against AIDS.* Chicago: University of Chicago Press, 2009.

Govindrajan, Radhika. *Animal Intimacies: Interspecies Relatedness in India's Central Himalayas.* Chicago: University of Chicago Press, 2018.

Gramsci, Antonio. *Selections from the Prison Notebooks.* Edited and translated by Quintin Hoare and Geoffrey Nowell Smith. New York: International Publishers, 1971.

Gruen, Lori. *Entangled Empathy: An Alternative Ethic for Our Relationships with Animals.* New York: Lantern Books, 2015.

Guenther, Katja M. "How Volunteerism Inhibits Mobilization: A Case Study of Shelter Animal Advocates." *Social Movement Studies* 16, no. 2 (2017): 240–53.

———. "The Impact of Emotional Opportunities on the Emotion Cultures of Feminist Organizations." *Gender and Society* 23, no. 3 (2009): 337–62.

———. "The Politics of Names: Rethinking the Methodological and Ethical Significance of Naming People, Organizations, and Places." *Qualitative Research* 9, no. 4 (2009): 411–21.

———. "Volunteers' Power and Resistance in the Struggle for Shelter Animal Survival." *Sociological Forum* 32, no. 4 (2017): 1–22.

Gunter, Lisa M., Rebecca T. Barber, and Clive D. L. Wynne. "What's in a Name? Effect of Breed Perceptions and Labeling on Attractiveness, Adoptions and Length of Stay for Pit-Bull-Type Dogs." *PLoS One* 11, no. 3 (2016).

Hancock, Ange-Marie. *The Politics of Disgust: The Public Identity of the Welfare Queen.* New York: New York University Press, 2004.

Hannah, Matthew G. "Biopower, Life, and Left Politics." *Antipode* 43, no. 4 (2011): 1034–55.

Haraway, Donna. *When Species Meet.* Minneapolis: University of Minnesota Press, 2008.

Harboldt, Tami L. *Bridging the Bond: The Cultural Construction of the Shelter Pet.* West Lafayette, IN: Purdue University Press, 2003.

Harper, A. Breeze, ed. *Sistah Vegan.* Brooklyn, NY: Lantern Books, 2009.

Hartsock, Nancy C. M. "The Feminist Standpoint: Developing the Ground for a Specifically Feminist Historical Materialism." In *Discovering Reality: Feminist Perspectives on Epistemology, Metaphysics, Methodology, and Philosophy of Science,* edited by Sandra Harding and Merrill B. Hintikka, 283–310. Dordrecht: Kluwer Academic Publishers, 1983.

Hebdige, Dick. *Subculture: The Meaning of Style.* London: Routledge, 1979.

Hoffman, Christy L., Natalie Harrison, London Wolff, and Carri Westgarth. "Is That Dog a Pit Bull? A Cross-country Comparison of Perceptions of Shelter Workers Regarding Breed Identification." *Journal of Applied Animal Welfare Science* 17, no. 4 (2014): 322–39.

Hollander, Jocelyn A., and Rachel L. Einwohner. "Conceptualizing Resistance." *Sociological Forum* 19, no. 4 (2004): 533–54.

Horowitz, Alexandra. "Behavior." In *Critical Terms for Animal Studies,* edited by Lori Gruen, 64–78. Chicago: University of Chicago Press, 2018.

Howe, Neil. "How Generational Change Boosts the Roaring Pet Care Market." *Forbes,* June 20, 2017.

Hribal, Jason. *Fear of the Animal Planet: The Hidden History of Animal Resistance.* Petrolia, CA: Counterpunch; Oakland, CA: AK Press, 2010.

Humane Society of the United States. "Ending Pet Homelessness." 2018. http://www .humanesociety.org/issues/pet_overpopulation/facts/pet_ownership_statistics .html.

———. "Our Policies." 2019. https://www.humanesociety.org/our-policies.

———. "Pets by the Numbers: U.S. Pet Ownership, Community Cat and Shelter Population Estimates." 2018. https://www.humanesociety.org/resources /pets-numbers.

———. "Puppy Mills: Facts and Figures." 2014. https://www.humanesociety.org/resources /fact-sheets-resources.

———. "Statement on Euthanasia." 2018. https://www.humanesociety.org/our-policies #statement-8.

Ignatiev, Noel. *How the Irish Became White*. New York: Routledge, 1995.

Irvine, Leslie. "Animal Problems/People Skills: Emotional and Interactional Strategies in Humane Education." *Society and Animals* 10, no. 1 (2002): 63–91.

———. "Animal Sheltering." In *The Oxford Handbook of Animal Studies*, edited by Linda Kalof, 98–112. Oxford: Oxford University Press, 2017.

———. *If You Tame Me: Understanding Our Connection with Animals*. Philadelphia: Temple University Press, 2004.

———. *My Dog Always Eats First: Homeless People and Their Animals*. Boulder, CO: Lynne Rienner, 2015.

———. "Pampered or Enslaved? The Moral Dilemmas of Pets." *International Journal of Sociology and Social Policy* 24, no. 9 (2014): 5–17.

———. "The Power of Play." *Anthrozoös* 14, no. 3 (2001): 151–60.

———. "The Problem of Unwanted Pets: A Case Study in How Institutions 'Think' about Clients' Needs." *Social Problems* 50, no. 4 (2003): 550–66.

Jackson-Schebetta, Lisa. "Mythologies and Commodifications of Dominion in 'The Dog Whisperer with Cesar Millan.'" *Journal for Critical Animal Studies* 7, no. 1 (2009): 107–31.

Jaskot, Colleen. "Closing the Door on the Gas Chamber." *Animal Sheltering*, January/February 2017. https://www.animalsheltering.org/magazine/articles/closing-door-gas-chamber.

Jerolmack, Colin. "Animal Practices, Ethnicity, and Community: The Turkish Pigeon Handlers of Berlin." *American Sociological Review* 72, no. 6 (2007): 874–94.

———. "Primary Groups and Cosmopolitan Ties: The Rooftop Pigeon Flyers of New York City." *Ethnography* 10, no. 4 (2009): 435–57.

Jerolmack, Colin, and Alexandra K. Murphy. "The Ethical Dilemmas and Social Scientific Trade-Offs of Masking in Ethnography." *Sociological Methods and Research* 48, no. 4 (2017): 1–27.

Jones, Keithly, Mildred Haley, and Alex Melton. "Per Capita Red Meat and Poultry Disappearance: Insights into Its Steady Growth." US Department of Agriculture, June 4, 2018. https://www.ers.usda.gov/amber-waves/2018/june/per-capita-red-meat-and-poultry-disappearance-insights-into-its-steady-growth/.

Joy, Melanie. *Why We Love Dogs, Eat Pigs, and Wear Cows: An Introduction to Carnism*. Newburyport, MA: Conari Press, 2009.

Junod, Tom. "The State of the American Dog." *Esquire*, August 2014. https://www.esquire.com/news-politics/a23731/american-dog-0814/.

Kalof, Linda, and Carl Taylor. "The Discourse of Dog Fighting." *Humanity and Society* 31, no. 4 (November 2007): 319–33.

Kaminski, Juliane, Sebastian Tempelmann, Josep Call, and Michael Tomasello. "Domestic Dogs Comprehend Human Communication with Iconic Signs." *Developmental Science* 12, no. 6 (2009): 831–37.

Kass, Philip H., Jr., John C. New, Janet M. Scarlett, and Mo D. Salman. "Understanding Animal Companion Surplus in the United States: Relinquishment of Nonadoptables to Animal Shelters for Euthanasia." *Journal of Applied Animal Welfare Science* 4, no. 4 (2001): 237–48.

Kemmerer, Lisa, ed. *Sister Species: Women, Animals, and Social Justice.* Urbana: University of Illinois Press, 2011.

Kim, Claire Jean. "Abolition." In *Critical Terms for Animal Studies*, edited by Lori Gruen, 15–32. Chicago: University of Chicago Press, 2018.

———. *Dangerous Crossings: Race, Species, and Nature in a Multicultural Age.* Cambridge: Cambridge University Press, 2015.

———. "Murder and Mattering in Harambe's House." *Politics and Animals* 3, no. 2 (2017): 37–51.

———. "The Wonderful, Horrible Life of Michael Vick." In *Ecofeminism: Feminist Intersections with Other Animals and the Earth*, edited by Carol J. Adams and Lori Gruen, 155–90. New York: Bloomsbury Academic, 2014.

Kirksey, S. Eben, and S. Helmreich. "The Emergence of Multispecies Ethnography." *Cultural Anthropology* 25, no. 4 (2010): 545–76.

Ko, Aph, and Syl Ko, eds. *Aphro-Ism: Essays on Pop Culture, Feminism, and Black Veganism from Two Sisters.* New York: Lantern Books, 2017.

Ko, Syl. "Black Veganism Revisited." In *Aphro-ism: Essays on Pop Culture, Feminism, and Black Veganism from Two Sisters*, edited by Aph Ko and Syl Ko, 120–26. Brooklyn, NY: Lantern Books, 2017.

Kustritz, Margaret V. Root. "Pros, Cons, and Techniques of Pediatric Neutering." In *Veterinary Clinics of North America: Small Animal Practice* 44, no. 2 (March 2014): 221–33.

Laland, Kevin N., and William Hoppitt. "Do Animals Have Culture?" *Evolutionary Anthropology* 12 (2003): 150–59.

Lambert, Susan, and Stefan Moore, dirs. *Tyke Elephant Outlaw.* DVD. Jumping Dog Productions, 2015.

Le Bon, Gustav. *The Crowd: A Study of the Popular Mind.* New York: Penguin, 1977.

Lee, Diana, and Marilee Geyer. *One at a Time: A Week in an American Animal Shelter.* Scotts Valley, CA: No Voice Unheard, 2005.

Lepper, Merry, Philip H. Kass, and Lynette A. Hart. "Prediction of Adoption versus Euthanasia among Dogs and Cats in a California Animal Shelter." *Journal of Applied Animal Welfare Science* 5, no. 1 (2002): 29–42.

Levine, Rachel, and Justyna Poray-Wybranowska. "American Bully: Fear, Paradox, and the New Family Dog." *Otherness: Essays and Studies* 5, no. 2 (2016): 151–200.

Lewis, Oscar. *La Vida: A Puerto Rican Family in the Culture of Poverty—San Juan and New York.* New York: Random House, 1966.

Los Angeles Homeless Services Authority. "2018 Greater Los Angeles Homeless Count—Data Summary." Los Angeles, 2018. https://www.lahsa.org/documents ?id=2000-2018-greater-los-angeles-homeless-count-data-summary-total-point -in-time-homeless-population-by-geographic-areas.pdf.

Loveman, Mara, and Jeronimo O. Muniz. "How Puerto Rico Became White: Boundary Dynamics and Intercensus Racial Reclassification." *American Sociological Review* 72, no. 6 (2007): 915–39.

Lukacs, Georg. *History and Class Consciousness.* Cambridge, MA: MIT Press, 1971.

MacKinnon, Catharine A. "Of Mice and Men: A Fragment on Animal Rights." In

The Feminist Care Tradition in Animal Ethics, edited by Josephine Donovan and Carol J. Adams, 316–32. New York: Columbia University Press, 2007.

MacLean, Evan L., Christopher Krupenye, and Brian Hare. "Dogs (*Canis Familiaris*) Account for Body Orientation but Not Visual Barriers When Responding to Pointing Gestures." *Journal of Comparative Psychology* 128, no. 3 (2014): 285–97.

Marder, Amy R., Anastasia Shabelansky, Gary J. Patronek, Seana Dowling-Guyer, and Sheila Segurson D'Arpino. "Food-Related Aggression in Shelter Dogs: A Comparison of Behavior Identified by a Behavior Evaluation in the Shelter and Owner Reports after Adoption." *Applied Animal Behaviour Science* 148, no. 1–2 (2013): 150–56.

Markovits, Andrei S., and Katherine N. Crosby. *From Property to Family: American Dog Rescue and the Discourse of Compassion*. Ann Arbor: University of Michigan Press, 2014.

Marlor, Chantelle. "Bureaucracy, Democracy, and Exclusion: Why Indigenous Knowledge Holders Have a Hard Time Being Taken Seriously." *Qualitative Sociology* 33 (2010): 513–31.

Marra, Peter P., and Chris Santella. *Cat Wars: The Devastating Consequences of a Cuddly Killer*. Princeton, NJ: Princeton University Press, 2016.

McCance, Dawne. *Critical Animal Studies: An Introduction*. Albany: SUNY Press, 2013.

McFarland, Sarah E, and Ryan Hediger. "Approaching the Agency of Other Animals: An Introduction." In *Animals and Agency: An Interdisciplinary Exploration*, edited by Sarah E. McFarland and Ryan Hediger, 1–20. Leiden: Brill, 2009.

McGrew, W. C. "Culture in Nonhuman Primates?" *Annual Review of Anthropology* 27 (1998): 301–28.

McKenzie, Brennen. "Evaluating the Benefits and Risks of Neutering Dogs and Cats." *CAB Reviews: Perspectives in Agriculture, Veterinary Science, Nutrition and Natural Resources* 5, no. 45 (2010): 1–18.

Medlin, Jamey. "Pit Bull Bans and the Human Factors Affecting Canine Behavior." *DePaul Law Review* 56 (2007): 1285–1320.

Meijer, Eva. "Political Animal Voices." PhD diss., University of Amsterdam, 2017.

———. *When Animals Speak: Towards an Interspecies Democracy*. New York: New York University Press, 2019.

Meltzer, Marissa. "The Trouble with Pibbles: Rebranding a Fearsome Dog." *New York Times*, January 5, 2019.

Millan, Cesar. *Be the Pack Leader: Use Cesar's Way to Transform Your Dog . . . and Your Life*. New York: Three Rivers Press, 2007.

Milliken, Jennifer, Sonya Humy, and Lucinda Woodward. "Give a Dog a Bad Name and Hang Him: Evaluating Big, Black Dog Syndrome." *Society and Animals* 20, no. 3 (2012): 236–53.

Mills, Charles W. *The Racial Contract*. Ithaca, NY: Cornell University Press, 1997.

Mohan-Gibbons, Heather, Emily D. Dolan, Pamela Reid, Margaret R. Slater, Hugh

Mulligan, and Emily Weiss. "The Impact of Excluding Food Guarding from a Standardized Behavioral Canine Assessment in Animal Shelters." *Animals* 8, no. 27 (2018).

Moore, Lisa Jean, and Mary Kosut. "Among the Colony: Ethnographic Fieldwork, Urban Bees, and Intra-species Mindfulness." *Ethnography* 15, no. 4 (2014): 516–39.

Morin, Karen M. "Carceral Space: Prisoners and Animals." *Antipode* 48, no. 5 (2016): 1317–36.

———. "Wildspace: The Cage, the Supermax, and the Zoo." In *Critical Animal Geographies: Politics, Intersections, and Hierarchies in a Multispecies World*, edited by Kathryn Gillespie and Rosemary-Claire Collard, 73–91. New York: Routledge, 2017.

Morris, Patricia. *Blue Juice: Euthanasia in Veterinary Medicine*. Philadelphia: Temple University Press, 2012.

Moynihan, Daniel P. *The Negro Family: The Case for National Action*. Washington, DC: Office of Policy Planning and Research, US Department of Labor, 1965.

Mumby, Dennis K. "Theorizing Resistance in Organization Studies: A Dialectical Approach." *Management Communication Quarterly* 19, no. 1 (2005): 19–44.

Nair, Yasmin. "Racism and the American Pit Bull." *Current Affairs*, September 2016. https://www.currentaffairs.org/2016/09/racism-and-the-american-pit-bull.

Nast, Heidi J. "Critical Pet Studies?" *Antipode* 38, no. 5 (2006): 894–906.

———. "Loving . . . Whatever: Alienation, Neoliberalism and Pet-Love in the Twenty-First Century." *ACME* 5, no. 2 (2015): 300–327.

———. "Pit Bulls, Slavery, and Whiteness in the Mid- to Late-Nineteenth Century US." In *Critical Animal Geographies: Politics, Intersections, and Hierarchies in a Multispecies World*, edited by Kathryn Gillespie and Rosemary-Claire Collard, 127–54. London: Routledge, 2015.

Neumann, Sandra. "Animal Welfare Volunteers: Who Are They and Why Do They Do What They Do." *Anthrozoös* 23, no. 4 (2010): 351–64.

Nilson, Finn, John Damsager, Jens Lauritsen, and Carl Bonander. "The Effect of Breed-Specific Dog Legislation on Hospital Treated Dog Bites in Odense, Denmark: A Time Series Intervention Study." *Plos One* 13, no. 12 (2018): e0208393.

Nocella, Anthony J., II, John Sorenson, Kim Socha, and Atsuko Matsuoka. "Introduction: The Emergence of Critical Animal Studies: The Rise of Intersectional Animal Liberation." *Counterpoints* 448 (2014): xix–xxvi.

No Kill Advocacy Center. "No Kill Equation." 2019. https://www.nokilladvocacycenter.org/no-kill-equation.html.

Ojakangas, Mika. "Impossible Dialogues on Bio-Power: Agamben and Foucault." *Foucault Studies* 2 (2005): 5–28.

Olson, K. R., J. K. Levy, B. Norby, M. M. Crandall, J. E. Broadhurst, S. Jacks, R. C. Barton, and M. S. Zimmerman. "Inconsistent Identification of Pit Bull-Type Dogs by Shelter Staff." *Veterinary Journal* 206, no. 2 (2015): 197–202.

Omi, Michael, and Howard Winant. *Racial Formation in the United States from the 1960s to the 1990s*. 2nd ed. New York: Routledge, 1994.

Ortiz, Vilma, and Edward Telles. "Racial Identity and Racial Treatment of Mexican Americans." *Race and Social Problems* 4, no. 1 (2012): 1–28.

Ortner, Sherry B. "Is Female to Male as Nature Is to Culture?" *Feminist Studies* 1, no. 2 (1972): 5–31.

Pachirat, Timothy. *Every Twelve Seconds: Industrialized Slaughter and the Politics of Sight*. New Haven, CT: Yale University Press, 2013.

Parlapiano, Alicia. "Spaying, Neutering and Rescuing Lead to Drop in Pet Euthanasia." *New York Times*, September 4, 2019.

Parreñas, Juno Salazar. *Decolonizing Extinction: The Work of Care in Orangutan Rehabilitation*. Durham, NC: Duke University Press, 2018.

Patronek, Gary J., and Janis Bradley. "No Better Than Flipping a Coin: Reconsidering Canine Behavior Evaluations in Animal Shelters." *Journal of Veterinary Behavior: Clinical Applications and Research* 15 (2016): 66–77.

Patronek, Gary J., Lawrence T. Glickman, Alan M. Beck, George P. McCabe, and Carol Ecker. "Risk Factors for Relinquishment of Cats to an Animal Shelter." *Journal of the American Veterinary Medical Association* 209, no. 3 (1996): 582–88.

Peirotti, Raymond, and Brandy R. Fogg. *The First Domestication: How Wolves and Humans Coevolved*. New Haven, CT: Yale University Press, 2017.

Peterson, Anna L. "Canine Rescue as a Social Movement: The Politics of Love." *Society and Animals* 26 (2018): 1–18.

Pierce, Jessica. *The Last Walk: Reflections on Our Pets at the End of Their Lives*. Chicago: University of Chicago Press, 2012.

Pilley, John W. *Chaser: Unlocking the Genius of the Dog Who Knows a Thousand Words*. Boston: Mariner, 2014.

Pitbullinfo.org. "Facts and Information about Pit Bull-Type Dogs." 2018. https://www.pitbullinfo.org/.

Potts, Annie, and Philip Armstrong. "Vegan." In *Critical Terms for Animal Studies*, edited by Lori Gruen, 395–409. Chicago: University of Chicago Press, 2018.

Pribac, Teya Brooks. "Grieving at a Distance." In *Mourning Animals: Rituals and Practices Surrounding Animal Deaths*, edited by Margo DeMello, 193–200. East Lansing: Michigan State University Press, 2016.

Probyn-Rapsey, Fiona. "Anthropocentrism." In *Critical Terms for Animal Studies*, edited by Lori Gruen, 47–63. Chicago: University of Chicago Press, 2018.

Protopopova, Alexandra, Amanda Joy Gilmour, Rebecca Hannah Weiss, Jacqueline Yontsye Shen, and Clive David Lawrence Wynne. "The Effects of Social Training and Other Factors on Adoption Success of Shelter Dogs." *Applied Animal Behaviour Science* 142 (2012): 61–68.

Rabinow, Paul, and Nikolas Rose. "Biopower Today." *BioSocieties* 1 (November 2006): 195–217.

Raissian, Kerri M., and Lindsey Rose Bullinger. "Money Matters: Does the Minimum Wage Affect Child Maltreatment Rates?" *Child and Youth Services Review* 72 (2017): 60–70.

Rayment, Diana J., Bert De Groef, Richard A. Peters, and Linda C. Marston. "Applied Personality Assessment in Domestic Dogs: Limitations and Caveats." *Applied Animal Behaviour Science* 163 (2015): 1–18.

Redmalm, David. "Pet Grief: When Is Non-human Life Grievable?" *Sociological Review* 63, no. 1 (2015): 19–35.

Reeve, Charlie L., Christiane Spitzmüller, and Natalie DiGiacomo. "The Caring-Killing Paradox: Euthanasia-Related Strain among Animal-Shelter Workers." *Journal of Applied Social Psychology* 35, no. 1 (2005): 119–43.

Rehn, Therese, and Linda J. Keeling. "The Effect of Time Left Alone at Home on Dog Welfare." *Applied Animal Behaviour Science* 129, no. 2–4 (2011): 129–35.

Robinson, Becky. *The Evolution of the Cat Revolution.* New York: Lantern Books, 2015.

Rosado, Belén, Sylvia García-Belenguer, Marta León, and Jorge Palacio. "Spanish Dangerous Animals Act: Effect on the Epidemiology of Dog Bites." *Journal of Veterinary Behavior: Clinical Applications and Research* 2, no. 5 (2007): 166–74.

Rosenberg, Meisha. "Golden Retrievers Are White, Pit Bulls Are Black, and Chihuahuas Are Hispanic: Representations of Breeds of Dog and Issues of Race in Popular Culture." In *Making Animal Meaning*, edited by Linda Kalof and Georgina M. Montgomery, 113–26. East Lansing: Michigan State University Press, 2011.

Rowan, Andrew, and Tamara Kartal. "Dog Population and Dog Sheltering Trends in the United States of America." *Animals* 8, no. 5 (2018): 1–20.

Safe Parking LA. "Safe Parking LA." 2019. https://www.safeparkingla.org.

Safina, Carl. *Beyond Words: What Animals Think and Feel.* New York: Picador, 2016.

Salman, M. D., John G. New Jr., Janet M. Scarlett, Philip H. Kass, Rebecca Ruch-Gallie, and Suzanne Hetts. "Human and Animal Factors Related to Relinquishment of Dogs and Cats in 12 Selected Animal Shelters in the United States." *Journal of Applied Animal Welfare Science* 1, no. 3 (1998): 207–26.

Sanders, Clinton R. "Understanding Dogs: Caretakers' Attributions of Mindedness in Canine-Human Relationships." *Journal of Contemporary Ethnography* 22, no. 2 (1993): 205–26.

Scarlett, Janet, and Naomi Johnston. "Impact of a Subsidized Spay Neuter Clinic on Impoundments and Euthanasia in a Community Shelter and on Service and Complaint Calls to Animal Control." *Journal of Applied Animal Welfare Science* 15 (2012): 53–69.

Scott, James C. *Weapons of the Weak: Everyday Forms of Peasant Resistance.* New Haven, CT: Yale University Press, 1987.

Scott, Shelly R. "The Racehorse as Protagonist: Agency, Independence, and Improvisation." In *Animals and Agency: An Interdisciplinary Exploration*, edited by Sarah E. McFarland and Ryan Hediger, 45–65. Leiden: Brill, 2009.

Sexton, Jared. "People-of-Color-Blindness: Notes on the Afterlife of Slavery." *Social Text* 28, no. 2 (2010): 31–56.

Shelter Animals Count. "2016 Animal Sheltering Statistics." 2016. https://shelteranimalscount.org/m/2016-animal-sheltering-statistics.

Silliman, Jael, Marlene Gerber Fried, Loretta Ross, and Elena Gutiérrez. *Undivided Rights: Women of Color Organize for Reproductive Justice*. Chicago: Haymarket, 2016.

Singer, Peter. *Animal Liberation: A New Ethics for Our Treatment of Animals*. New York: Avon Books, 1975.

Spade, Dean. *Normal Life: Administrative Violence, Critical Trans Politics, and the Limits of Law*. Boston: South End Press, 2011.

Sparks, Jessica L. Decker, Bridget Camacho, Philip Tedeschi, and Kevin N. Morris. "Race and Ethnicity Are Not Primary Determinants in Utilizing Veterinary Services in Underserved Communities in the United States." *Journal of Applied Animal Welfare Science* 21, no. 2 (2018): 120–29.

Srinivasan, Krithika. "The Biopolitics of Animal Being and Welfare: Dog Control and Care in the UK and India." *Transactions of the Institute of British Geographers* 38 (2013): 106–19.

Stanescu, James. "Species Trouble: Judith Butler, Mourning, and the Precarious Lives of Animals." *Hypatia* 27, no. 3 (2012): 567–82.

State of California. SB 1785, 1998. http://www.leginfo.ca.gov/pub/97-98/bill/sen/sb_1751-1800/sb_1785_bill_19980923_chaptered.html.

Striffler, Steve. *Chicken: The Dangerous Transformation of America's Favorite Food*. New Haven, CT: Yale University Press, 2007.

Tarver, Erin C. "The Dangerous Individual('s) Dog: Race, Criminality and the 'Pit Bull.'" *Culture, Theory and Critique* 55, no. 3 (2014): 273–85.

Taylor, Nicola. "In It for the Nonhuman Animals: Animal Welfare, Moral Certainty, and Disagreements." *Society and Animals* 12, no. 4 (2004): 317–39.

Taylor, Sunaura. *Beasts of Burden: Animal and Disability Liberation*. New York: New Press, 2017.

Telles, Edward E., and Vilma Ortiz. *Generations of Exclusion: Mexican Americans, Assimilation, and Race*. New York: Russell Sage Foundation, 2008.

Thierman, Stephen. "Apparatuses of Animality: Foucault Goes to a Slaughterhouse." *Foucaultian Studies* 21, no. 9 (2010): 89–110.

Tolich, Martin. "Internal Confidentiality: When Confidentiality Assurances Fail Relational Informants." *Qualitative Sociology* 27, no. 1 (2004): 101–6.

Tullis, Paul. "The Softer Side of Pit Bulls." *Time*, July 22, 2013. http://time.com/600/the-softer-side-of-pit-bulls/.

Twine, France Winddance, and Charles Gallagher. "The Future of Whiteness: A Map of the 'Third Wave.'" *Ethnic and Racial Studies* 31, no. 1 (2008): 4–24.

Twining, Hilary, Arnold Arluke, and Gary Patronek. "Managing the Stigma of Outlaw Breeds: A Case Study of Pit Bull Owners." *Society and Animals* 8, no. 1 (2000): 25–52.

Tyler, Tom. *CIFERAE: A Bestiary in Five Fingers*. Minneapolis: University of Minnesota Press, 2012.

UC Davis Koret Center for Shelter Medicine. "Facility Design and Animal Housing." 2015. https://www.sheltermedicine.com/library/resources/?utf8=?&search%5Bslug%5D=facility-design-and-animal-housing.

US Department of Housing and Urban Development. *The 2015 Annual Homeless Assessment Report to Congress*. Washington, DC, 2015.

Vinthagen, Stellan, and Anna Johansson. "'Everyday Resistance': Exploration of a Concept and Its Theories." *Resistance Studies Magazine*, no. 1 (2013): 1–46.

Voith, Victoria L., Elizabeth Ingram, Katherine Mitsouras, and Kristopher Irizarry. "Comparison of Adoption Agency Breed Identification and DNA Breed Identification of Dogs." *Journal of Applied Animal Welfare Science* 12, no. 3 (2009): 253–62.

Voith, Victoria L., Rosalie Trevejo, Colette Dowling-Guyer, Seana Chadik, Amy Marder, Vanessa Johnson, and Kristopher Irizarry. "Comparison of Visual and DNA Breed Identification of Dogs and Inter-observer Reliability." *American Journal of Sociological Research* 3, no. 2 (2013): 17–129.

Wacquant, Loïc. "From Slavery to Mass Incarceration." *New Left Review*, January/ February 2002, 41–60.

Wadiwel, Dinesh Joseph. "Biopolitics." In *Critical Terms for Animal Studies*, edited by Lori Gruen, 79–98. Chicago: University of Chicago Press, 2018.

———. "Cows and Sovereignty: Biopower and Animal Life." *Borderlands E-Journal* 1, no. 2 (2002): 1–8.

———. *The War against Animals*. Leiden: Brill, 2015.

Wagner, Denae, Kate Hurley, and Jenny Stavisky. "Shelter Housing for Cats: Principles of Design for Health, Welfare and Rehoming." *Journal of Feline Medicine and Surgery* 20 (2018): 635–42.

Wang, Xiaoming, Richard Tedford, and Mauricio Antón. *Dogs: Their Fossil Relatives and Evolutionary History*. New York: Columbia University Press, 2008.

Warkentin, Traci. "Must Every Animal Studies Scholar Be Vegan?" *Hypatia* 27, no. 3 (2012): 499–504.

———. "Whale Agency: Affordances and Acts of Resistance in Captive Environments." In *Animals and Agency: An Interdisciplinary Exploration*, edited by Sarah E. McFarland and Ryan Hediger, 23–43. Leiden: Brill, 2009.

Weaver, Harlan. "'Becoming in Kind': Race, Class, Gender, and Nation in Cultures of Dog Rescue and Dogfighting." *American Quarterly* 65, no. 2–3 (2013): 689–709.

———. "Pit Bull Promises: Inhuman Intimacies and Queer Kinships in an Animal Shelter." *GLQ: A Journal of Lesbian and Gay Studies* 21, no. 2–3 (2015): 343–63.

Weiner, Melissa F. "Whitening a Diverse Dutch Classroom: White Cultural Discourses in an Amsterdam Primary School." *Ethnic and Racial Studies* 38, no. 2 (2015): 359–76.

Weiss, Emily. "Filling the Pit." *ASPCA Pro*, May 15, 2014. https://www.aspcapro .org/blog/2014/05/15/filling-pit [no longer accessible].

———. "Rising from the Pit." *ASPCA Pro*, May 19, 2017. https://www.aspcapro.org /blog/2017/05/19/rising-pit [no longer accessible].

Whitehead, Hal, and Luke Rendell. *The Cultural Lives of Whales and Dolphins*. Chicago: University of Chicago Press, 2015.

Wilderson, Frank B., III. *Red, White, and Black: Cinema and the Structure of US Antagonisms*. Durham, NC: Duke University Press, 2010.

Winograd, Nathan. *Irreconcilable Differences: The Battle for the Heart and Soul of America's Animal Shelters*. CreateSpace Independent Publishing Platform, 2009.

———. *Redemption: The Myth of Pet Overpopulation and the No Kill Revolution in America*. Los Angeles: Almaden Books, 2009.

Wolch, Jennifer, Alec Brownlow, and Unna Lassiter. "Constructing the Animal Worlds of Inner-City Los Angeles." In *Animal Spaces, Beastly Places: New Geographies of Human-Animal Relations*, edited by Chris Wilbert, 71–97. Oxford: Taylor and Francis, 2000.

Young, Iris Marion. *Justice and the Politics of Difference*. Princeton, NJ: Princeton University Press, 1990.

Zawistowski, Stephen, Julie Morris, M. D. Salman, and Rebecca Ruch-Gallie. "Population Dynamics, Overpopulation, and the Welfare of Companion Animals: New Insights on Old and New Data." *Journal of Applied Animal Welfare Science* 1, no. 3 (1998): 193–206.

Zheutlin, Peter. *Rescue Road: One Man, Thirty Thousand Dogs, and a Million Miles on the Last Hope Highway*. Naperville, IL: Sourcebooks, 2015.

Index

abortion, 60, 88–89
abolition, 236, 241, 268n11
abuse. *See* neglect and abuse
Adams, Carol J., 250n50
AdoptAPet, 131, 133
adoption and adoptability: and
  commodification, 131–32, 199–200;
  desirable *vs.* undesirable criteria,
  overview, 99, 104, 108–9, 257n12,
  258n16; individuation strategies,
  124–25, 130–31, 132–34; off-site
  events, 41, 218; promotion strategies
  for pit bulls, 178–84; and relational
  resistance, 104–5; resistance to
  breed and behavior criteria, 110–11;
  resistance to health-based criteria,
  111–16; statistics, 16, 249n39;
  temperament tests, 164–68, 170,
  263–64n58; time lines, 215–19,
  221–22; types of adopters, 266n38.
  See also fostering
African Americans. *See* Black
  community
Afropessimism, 159, 262n40
Agamben, Giorgio, 17, 195

aggression. *See* behavior and aggression
Alley Cat Allies, 13
alopecia, 112–13
Angel City Pit Bulls, 161
animality, 6, 16–18, 153, 199, 209, 245
Animal Liberation (Singer), 14
animal practices: and acculturation, 89;
  as basis for judgment, 46, 60, 61, 91;
  as concept, 3; conflict over, 4, 85, 122,
  123, 259n31; and dogfighting, 155;
  ethnic and class differences in, 8, 83,
  89, 155, 157–58, 175–77, 178, 199; at
  PAW, 6, 43, 90; in PAW's service area,
  85, 87; and pit bulls, 155, 175–77, 184;
  and whiteness, 175, 181, 184, 188
animal studies, 14–22
animal welfare. *See* welfare
anthrocentrism, 14, 126, 150, 192
anthroparchal state, as concept, 35. *See*
  also killing; power
anthroparchy, 200, 209, 239, 247n2,
  251n6
anthropological machine, 217
Asian American community, 39, 78, 83,
  89, 158–59, 173

The authorized representative in the EU for product safety and compliance is:
Mare Nostrum Group
B.V Doelen 72
4831 GR Breda
The Netherlands

www.ingramcontent.com/pod-product-compliance
Lightning Source LLC
Chambersburg PA
CBHW020502270326
41926CB00008B/707